Getting Started

CFA® 2017

Level I CFA® Exam

Welcome

As the VP of Advanced Designations at Kaplan Schweser, I am pleased to have the opportunity to help you prepare for the 2017 CFA® exam. Getting an early start on your study program is important for you to sufficiently **prepare**, **practice**, and **perform** on exam day. Proper planning will allow you to set aside enough time to master the Learning Outcome Statements (LOS) in the Level I curriculum.

Now that you've received your SchweserNotes™, here's how to get started:

Step 1: Access Your Online Tools
Visit www.schweser.com and log in to your online account using the button located in the top navigation bar. After logging in, select the appropriate level and proceed to the dashboard where you can access your online products.

Step 2: Create a Study Plan
Create a study plan with the Study Calendar (located on the Schweser dashboard) and familiarize yourself with your financial calculator. Check out our calculator videos in the Candidate Resource Library (also found on the dashboard).

Step 3: Prepare and Practice
Read your SchweserNotes™ Volumes 1–5
At the end of each reading, you can answer the Concept Checker questions for better understanding of the curriculum.

Attend a Weekly Class
Attend live classes online or take part in our live classroom courses in select cities around the world. Our expert faculty will guide you through the curriculum with a structured approach to help you prepare for the CFA® exam. The Schweser On-Demand Video Lectures, in combination with the Weekly Class, offer a blended learning approach that covers every LOS in the CFA curriculum. (See our instruction packages to the right. Visit www.schweser.com/cfa to order.)

Practice with SchweserPro™ QBank
Maximize your retention of important concepts by answering questions in the SchweserPro™ QBank and taking several Practice Exams. Use Schweser's QuickSheet for continuous review on the go. (Visit www.schweser.com/cfa to order.)

Step 4: Attend a 3-Day, 5-Day, or WindsorWeek™ Review Workshop
Schweser's late-season review workshops are designed to drive home the CFA® material, which is critical for CFA exam success. Review key concepts in every topic, **perform** by working through demonstration problems, and **practice** your exam techniques. (See review options to the right.)

Step 5: Perform
Take a Live or Live Online Schweser Mock Exam to ensure you are ready to **perform** on the actual CFA® exam. Put your skills and knowledge to the test and gain confidence before the exam. (See exam options to the right.)

Again, thank you for trusting Kaplan Schweser with your CFA exam preparation!

Sincerely,

Tim Smaby
Tim Smaby, PhD, CFA, FRM
Vice President, Advanced Designations, Kaplan Schweser

The Kaplan Way for Learning

PREPARE
Acquire new knowledge through demonstration and examples.

PRACTICE
Apply new knowledge through simulation and practice.

PERFORM
Evaluate mastery of new knowledge and identify achieved outcomes.

CFA® Instruction Packages:
- Premium Instruction Package
- PremiumPlus™ Package

Final Review Options:
- Live 3-Day Review Workshop (held in select cities)
- Live Online 3-Day Review Workshop
- NYC 5-Day Review Workshop
- DFW 5-Day Review Workshop*
- WindsorWeek™*
- Live Schweser Mock Exam (offered in select cities worldwide)
- Live Online Schweser Mock Exam

*Only offered for June exam

Contact us for questions about your study package, upgrading your package, purchasing additional study materials, or for additional information:

888.325.5072 (U.S.) | +1 608.779.8327 (Int'l.)

staff@schweser.com | www.schweser.com/cfa

Book 4 – Corporate Finance, Portfolio Management, and Equity Investments

Reading Assignments and Learning Outcome Statements v

Study Session 10 – Corporate Finance: Corporate Governance, Capital Budgeting, and Cost of Capital 1

Study Session 11 – Corporate Finance: Leverage, Dividends and Share Repurchases, and Working Capital Management 66

Study Session 12 – Portfolio Management 112

Study Session 13 – Equity: Market Organization, Market Indices, and Market Efficiency 196

Study Session 14 – Equity Analysis and Valuation 257

Formulas 320

Index 325

SCHWESERNOTES™ 2017 LEVEL I CFA® BOOK 4: CORPORATE FINANCE, PORTFOLIO MANAGEMENT, AND EQUITY INVESTMENTS

©2016 Kaplan, Inc. All rights reserved.

Published in 2016 by Kaplan, Inc.

Printed in China.

ISBN: 978-1-4754-4096-6

If this book does not have the hologram with the Kaplan Schweser logo on the back cover, it was distributed without permission of Kaplan Schweser, a Division of Kaplan, Inc., and is in direct violation of global copyright laws. Your assistance in pursuing potential violators of this law is greatly appreciated.

Required CFA Institute disclaimer: "CFA Institute does not endorse, promote, or warrant the accuracy or quality of the products or services offered by Kaplan Schweser. CFA® and Chartered Financial Analyst® are trademarks owned by CFA Institute."

Certain materials contained within this text are the copyrighted property of CFA Institute. The following is the copyright disclosure for these materials: "Copyright, 2016, CFA Institute. Reproduced and republished from 2017 Learning Outcome Statements, Level I, II, and III questions from CFA® Program Materials, CFA Institute Standards of Professional Conduct, and CFA Institute's Global Investment Performance Standards with permission from CFA Institute. All Rights Reserved."

These materials may not be copied without written permission from the author. The unauthorized duplication of these notes is a violation of global copyright laws and the CFA Institute Code of Ethics. Your assistance in pursuing potential violators of this law is greatly appreciated.

Disclaimer: The Schweser Notes should be used in conjunction with the original readings as set forth by CFA Institute in their 2017 Level I CFA Study Guide. The information contained in these Notes covers topics contained in the readings referenced by CFA Institute and is believed to be accurate. However, their accuracy cannot be guaranteed nor is any warranty conveyed as to your ultimate exam success. The authors of the referenced readings have not endorsed or sponsored these Notes.

Reading Assignments and Learning Outcome Statements

The following material is a review of the Corporate Finance, Portfolio Management, and Equity Investments principles designed to address the learning outcome statements set forth by CFA Institute.

Study Session 10

Reading Assignments
Corporate Finance and Portfolio Management, CFA Program Level I 2017 Curriculum (CFA Institute, 2016)
- 34. Corporate Governance and ESG: An Introduction — page 1
- 35. Capital Budgeting — page 18
- 36. Cost of Capital — page 41

Study Session 11

Corporate Finance and Portfolio Management, CFA Program Level I 2017 Curriculum (CFA Institute, 2016)
- 37. Measures of Leverage — page 66
- 38. Dividends and Share Repurchases: Basics — page 81
- 39. Working Capital Management — page 95

Study Session 12

Reading Assignments
Corporate Finance and Portfolio Management, CFA Program Level I 2017 Curriculum (CFA Institute, 2016)
- 40. Portfolio Management: An Overview — page 112
- 41. Risk Management: An Introduction — page 124
- 42. Portfolio Risk and Return: Part I — page 135
- 43. Portfolio Risk and Return: Part II — page 158
- 44. Basics of Portfolio Planning and Construction — page 184

Study Session 13

Reading Assignments
Equity and Fixed Income, CFA Program Level I 2017 Curriculum (CFA Institute, 2016)
- 45. Market Organization and Structure — page 196
- 46. Security Market Indices — page 225
- 47. Market Efficiency — page 244

Book 4 – Corporate Finance, Portfolio Management, and Equity Investments
Reading Assignments and Learning Outcome Statements

STUDY SESSION 14

Reading Assignments
Equity and Fixed Income, CFA Program Level I 2017 Curriculum (CFA Institute, 2016)

48. Overview of Equity Securities	page 257
49. Introduction to Industry and Company Analysis	page 270
50. Equity Valuation: Concepts and Basic Tools	page 290

Book 4 – Corporate Finance, Portfolio Management, and Equity Investments
Reading Assignments and Learning Outcome Statements

LEARNING OUTCOME STATEMENTS (LOS)

STUDY SESSION 10

The topical coverage corresponds with the following CFA Institute assigned reading:

34. Corporate Governance and ESG: An Introduction

The candidate should be able to:

a. describe corporate governance. (page 1)
b. describe a company's stakeholder groups and compare interests of stakeholder groups. (page 2)
c. describe principal–agent and other relationships in corporate governance and the conflicts that may arise in these relationships. (page 3)
d. describe stakeholder management. (page 4)
e. describe mechanisms to manage stakeholder relationships and mitigate associated risks. (page 4)
f. describe functions and responsibilities of a company's board of directors and its committees. (page 5)
g. describe market and non-market factors that can affect stakeholder relationships and corporate governance. (page 7)
h. identify potential risks of poor corporate governance and stakeholder management and identify benefits from effective corporate governance and stakeholder management. (page 9)
i. describe factors relevant to the analysis of corporate governance and stakeholder management. (page 9)
j. describe environmental and social considerations in investment analysis. (page 11)
k. describe how environmental, social, and governance factors may be used in investment analysis. (page 12)

The topical coverage corresponds with the following CFA Institute assigned reading:

35. Capital Budgeting

The candidate should be able to:

a. describe the capital budgeting process and distinguish among the various categories of capital projects. (page 18)
b. describe the basic principles of capital budgeting. (page 19)
c. explain how the evaluation and selection of capital projects is affected by mutually exclusive projects, project sequencing, and capital rationing. (page 21)
d. calculate and interpret net present value (NPV), internal rate of return (IRR), payback period, discounted payback period, and profitability index (PI) of a single capital project. (page 21)
e. explain the NPV profile, compare the NPV and IRR methods when evaluating independent and mutually exclusive projects, and describe the problems associated with each of the evaluation methods. (page 29)
f. describe expected relations among an investment's NPV, company value, and share price. (page 32)

Book 4 – Corporate Finance, Portfolio Management, and Equity Investments
Reading Assignments and Learning Outcome Statements

The topical coverage corresponds with the following CFA Institute assigned reading:

36. **Cost of Capital**
    The candidate should be able to:
    a. calculate and interpret the weighted average cost of capital (WACC) of a company. (page 41)
    b. describe how taxes affect the cost of capital from different capital sources. (page 41)
    c. describe the use of target capital structure in estimating WACC and how target capital structure weights may be determined. (page 43)
    d. explain how the marginal cost of capital and the investment opportunity schedule are used to determine the optimal capital budget. (page 44)
    e. explain the marginal cost of capital's role in determining the net present value of a project. (page 45)
    f. calculate and interpret the cost of debt capital using the yield-to-maturity approach and the debt-rating approach. (page 45)
    g. calculate and interpret the cost of noncallable, nonconvertible preferred stock. (page 46)
    h. calculate and interpret the cost of equity capital using the capital asset pricing model approach, the dividend discount model approach, and the bond-yield-plus risk-premium approach. (page 47)
    i. calculate and interpret the beta and cost of capital for a project. (page 49)
    j. describe uses of country risk premiums in estimating the cost of equity. (page 51)
    k. describe the marginal cost of capital schedule, explain why it may be upward-sloping with respect to additional capital, and calculate and interpret its break-points. (page 52)
    l. explain and demonstrate the correct treatment of flotation costs. (page 54)

STUDY SESSION 11

The topical coverage corresponds with the following CFA Institute assigned reading:

37. **Measures of Leverage**
    The candidate should be able to:
    a. define and explain leverage, business risk, sales risk, operating risk, and financial risk and classify a risk. (page 66)
    b. calculate and interpret the degree of operating leverage, the degree of financial leverage, and the degree of total leverage. (page 67)
    c. analyze the effect of financial leverage on a company's net income and return on equity. (page 70)
    d. calculate the breakeven quantity of sales and determine the company's net income at various sales levels. (page 72)
    e. calculate and interpret the operating breakeven quantity of sales. (page 72)

The topical coverage corresponds with the following CFA Institute assigned reading:

38. **Dividends and Share Repurchases: Basics**
    The candidate should be able to:
    a. describe regular cash dividends, extra dividends, liquidating dividends, stock dividends, stock splits, and reverse stock splits, including their expected effect on shareholders' wealth and a company's financial ratios. (page 81)

b. describe dividend payment chronology, including the significance of declaration, holder-of-record, ex-dividend, and payment dates. (page 84)
   c. compare share repurchase methods. (page 85)
   d. calculate and compare the effect of a share repurchase on earnings per share when 1) the repurchase is financed with the company's excess cash and 2) the company uses debt to finance the repurchase. (page 85)
   e. calculate the effect of a share repurchase on book value per share. (page 88)
   f. explain why a cash dividend and a share repurchase of the same amount are equivalent in terms of the effect on shareholders' wealth, all else being equal. (page 88)

The topical coverage corresponds with the following CFA Institute assigned reading:
39. **Working Capital Management**
    The candidate should be able to:
    a. describe primary and secondary sources of liquidity and factors that influence a company's liquidity position. (page 95)
    b. compare a company's liquidity measures with those of peer companies. (page 96)
    c. evaluate working capital effectiveness of a company based on its operating and cash conversion cycles and compare the company's effectiveness with that of peer companies. (page 98)
    d. describe how different types of cash flows affect a company's net daily cash position. (page 98)
    e. calculate and interpret comparable yields on various securities, compare portfolio returns against a standard benchmark, and evaluate a company's short-term investment policy guidelines. (page 99)
    f. evaluate a company's management of accounts receivable, inventory, and accounts payable over time and compared to peer companies. (page 101)
    g. evaluate the choices of short-term funding available to a company and recommend a financing method. (page 104)

STUDY SESSION 12

The topical coverage corresponds with the following CFA Institute assigned reading:
40. **Portfolio Management: An Overview**
    The candidate should be able to:
    a. describe the portfolio approach to investing. (page 112)
    b. describe types of investors and distinctive characteristics and needs of each. (page 113)
    c. describe defined contribution and defined benefit pension plans. (page 114)
    d. describe the steps in the portfolio management process. (page 115)
    e. describe mutual funds and compare them with other pooled investment products. (page 115)

The topical coverage corresponds with the following CFA Institute assigned reading:
41. **Risk Management: An Introduction**
    The candidate should be able to:
    a. define risk management. (page 124)
    b. describe features of a risk management framework. (page 125)
    c. define risk governance and describe elements of effective risk governance. (page 125)

d. explain how risk tolerance affects risk management. (page 125)
e. describe risk budgeting and its role in risk governance. (page 126)
f. identify financial and non-financial sources of risk and describe how they may interact. (page 126)
g. describe methods for measuring and modifying risk exposures and factors to consider in choosing among the methods. (page 127)

The topical coverage corresponds with the following CFA Institute assigned reading:

42. Portfolio Risk and Return: Part I
The candidate should be able to:
a. calculate and interpret major return measures and describe their appropriate uses. (page 135)
b. describe characteristics of the major asset classes that investors consider in forming portfolios. (page 138)
c. calculate and interpret the mean, variance, and covariance (or correlation) of asset returns based on historical data. (page 139)
d. explain risk aversion and its implications for portfolio selection. (page 142)
e. calculate and interpret portfolio standard deviation. (page 143)
f. describe the effect on a portfolio's risk of investing in assets that are less than perfectly correlated. (page 144)
g. describe and interpret the minimum-variance and efficient frontiers of risky assets and the global minimum-variance portfolio. (page 146)
h. explain the selection of an optimal portfolio, given an investor's utility (or risk aversion) and the capital allocation line. (page 147)

The topical coverage corresponds with the following CFA Institute assigned reading:

43. Portfolio Risk and Return: Part II
The candidate should be able to:
a. describe the implications of combining a risk-free asset with a portfolio of risky assets. (page 158)
b. explain the capital allocation line (CAL) and the capital market line (CML). (page 159)
c. explain systematic and nonsystematic risk, including why an investor should not expect to receive additional return for bearing nonsystematic risk. (page 163)
d. explain return generating models (including the market model) and their uses. (page 165)
e. calculate and interpret beta. (page 166)
f. explain the capital asset pricing model (CAPM), including its assumptions, and the security market line (SML). (page 168)
g. calculate and interpret the expected return of an asset using the CAPM. (page 172)
h. describe and demonstrate applications of the CAPM and the SML. (page 173)

The topical coverage corresponds with the following CFA Institute assigned reading:

44. Basics of Portfolio Planning and Construction
The candidate should be able to:
a. describe the reasons for a written investment policy statement (IPS). (page 184)
b. describe the major components of an IPS. (page 184)
c. describe risk and return objectives and how they may be developed for a client. (page 185)

d. distinguish between the willingness and the ability (capacity) to take risk in analyzing an investor's financial risk tolerance. (page 186)
e. describe the investment constraints of liquidity, time horizon, tax concerns, legal and regulatory factors, and unique circumstances and their implications for the choice of portfolio assets. (page 186)
f. explain the specification of asset classes in relation to asset allocation. (page 188)
g. describe the principles of portfolio construction and the role of asset allocation in relation to the IPS. (page 189)

Study Session 13

The topical coverage corresponds with the following CFA Institute assigned reading:
45. Market Organization and Structure
The candidate should be able to:
a. explain the main functions of the financial system. (page 196)
b. describe classifications of assets and markets. (page 198)
c. describe the major types of securities, currencies, contracts, commodities, and real assets that trade in organized markets, including their distinguishing characteristics and major subtypes. (page 199)
d. describe types of financial intermediaries and services that they provide. (page 202)
e. compare positions an investor can take in an asset. (page 205)
f. calculate and interpret the leverage ratio, the rate of return on a margin transaction, and the security price at which the investor would receive a margin call. (page 207)
g. compare execution, validity, and clearing instructions. (page 208)
h. compare market orders with limit orders. (page 208)
i. define primary and secondary markets and explain how secondary markets support primary markets. (page 212)
j. describe how securities, contracts, and currencies are traded in quote-driven, order-driven, and brokered markets. (page 213)
k. describe characteristics of a well-functioning financial system. (page 215)
l. describe objectives of market regulation. (page 216)

The topical coverage corresponds with the following CFA Institute assigned reading:
46. Security Market Indices
The candidate should be able to:
a. describe a security market index. (page 225)
b. calculate and interpret the value, price return, and total return of an index. (page 225)
c. describe the choices and issues in index construction and management. (page 226)
d. compare the different weighting methods used in index construction. (page 226)
e. calculate and analyze the value and return of an index given its weighting method. (page 228)
f. describe rebalancing and reconstitution of an index. (page 232)
g. describe uses of security market indices. (page 233)
h. describe types of equity indices. (page 233)
i. describe types of fixed-income indices. (page 234)
j. describe indices representing alternative investments. (page 235)
k. compare types of security market indices. (page 236)

Book 4 – Corporate Finance, Portfolio Management, and Equity Investments
Reading Assignments and Learning Outcome Statements

The topical coverage corresponds with the following CFA Institute assigned reading:
47. Market Efficiency
The candidate should be able to:
a. describe market efficiency and related concepts, including their importance to investment practitioners. (page 244)
b. distinguish between market value and intrinsic value. (page 245)
c. explain factors that affect a market's efficiency. (page 245)
d. contrast weak-form, semi-strong-form, and strong-form market efficiency. (page 246)
e. explain the implications of each form of market efficiency for fundamental analysis, technical analysis, and the choice between active and passive portfolio management. (page 247)
f. describe market anomalies. (page 248)
g. describe behavioral finance and its potential relevance to understanding market anomalies. (page 251)

STUDY SESSION 14

The topical coverage corresponds with the following CFA Institute assigned reading:
48. Overview of Equity Securities
The candidate should be able to:
a. describe characteristics of types of equity securities. (page 257)
b. describe differences in voting rights and other ownership characteristics among different equity classes. (page 258)
c. distinguish between public and private equity securities. (page 259)
d. describe methods for investing in non-domestic equity securities. (page 260)
e. compare the risk and return characteristics of different types of equity securities. (page 261)
f. explain the role of equity securities in the financing of a company's assets. (page 262)
g. distinguish between the market value and book value of equity securities. (page 262)
h. compare a company's cost of equity, its (accounting) return on equity, and investors' required rates of return. (page 263)

The topical coverage corresponds with the following CFA Institute assigned reading:
49. Introduction to Industry and Company Analysis
The candidate should be able to:
a. explain uses of industry analysis and the relation of industry analysis to company analysis. (page 270)
b. compare methods by which companies can be grouped, current industry classification systems, and classify a company, given a description of its activities and the classification system. (page 270)
c. explain the factors that affect the sensitivity of a company to the business cycle and the uses and limitations of industry and company descriptors such as "growth," "defensive," and "cyclical". (page 273)
d. explain how a company's industry classification can be used to identify a potential "peer group" for equity valuation. (page 274)
e. describe the elements that need to be covered in a thorough industry analysis. (page 275)

Book 4 – Corporate Finance, Portfolio Management, and Equity Investments
Reading Assignments and Learning Outcome Statements

    f. describe the principles of strategic analysis of an industry. (page 275)
    g. explain the effects of barriers to entry, industry concentration, industry capacity, and market share stability on pricing power and price competition. (page 277)
    h. describe industry life cycle models, classify an industry as to life cycle stage, and describe limitations of the life-cycle concept in forecasting industry performance. (page 279)
    i. compare characteristics of representative industries from the various economic sectors. (page 281)
    j. describe macroeconomic, technological, demographic, governmental, and social influences on industry growth, profitability, and risk. (page 281)
    k. describe the elements that should be covered in a thorough company analysis. (page 282)

The topical coverage corresponds with the following CFA Institute assigned reading:
50. Equity Valuation: Concepts and Basic Tools
The candidate should be able to:
    a. evaluate whether a security, given its current market price and a value estimate, is overvalued, fairly valued, or undervalued by the market. (page 290)
    b. describe major categories of equity valuation models. (page 291)
    c. explain the rationale for using present value models to value equity and describe the dividend discount and free-cash-flow-to-equity models. (page 292)
    d. calculate the intrinsic value of a non-callable, non-convertible preferred stock. (page 295)
    e. calculate and interpret the intrinsic value of an equity security based on the Gordon (constant) growth dividend discount model or a two-stage dividend discount model, as appropriate. (page 296)
    f. identify characteristics of companies for which the constant growth or a multistage dividend discount model is appropriate. (page 301)
    g. explain the rationale for using price multiples to value equity, how the price to earnings multiple relates to fundamentals, and the use of multiples based on comparables. (page 302)
    h. calculate and interpret the following multiples: price to earnings, price to an estimate of operating cash flow, price to sales, and price to book value. (page 302)
    i. describe enterprise value multiples and their use in estimating equity value. (page 307)
    j. describe asset-based valuation models and their use in estimating equity value. (page 308)
    k. explain advantages and disadvantages of each category of valuation model. (page 310)

The following is a review of the Corporate Finance principles designed to address the learning outcome statements set forth by CFA Institute. Cross-Reference to CFA Institute Assigned Reading #34.

Corporate Governance and ESG: An Introduction

Study Session 10

Exam Focus

Candidates should understand the idea of a firm's stakeholders, how conflicts can arise between stakeholders, and how effective corporate governance can mitigate problems arising from these conflicts. Other important points are the election of the board of directors, the board's duties, and important factors in board composition. Finally, the rationale for incorporating environmental, social, and governance factors into the portfolio selection process is presented.

LOS 34.a: Describe corporate governance.

In the CFA Institute publication, *The Corporate Governance of Listed Companies: A Manual for Investors*[1], corporate governance is described as "the system of internal controls and procedures by which individual companies are managed. It provides a framework that defines the rights, roles and responsibilities of various groups . . . within an organization. At its core, corporate governance is the arrangement of checks, balances, and incentives a company needs in order to minimize and manage the conflicting interests between insiders and external shareowners."

Under **shareholder theory**, the primary focus of a system of corporate governance is the interests of the firm's shareholders, which are taken to be the maximization of the market value of the firm's common equity. Under this theory, corporate governance is primarily concerned with the conflict of interest between the firm's managers and its owners (shareholders).

The focus of corporate governance under **stakeholder theory** is broader; it considers conflicts among the several groups that have an interest in the activities and performance of the firm. These groups include shareholders, employees, suppliers, and customers, among others.

---

1. https://www.cfainstitute.org/learning/products/publications/readings/Pages/the_corporate_governance_of_listed_companies__a_manual_for_investors.aspx

LOS 34.b: Describe a company's stakeholder groups and compare interests of stakeholder groups.

The following have been identified as the primary stakeholders of a corporation.

Shareholders have a residual interest in the corporation in that they have claim to the net assets of the corporation after all liabilities have been settled. Shareholders have voting rights for the election of the board of directors and for other important corporate matters, which gives them effective control of the firm and its management. They have an interest in the ongoing profitability and growth of the firm, both of which can increase the value of their ownership shares.

The **board of directors** has a responsibility to protect the interests of shareholders; to hire, fire, and set the compensation of the firm's senior managers; to set the strategic direction of the firm; and to monitor financial performance and other aspects of the firm's ongoing activities.

Typically, the firm's executives (most-senior managers) serve on the board of directors, along with directors who are not otherwise employed by the firm. In a one-tier board structure, both company executives and non-executive board members serve on a single board of directors. In some countries, boards have a two-tier structure in which the non-executive board members serve on a supervisory board that oversees a management board, made up of company executives.

Senior managers typically receive compensation (remuneration) that is made up of a salary, a bonus based on some measure of company performance, and perquisites (e.g., expense accounts, use of company planes, special retirement benefits, vacation time off). Their interests can be expected to include continued employment and maximizing the total value of their compensation. Executive bonuses are typically tied to some measure of firm performance, giving senior managers a strong interest in the financial success of the firm.

Employees also have an interest in the sustainability and success of the firm. They have an interest in their rate of pay, opportunities for career advancement, training, and working conditions.

Creditors supply debt capital to the firm and are primarily owners of the firm's outstanding bonds and banks that have made loans to the firm. Providers of debt capital to the firm do not typically have a vote in firm management and do not participate in firm growth beyond receiving their promised interest and principal payments. The interests of creditors are protected to varying degrees by covenants in their debt agreements with the firm.

Suppliers of resources to the firm have an interest preserving an ongoing relationship with the firm, in the profitability of their trade with the firm, and in the growth and ongoing stability of the firm. As they are typically short-term creditors of the firm, they also have an interest in the firm's solvency and on-going financial strength.

Study Session 10
Cross-Reference to CFA Institute Assigned Reading #34 – Corporate Governance and ESG: An Introduction

LOS 34.c: Describe principal–agent and other relationships in corporate governance and the conflicts that may arise in these relationships.

The **principal-agent conflict** arises because an agent is hired to act in the interest of the principal, but an agent's interests may not coincide exactly with those of the principal. Consider an insurance agent who is paid a commission on policies written. It would be in the agent's interest to write insurance policies on people or property that are not good risks, in order to maximize commission income. The principal (the owners of the insurance company) does not want to issue policies that are bad risks as that is a money-losing proposition. Insurance companies mitigate this conflict by imposing underwriting standards for the policies they will issue and by continuing to work only with agents who consistently act in the company's best interest.

Conflicts of interest between shareholders and managers or directors

In the context of a corporation, shareholders are the principals (owners), and firm management and board members (directors) are their agents. Managers and directors may choose a lower level of business risk than shareholders would. This conflict can arise because the risk of company managers and directors is more dependent of firm performance compared to the risk of shareholders, who hold diversified portfolios of stocks and are not dependent on the firm for employment.

Conflicts may also arise when directors who are also managers favor management interests at the expense of shareholders or when directors favor one group of shareholders at the expense of another.

There is also an **information asymmetry** between shareholders and managers because managers have more and better information about the functioning of the firm and its strategic direction than shareholders do. This decreases the ability of shareholders or non-executive directors to monitor and evaluate whether managers are acting in the best interests of shareholders.

Conflicts between groups of shareholders

A single shareholder or group of shareholders may hold a majority of the votes and act against the interests of the minority shareholders. Some firms have different classes of common stock outstanding, some with more voting power than others. A group of shareholders may have effective control of the company although they have a claim to less than 50% of the earnings and assets of the company.

In the event of an acquisition of the company, controlling shareholders may be in a position to get better terms for themselves relative to the terms forced on minority shareholders. Majority shareholders may cause the company to enter into **related party transactions**, agreements or specific transactions that benefit entities in which they have a financial interest, to the detriment of minority shareholders.

Conflicts of interest between creditors and shareholders

Shareholders may prefer more business risk than creditors do because creditors have a limited upside from good results compared to shareholders. Equity owners could also act against the interests of creditors by issuing new debt that increases the default risk faced by existing debt holders, or by the company paying greater dividends to equity holders, thereby increasing creditors' risk of default.

Conflicts of interest between shareholders and other stakeholders

The company may decide to raise prices or reduce product quality in order to increase profits to the detriment of customers. The company may employ strategies that significantly reduce the taxes they pay to the government.

LOS 34.d: Describe stakeholder management.

LOS 34.e: Describe mechanisms to manage stakeholder relationships and mitigate associated risks.

Stakeholder management refers to the management of company relations with stakeholders and is based on having a good understanding of stakeholder interests and maintaining effective communication with stakeholders. The management of stakeholder relationships is based on four types of infrastructures:

1. The **legal infrastructure** identifies the laws relevant to and the legal recourse of stakeholders when their rights are violated.

2. The **contractual infrastructure** refers to the contracts between the company and its stakeholders that spell out the rights and responsibilities of the company and the stakeholders.

3. The **organizational infrastructure** refers to a company's corporate governance procedures, including its internal systems and practices that address how it manages its stakeholder relationships.

4. **Governmental infrastructure** comprises the regulations to which companies are subject.

With respect to the company's relationship with shareholders, there are standard practices. These practices are required by corporate laws and similar in many jurisdictions, although there are some differences across countries.

Corporations typically hold an **annual general meeting** after the end of the firm's fiscal year. At the general meeting, company management provides shareholders with the audited financial statements for the year, addresses the company's performance and significant actions over the period, and answers shareholder questions.

Corporate laws dictate when the annual general meeting may occur and how the meeting must be communicated to shareholders. Typically, anyone owning shares is permitted to attend the annual general meeting, to speak or ask questions, and to vote their shares. A shareholder who does not attend the annual general meeting can vote her shares by **proxy**, meaning she assigns her right to vote to another who will attend the meeting, often a director, member of management, or the shareholder's investment advisor. A proxy may specify the shareholder's vote on specific issues or leave the vote to the discretion of the person to whom the proxy is assigned.

Ordinary resolutions, such as approval of auditor and the election of directors, require a simple majority of the votes cast. Other resolutions, such as those regarding a merger or takeover, or that require amendment of corporate bylaws, are termed **special resolutions** and may require a supermajority vote for passage, typically two-thirds or three-fourths of the votes cast. Such special resolutions can also be addressed at **extraordinary general meetings**, which can be called anytime there is a resolution about a matter that requires a vote of the shareholders.

When there are multiple board member elections at one meeting, some companies use majority voting and some use cumulative voting. With **majority voting**, the candidate with the most votes for each single board position is elected. With **cumulative voting**, shareholders can cast all their votes (shares times number of board position elections) for a single board candidate or divide them among board candidates. Cumulative voting can result in greater minority shareholder representation on the board compared to majority voting.

Minority shareholders may have special rights by law when the company is acquired by another company.

LOS 34.f: Describe functions and responsibilities of a company's board of directors and its committees.

Board structure

A company may have any number of directors on its board. Companies often have directors with expertise in specific areas of the firm's business, such as risk management, finance, or industry strategy. In a **one-tier board**, there is a single board of directors that includes both internal and external directors. Internal directors (also called executive directors) are typically senior managers employed by the firm. External board members (also called non-executive directors) are those who are not company management. Non-executive directors who have no other relationship with the company are termed **independent directors**. Employee board representatives may be a significant portion of the non-executive directors.

In a **two-tier board** structure, there is a supervisory board that typically excludes executive directors. The supervisory board and the management board (made up of executive directors) operate independently. The management board is typically led by the company's CEO.

With a one-tier board, the chairman of the board is sometimes the company CEO. While this was common practice in the United States historically, separation of the

CEO and chairman of the board functions has become more common in recent years. When a **lead independent director** is appointed, he has the ability to call meetings of the independent directors, separate from meetings of the full board.

Currently, the general practice is for all board member elections to be held at the same meeting and each election to be for multiple years. With a **staggered board**, elections for some board positions are held each year. This structure limits the ability of shareholders to replace board members in any one year and is used less now than it has been historically.

Board responsibilities

The board of directors is elected by shareholders to act in their interest. Board members are typically mandated by corporate law to be fully informed and to use due diligence and their expertise in fulfilling their obligation to act in the interests of the company and its shareholders.

The board of directors is not involved in the day-to-day management of the company; that responsibility rests with senior management. The duties of the board include responsibility for:

- Selecting senior management, setting their compensation and bonus structure, evaluating their performance, and replacing them as needed.
- Setting the strategic direction for the company and making sure that management implements the strategy approved by the board.
- Approving capital structure changes, significant acquisitions, and large investment expenditures.
- Reviewing company performance and implementing any necessary corrective steps.
- Planning for continuity of management and the succession of the CEO and other senior managers.
- Establishing, monitoring, and overseeing the firm's internal controls and risk management system.
- Ensuring the quality of the firm's financial reporting and internal audit, as well as oversight of the external auditors.

Board committees

A board of directors typically has committees made up of board members with particular expertise. These committees report to the board, which retains the overall responsibility for the various board functions. The following are examples of typical board committees.

An **audit committee** is responsible for:

- Oversight of the financial reporting function and implementation of accounting policies.
- Effectiveness of the company's internal controls and the internal audit function.
- Recommending an external auditor and its compensation.
- Proposing remedies based on their review of internal and external audits.

A **governance committee** is responsible for:

- Oversight of the company's corporate governance code.
- Implementing the company's code of ethics and policies regarding conflicts of interest.
- Monitoring changes in relevant laws and regulations.
- Ensuring that the company is in compliance with all applicable laws and regulations, as well as with the company's governance policies.

A **nominations committee** proposes qualified candidates for election to the board, manages the search process, and attempts to align the board's composition with the company's corporate governance policies.

A **compensation committee** or **remuneration committee** recommends to the board the amounts and types of compensation to be paid to directors and senior managers. This committee may also be responsible for oversight of employee benefit plans and evaluation of senior managers.

A **risk committee** informs the board about appropriate risk policy and risk tolerance of the organization, and oversees the enterprise-wide risk management processes of the organization.

An **investment committee** reviews and reports to the board on management proposals for large acquisitions or projects, sale or other disposal of company assets or segments, and the performance of acquired assets and other large capital expenditures.

The number and size of board committees will depend on the size, complexity, and nature of the business. Regulations often require that firms have audit committees. Financial services firms are often required to have a risk committee as well. Some companies combine two functions into one committee. The composition of a board committee is often based on its function, with audit committees, compensation committees, and governance committees often made up of only non-executive or independent directors.

LOS 34.g: Describe market and non-market factors that can affect stakeholder relationships and corporate governance.

Several capital market factors can affect corporate governance and stakeholder relationships. Companies that work to have more communication and contact with shareholders, in addition to annual meetings and analyst meetings, have improved relations with shareholders who may be more likely to support management proposals and positions in the event of negative comments or pressure for change from dissident shareholder groups.

Activist shareholders pressure companies in which they hold a significant number of shares for changes, often changes they believe will increase shareholder value. They may bring pressure for change by initiating shareholder lawsuits or by seeking representation on the board of directors. Other activist tactics include proposing shareholder resolutions for a vote and raising their issues to all shareholders or the public to gain wider support. Hedge funds have, more and more, engaged in shareholder activism to increase the market values of firms in which they hold significant stakes.

A group may initiate a **proxy fight**, in which they seek the proxies of shareholders to vote in favor of their alternative proposals and policies. An activist group may make a **tender offer** for a specific number of shares of a company to gain enough votes to take over the company.

Both senior managers and boards of directors can be replaced by shareholders if they believe company performance is poor and would be improved by a change. The threat of a **hostile takeover**, one not supported by the company's management, can act as an incentive to influence company managements and boards to pursue policies more in alignment with the interests of shareholders and oriented toward increasing shareholder value.

Issues of corporate governance and conflicts of interest arise when company management proposes and the board passes anti-takeover measures to protect their jobs. Staggered board elections make a hostile takeover more costly and difficult.

An important non-market factor that can affect stakeholder relationships is the legal environment within which the company operates. Shareholders' and creditors' interests are considered to be better protected in countries with a **common-law system** under which judges' rulings become law in some instances. In a **civil law system**, judges are bound to rule based only on specifically enacted laws. In general, the rights of creditors are more clearly defined than those of shareholders and, therefore, are not as difficult to enforce through the courts.

In the past, corporate boards and managements have had an advantage in communicating through the media to influence shareholders or to shape public opinion. Advances in communications, especially through internet outlets and social media sites, have levelled the playing fields to a significant degree. It has become much easier for dissident shareholders to bring issues to the attention of other shareholders and to influence public opinion about certain issues. Among senior managers and board members, concern about their professional reputations has increased as a result. Media exposure can act as an important incentive for management to pursue policies that are consistent with the interests of shareholders and avoid egregious related-party transactions.

In 2003, the U.S. SEC mandated that U.S.-registered mutual funds institute policies and procedures to ensure that the proxies they hold for investors in their funds are voted in the best interests of fund investors. Prior to this, many funds that held shares for investors failed to devote resources to fulfill their responsibility to vote proxies. U.S. funds are also required to disclose their proxy voting records.

Overall, the increased focus on the importance of good corporate governance has given rise to a new industry focused on corporate governance, which includes firms that advise funds on proxy voting and corporate governance matters. Firms that provide ratings of companies' corporate governance practices offer another avenue to influence managements to better address the interests of shareholders.

LOS 34.h: Identify potential risks of poor corporate governance and stakeholder management and identify benefits from effective corporate governance and stakeholder management.

Risks of poor governance and stakeholder management

When corporate governance is weak, the control functions of audits and board oversight may be weak as well. The risk is that some stakeholders can gain an advantage, to the disadvantage of other stakeholders. Accounting fraud, or simply poor recordkeeping, will have negative implications for company performance and value.

When governance is weak and managers are not monitored, they may choose lower-than-optimal risk, reducing company value. Without proper monitoring and oversight, management may have incentive compensation that causes them to pursue their own benefit rather than the company's benefit. If they are allowed to engage in related-party transactions that benefit their friends or family, this will decrease company value.

Poor compliance procedures with respect to regulation and reporting can easily lead to legal and reputational risks. Violating stakeholder rights can lead to stakeholder lawsuits. A company's reputation can be damaged by failure to comply with governmental regulations. Failure to manage creditors' rights can lead to debt default and bankruptcy.

Benefits of effective governance and stakeholder management

Effective corporate governance can improve operational efficiency by ensuring that management and board member incentives align their interests well with those of shareholders. Effective governance implies effective control and monitoring. Just as weak control can lead to abuses, a strong system of controls and compliance with laws and regulations can avoid many legal and regulatory risks.

Formal policies regarding conflicts of interest and related party transactions can also lead to better operating results. Proper governance with respect to the interests of creditors can reduce the risk of debt default or bankruptcy, thereby reducing the cost of debt financing. Alignment of management interests with those of shareholders leads to better financial performance and greater company value.

LOS 34.i: Describe factors relevant to the analysis of corporate governance and stakeholder management.

In recent years, both analysts and markets have had an increased focus on effective corporate governance as an important factor in operational and financial performance. Elements of corporate governance that analysts have focused on include ownership and voting structures, board composition, management remuneration, the composition of shareholders, strength of shareholder rights, and management of long-term risks.

Company ownership and voting structure

Voting control of companies is typically proportional to share ownership because each share entitles its holder to one vote. In a **dual class structure**, one class of shares may be entitled to several votes per share, while another class of shares is entitled to one vote per share. This structure is often used to ensure that founding shareholders (and, later, their heirs) can maintain control of the board of directors even when their economic ownership is significantly less than 50%. Companies with a dual-class share structure have traded, on average, at a discount to comparable companies with a single class of shares.

Clearly, the interests of the owners of shares with multiple votes will take precedence over the interests of shareholders in general. Analysts will consider what the interests of the controlling shareholders are and how the ownership of the controlling shares is expected to change over time.

Composition of a company's board

Analysts may want to consider carefully the make-up of a company's board of directors. Important considerations are whether directors:

- Are executive, non-executive, or independent directors.
- Are involved in related-party transactions with the company.
- Have the diversity of expertise that suits the company's current strategy and challenges.
- Have served for many years and may have become too close to the company's management.

Overall, an analyst must decide if the board is responsive to shareholder interests or has conflicts of interest, and if the board has the mix of expertise that is needed to deal with challenges and pursue the best strategy for the company.

Management incentives and remuneration

In addition to salary, senior corporate managers often receive cash bonuses based on short-term performance metrics and bonuses based on longer-term equity performance, such as company shares or options to be awarded at future dates. While such plans are typically described as being a mechanism to align the interests of management and shareholders more closely, in many cases they may not do that well. Analysts may be concerned if:

- The remuneration plan seems to offer greater incentives, paid in cash, to achieve short-term performance goals at the expense of building long-term company value through equity-based incentives.
- Performance-based incentive pay is fairly stable over time, indicating that the performance targets are possibly easy to achieve.
- Management remuneration is very high relative to that of comparable companies in the industry.
- Management incentives are not aligned with current company strategy and objectives.

Composition of shareholders

If a significant portion of a company's outstanding shares are held by an affiliated company or institution, those shareholders may be able to exert enough influence to dictate the company's policies and direction. In some countries, it is quite common for one company to hold a large minority stake in another company. Some claim that such cross-holdings between companies lead to greater stability, better cooperation between the two companies, and a longer-term perspective on company performance. However, when the shareholder company tends to vote with management and to support board members with long tenure, it can hinder change by protecting the company from potential hostile takeovers and activist shareholders.

Activist shareholders and investors who buy shares in an attempt to profit from their activism can cause changes in the composition of a firm's shareholders, its board membership, and its corporate strategy in a relatively short period of time.

Relative strength of shareholders' rights

If the rights of shareholders are weak, perceived increases in shareholder returns from being acquired or from significant changes in corporate strategy may be difficult or impossible to realize. Examples of weak shareholders' rights are the existence of anti-takeover provisions in the corporate charter or bylaws, staggered boards, and a class of super voting shares, which all restrict the rights of shareholders to effect change.

Management of long-term risks

Analysts should be concerned if a company does not manage the risks of stakeholder conflicts well over time. A failure to manage stakeholder issues well or a failure to manage other long-term risks to the company's sustainability can have disastrous consequences for shareholders and others with interests tied to company results.

LOS 34.j: Describe environmental and social considerations in investment analysis.

Recently, investors have begun to consider environmental and social factors in making investment decisions. The use of environmental, social, and governance factors in making investment decisions is referred to as **ESG integration** or **ESG investing**. Many issues can be considered in this context, including harm or potential harm to the environment, risk of loss due to environmental accidents, the changing demographics of the workforce, and changing worker preferences.

ESG integration is also termed **sustainable investing** or **responsible investing** and sometimes **socially responsible investing**, although that term has previously referred to investing that integrates ethical or moral concerns into the portfolio selection process.

LOS 34.k: Describe how environmental, social, and governance factors may be used in investment analysis.

The most frequently used method of integrating ESG concerns into portfolio construction is **negative screening**, in which certain companies and certain sectors are excluded from portfolios. The mining and oil production sectors and companies that do not adhere to high standards of human rights may be excluded, for example.

In using the method of **positive screening**, no specific sectors are excluded from portfolios, but investors attempt to identify the companies with the best practices across environmental sustainability, employee rights and safety, and overall governance practices.

Impact investing refers to investing in order to promote specific social or environmental goals. This can be an investment in a specific company or project. Investors seek to make a profit while, at the same time, having a positive impact on society or the environment.

Thematic investing refers to investing based on a single goal, such as the development of alternative energy sources or clean water resources.

Key Concepts

LOS 34.a
Corporate governance refers to the internal controls and procedures of a company that delineate the rights and responsibilities of various groups and how conflicts of interest among the various groups are to be resolved.

LOS 34.b
The primary stakeholders of a corporation include shareholders, the board of directors, senior management, employees, creditors, and suppliers.

LOS 34.c
The principal-agent relationship refers to owners employing agents to act in their interests. Conflicts can arise because the agent's incentives may not align with those of the owner or, more generally, because the interests of one group within a corporation are not the same as those of other groups.

LOS 34.d
Stakeholder management refers to the management of the company relations with stakeholders and is based on having a good understanding of stakeholder interests and maintaining effective communication with stakeholders.

LOS 34.e
The management of stakeholder relationships is based on a company's legal, contractual, organizational, and government infrastructures.

LOS 34.f
The duties of a board of directors include:
- Selecting senior management, setting their compensation, and evaluating their performance.
- Setting the strategic direction for the company.
- Approving capital structure changes, significant acquisitions, and large investment expenditures.
- Reviewing company performance and implementing any necessary corrective steps.
- Planning for continuity of management and the succession of the CEO.
- Establishing, monitoring, and overseeing the firm's internal controls and risk management.
- Ensuring the quality of the firm's financial reporting and internal audit.

LOS 34.g
Factors that can affect stakeholder relationships and corporate governance include:
- Communication and engagement with shareholders.
- Shareholder activism.
- Threat of hostile takeover and existence of anti-takeover provisions.
- Company's legal environment.
- Growth of firms that advise funds on proxy voting and rate companies' corporate governance.

LOS 34.h
The risks of poor governance include weak control systems, poor decision making, legal risk, reputational risk, and default risk. Good corporate governance can improve operational efficiency and performance, reduce default risk, reduce the cost of debt, improve financial performance, and increase firm value.

LOS 34.i
Elements of corporate governance that analysts have found to be relevant include ownership and voting structures, board composition, management remuneration, the composition of shareholders, strength of shareholder rights, and management of long-term risks.

LOS 34.j
The use of environmental, social, and governance factors in making investment decisions is referred to as ESG integration or ESG investing. Many issues can be considered in this context, including harm or potential harm to the environment, risk of loss due to environmental accidents, the changing demographics of the workforce, and changing worker preferences.

LOS 34.k
Methods of integrating ESG concerns into portfolio construction are negative screening, positive screening, impact investing, and thematic investing.

Concept Checkers

1. The theory that deals with conflicts of interest between a company's owners and its creditors is *most appropriately* called:
   A. structure theory.
   B. stakeholder theory.
   C. shareholder theory.

2. For which two of a company's stakeholders does information asymmetry *most likely* make monitoring more difficult?
   A. Suppliers and employees.
   B. Employees and managers.
   C. Managers and shareholders.

3. The *least likely* item to be a requirement for good stakeholder management is:
   A. maintaining effective communication with other stakeholders.
   B. an understanding of the interests of several stakeholder groups.
   C. the ability to put aside the interests of one's stakeholder group.

4. An agreement between a company and a labor union that represents most of its employees would be *most appropriately* considered part of a company's:
   A. legal infrastructure.
   B. contractual infrastructure.
   C. organizational infrastructure.

5. The type of voting that is *most likely* to allow minority stockholders a greater representation on the board of directors is:
   A. majority voting.
   B. staggered voting.
   C. cumulative voting.

6. The type of resolution *most likely* to require a supermajority of shareholder votes for passage is a resolution to:
   A. acquire a company.
   B. choose a board member.
   C. approve the choice of an auditor.

7. The board of directors committee *most likely* to be responsible for monitoring the performance of a project that requires a large capital expenditure is the:
   A. risk committee.
   B. audit committee.
   C. investment committee.

8. The method of ESG integration that does not exclude any sectors but seeks to invest in the companies with the best practices regarding employee rights and environmental sustainability is:
   A. impact investing.
   B. positive screening.
   C. negative screening.

For more questions related to this topic review, log in to your Schweser online account and launch SchweserPro™ QBank; and for video instruction covering each LOS in this topic review, log in to your Schweser online account and launch the OnDemand video lectures, if you have purchased these products.

Study Session 10
Cross-Reference to CFA Institute Assigned Reading #34 – Corporate Governance and ESG: An Introduction

Answers – Concept Checkers

1. **B** Stakeholder theory focuses on the conflicts of interest among owners and several groups that have an interest in a company's activities, including creditors.

2. **C** Information asymmetry can exist between a company's shareholders and its managers because the company's managers may be much more knowledgeable about the company's functioning and strategic direction. This makes it more difficult for shareholders to monitor the firm's managers and determine whether they are acting in shareholders' interests.

3. **C** The ability to manage the conflicting interests of company relations with stakeholders requires good communication with stakeholders and a good understanding of their various interests.

4. **B** A company's contractual infrastructure refers to the contracts between the company and its stakeholders that specify the rights and responsibilities of each party.

5. **C** With cumulative voting, shareholders get a vote for each share they own times the number of director elections each year and can give all their votes to a single candidate for the board. This helps minority stockholders to get more proportional representation on the board of directors.

6. **A** Ordinary resolutions, such as those to appoint an auditor or elect a board member, require a simple majority. Acquisitions, mergers, takeovers, and amendments to the company bylaws often require a supermajority of more than 50% for passage.

7. **C** The investment committee reviews proposals for large acquisitions or projects and also monitors the performance of acquired assets and of projects requiring large capital expenditures.

8. **B** Positive screening does not exclude any sectors but seeks to invest in the companies with the best practices. Negative screening typically excludes some sectors. Impact investing refers to making an investment in a company or project in order to advance specific social or environmental goals.

The following is a review of the Corporate Finance principles designed to address the learning outcome statements set forth by CFA Institute. Cross-Reference to CFA Institute Assigned Reading #35.

CAPITAL BUDGETING

Study Session 10

EXAM FOCUS

If you recollect little from your basic financial management course in college (or if you didn't take one), you will need to spend some time on this review and go through the examples quite carefully. To be prepared for the exam, you need to know how to calculate all of the measures used to evaluate capital projects and the decision rules associated with them. Be sure you can interpret an NPV profile; one could be given as part of a question. Finally, know the reasoning behind the facts that (1) IRR and NPV give the same accept/reject decision for a single project and (2) IRR and NPV can give conflicting rankings for mutually exclusive projects.

LOS 35.a: Describe the capital budgeting process and distinguish among the various categories of capital projects.

The **capital budgeting process** is the process of identifying and evaluating capital projects, that is, projects where the cash flow to the firm will be received over a period longer than a year. Any corporate decisions with an impact on future earnings can be examined using this framework. Decisions about whether to buy a new machine, expand business in another geographic area, move the corporate headquarters to Cleveland, or replace a delivery truck, to name a few, can be examined using a capital budgeting analysis.

For a number of good reasons, capital budgeting may be the most important responsibility that a financial manager has. First, because a capital budgeting decision often involves the purchase of costly long-term assets with lives of many years, the decisions made may determine the future success of the firm. Second, the principles underlying the capital budgeting process also apply to other corporate decisions, such as working capital management and making strategic mergers and acquisitions. Finally, making good capital budgeting decisions is consistent with management's primary goal of maximizing shareholder value.

The capital budgeting process has four administrative steps:

Step 1: Idea generation. The most important step in the capital budgeting process is generating good project ideas. Ideas can come from a number of sources including senior management, functional divisions, employees, or sources outside the company.

Step 2: Analyzing project proposals. Because the decision to accept or reject a capital project is based on the project's expected future cash flows, a cash flow forecast must be made for each product to determine its expected profitability.

Step 3: Create the firm-wide capital budget. Firms must prioritize profitable projects according to the timing of the project's cash flows, available company resources, and the company's overall strategic plan. Many projects that are attractive individually may not make sense strategically.

Step 4: Monitoring decisions and conducting a post-audit. It is important to follow up on all capital budgeting decisions. An analyst should compare the actual results to the projected results, and project managers should explain why projections did or did not match actual performance. Because the capital budgeting process is only as good as the estimates of the inputs into the model used to forecast cash flows, a post-audit should be used to identify systematic errors in the forecasting process and improve company operations.

Categories of Capital Budgeting Projects

Capital budgeting projects may be divided into the following categories:

- *Replacement projects to maintain the business* are normally made without detailed analysis. The only issues are whether the existing operations should continue and, if so, whether existing procedures or processes should be maintained.
- *Replacement projects for cost reduction* determine whether equipment that is obsolete, but still usable, should be replaced. A fairly detailed analysis is necessary in this case.
- *Expansion projects* are taken on to grow the business and involve a complex decision-making process because they require an explicit forecast of future demand. A very detailed analysis is required.
- *New product or market development* also entails a complex decision-making process that will require a detailed analysis due to the large amount of uncertainty involved.
- *Mandatory projects* may be required by a governmental agency or insurance company and typically involve safety-related or environmental concerns. These projects typically generate little to no revenue, but they accompany new revenue-producing projects undertaken by the company.
- *Other projects.* Some projects are not easily analyzed through the capital budgeting process. Such projects may include a pet project of senior management (e.g., corporate perks) or a high-risk endeavor that is difficult to analyze with typical capital budgeting assessment methods (e.g., research and development projects).

LOS 35.b: Describe the basic principles of capital budgeting.

The capital budgeting process involves five key principles:

1. *Decisions are based on cash flows, not accounting income.* The relevant cash flows to consider as part of the capital budgeting process are **incremental cash flows**, the changes in cash flows that will occur if the project is undertaken.

   Sunk costs are costs that cannot be avoided, even if the project is not undertaken. Because these costs are not affected by the accept/reject decision, they should not be included in the analysis. An example of a sunk cost is a consulting fee paid to a marketing research firm to estimate demand for a new product prior to a decision on the project.

Externalities are the effects the acceptance of a project may have on other firm cash flows. The primary one is a negative externality called **cannibalization**, which occurs when a new project takes sales from an existing product. When considering externalities, the full implication of the new project (loss in sales of existing products) should be taken into account. An example of cannibalization is when a soft drink company introduces a diet version of an existing beverage. The analyst should subtract the lost sales of the existing beverage from the expected new sales of the diet version when estimated incremental project cash flows. A positive externality exists when doing the project would have a positive effect on sales of a firm's other product lines.

A project has a **conventional cash flow pattern** if the sign on the cash flows changes only once, with one or more cash outflows followed by one or more cash inflows. An **unconventional cash flow pattern** has more than one sign change. For example, a project might have an initial investment outflow, a series of cash inflows, and a cash outflow for asset retirement costs at the end of the project's life.

2. *Cash flows are based on opportunity costs.* **Opportunity costs** are cash flows that a firm will lose by undertaking the project under analysis. These are cash flows generated by an asset the firm already owns that would be forgone if the project under consideration is undertaken. Opportunity costs should be included in project costs. For example, when building a plant, even if the firm already owns the land, the cost of the land should be charged to the project because it could be sold if not used.

3. *The timing of cash flows is important.* Capital budgeting decisions account for the time value of money, which means that cash flows received earlier are worth more than cash flows to be received later.

4. *Cash flows are analyzed on an after-tax basis.* The impact of taxes must be considered when analyzing all capital budgeting projects. Firm value is based on cash flows they get to keep, not those they send to the government.

5. *Financing costs are reflected in the project's required rate of return.* Do not consider financing costs specific to the project when estimating incremental cash flows. The discount rate used in the capital budgeting analysis takes account of the firm's cost of capital. Only projects that are expected to return more than the cost of the capital needed to fund them will increase the value of the firm.

LOS 35.c: Explain how the evaluation and selection of capital projects is affected by mutually exclusive projects, project sequencing, and capital rationing.

Independent vs. Mutually Exclusive Projects

Independent projects are projects that are unrelated to each other and allow for each project to be evaluated based on its own profitability. For example, if projects A and B are independent, and both projects are profitable, then the firm could accept both projects. **Mutually exclusive** means that only one project in a set of possible projects can be accepted and that the projects compete with each other. If projects A and B were mutually exclusive, the firm could accept either Project A or Project B, but not both. A capital budgeting decision between two different stamping machines with different costs and output would be an example of choosing between two mutually exclusive projects.

Project Sequencing

Some projects must be undertaken in a certain order, or sequence, so that investing in a project today creates the opportunity to invest in other projects in the future. For example, if a project undertaken today is profitable, that may create the opportunity to invest in a second project a year from now. However, if the project undertaken today turns out to be unprofitable, the firm will not invest in the second project.

Unlimited Funds vs. Capital Rationing

If a firm has unlimited access to capital, the firm can undertake all projects with expected returns that exceed the cost of capital. Many firms have constraints on the amount of capital they can raise and must use *capital rationing*. If a firm's profitable project opportunities exceed the amount of funds available, the firm must ration, or prioritize, its capital expenditures with the goal of achieving the maximum increase in value for shareholders given its available capital.

LOS 35.d: Calculate and interpret net present value (NPV), internal rate of return (IRR), payback period, discounted payback period, and profitability index (PI) of a single capital project.

Net Present Value (NPV)

We first examined the calculation of net present value (NPV) in Quantitative Methods. The NPV is the sum of the present values of all the expected incremental cash flows if a project is undertaken. The discount rate used is the firm's cost of capital, adjusted for the risk level of the project. For a normal project, with an initial cash outflow followed by a series of expected after-tax cash inflows, the NPV is the present value of the expected inflows minus the initial cost of the project.

$$NPV = CF_0 + \frac{CF_1}{(1+k)^1} + \frac{CF_2}{(1+k)^2} + ... + \frac{CF_n}{(1+k)^n} = \sum_{t=0}^{n} \frac{CF_t}{(1+k)^t}$$

where:
CF_0 = initial investment outlay (a negative cash flow)
CF_t = after-tax cash flow at time t
k = required rate of return for project

A positive NPV project is expected to increase shareholder wealth, a negative NPV project is expected to decrease shareholder wealth, and a zero NPV project has no expected effect on shareholder wealth.

For *independent* projects, the *NPV decision rule* is simply to accept any project with a positive NPV and to reject any project with a negative NPV.

Example: NPV analysis

Using the project cash flows presented in Table 1, compute the NPV of each project's cash flows and determine for each project whether it should be accepted or rejected. Assume that the cost of capital is 10%.

Table 1: Expected Net After-Tax Cash Flows

Year (t)	Project A	Project B
0	−$2,000	−$2,000
1	1,000	200
2	800	600
3	600	800
4	200	1,200

Answer:

$$NPV_A = -2,000 + \frac{1,000}{(1.1)^1} + \frac{800}{(1.1)^2} + \frac{600}{(1.1)^3} + \frac{200}{(1.1)^4} = \$157.64$$

$$NPV_B = -2,000 + \frac{200}{(1.1)^1} + \frac{600}{(1.1)^2} + \frac{800}{(1.1)^3} + \frac{1,200}{(1.1)^4} = \$98.36$$

Both Project A and Project B have positive NPVs, so both should be accepted.

You may calculate the NPV directly by using the cash flow (CF) keys on your calculator. The process is illustrated in Table 2 and Table 3 for Project A.

Table 2: Calculating NPV$_A$ With the TI Business Analyst II Plus

Key Strokes	Explanation	Display
[CF] [2nd] [CLR WORK]	Clear memory registers	CF0 = 0.00000
2,000 [+/−] [ENTER]	Initial cash outlay	CF0 = −2,000.00000
[↓] 1,000 [ENTER]	Period 1 cash flow	C01 = 1,000.00000
[↓]	Frequency of cash flow 1	F01 = 1.00000
[↓] 800 [ENTER]	Period 2 cash flow	C02 = 800.00000
[↓]	Frequency of cash flow 2	F02 = 1.00000
[↓] 600 [ENTER]	Period 3 cash flow	C03 = 600.00000
[↓]	Frequency of cash flow 3	F03 = 1.00000
[↓] 200 [ENTER]	Period 4 cash flow	C04 = 200.00000
[↓]	Frequency of cash flow 4	F04 = 1.00000
[NPV] 10 [ENTER]	10% discount rate	I = 10.00000
[↓] [CPT]	Calculate NPV	NPV = 157.63951

Table 3: Calculating NPV$_A$ With the HP12C

Key Strokes	Explanation	Display
[f]→[FIN] → [f] → [REG]	Clear memory registers	0.00000
[f] [5]	Display 5 decimals. You only need to do this once.	0.00000
2,000 [CHS] [g] [CF0]	Initial cash outlay	−2,000.00000
1,000 [g] [CFj]	Period 1 cash flow	1,000.00000
800 [g] [CFj]	Period 2 cash flow	800.00000
600 [g] [CFj]	Period 3 cash flow	600.00000
200 [g] [CFj]	Period 4 cash flow	200.00000
10 [i]	10% discount rate	10.00000
[f] [NPV]	Calculate NPV	157.63951

Internal Rate of Return (IRR)

For a normal project, the **internal rate of return** (IRR) is the discount rate that makes the present value of the expected incremental after-tax cash inflows just equal to the initial cost of the project. More generally, the IRR is the discount rate that makes the present values of a project's estimated cash inflows equal to the present value of the project's estimated cash outflows. That is, IRR is the discount rate that makes the following relationship hold:

PV (inflows) = PV (outflows)

The IRR is also the discount rate for which the NPV of a project is equal to zero:

$$NPV = 0 = CF_0 + \frac{CF_1}{(1+IRR)^1} + \frac{CF_2}{(1+IRR)^2} + \ldots + \frac{CF_n}{(1+IRR)^n} = \sum_{t=0}^{n} \frac{CF_t}{(1+IRR)^t}$$

To calculate the IRR, you may use the trial-and-error method. That is, just keep guessing IRRs until you get the right one, or you may use a financial calculator.

IRR decision rule: First, determine the required rate of return for a given project. This is usually the firm's cost of capital. Note that the required rate of return may be higher or lower than the firm's cost of capital to adjust for differences between project risk and the firm's average project risk.

If IRR > the required rate of return, accept the project.

If IRR < the required rate of return, reject the project.

Example: IRR

Continuing with the cash flows presented in Table 1 for projects A and B, compute the IRR for each project and determine whether to accept or reject each project under the assumptions that the projects are independent and that the required rate of return is 10%.

Answer:

$$\text{Project A: } 0 = -2{,}000 + \frac{1{,}000}{(1+IRR_A)^1} + \frac{800}{(1+IRR_A)^2} + \frac{600}{(1+IRR_A)^3} + \frac{200}{(1+IRR_A)^4}$$

$$\text{Project B: } 0 = -2{,}000 + \frac{200}{(1+IRR_B)^1} + \frac{600}{(1+IRR_B)^2} + \frac{800}{(1+IRR_B)^3} + \frac{1{,}200}{(1+IRR_B)^4}$$

The cash flows should be entered as in Table 2 and Table 3 (if you haven't changed them, they are still there from the calculation of NPV).

With the TI calculator, the IRR can be calculated with:

[IRR] [CPT] to get 14.4888(%) for Project A and 11.7906(%) for Project B.

With the HP12C, the IRR can be calculated with:

[f] [IRR]

Both projects should be accepted because their IRRs are greater than the 10% required rate of return.

Payback Period

The **payback period** (PBP) is the number of years it takes to recover the initial cost of an investment.

Example: Payback period

Calculate the payback periods for the two projects that have the cash flows presented in Table 1. Note the Year 0 cash flow represents the initial cost of each project.

Answer:

Note that the cumulative net cash flow (NCF) is just the running total of the cash flows at the end of each time period. Payback will occur when the cumulative NCF equals zero. To find the payback periods, construct Table 4.

Table 4: Cumulative Net Cash Flows

	Year (t)	0	1	2	3	4
Project A	Net cash flow	–2,000	1,000	800	600	200
	Cumulative NCF	–2,000	–1,000	–200	400	600
Project B	Net cash flow	–2,000	200	600	800	1,200
	Cumulative NCF	–2,000	–1,800	–1,200	–400	800

The payback period is determined from the cumulative net cash flow table as follows:

$$\text{payback period} = \text{full years until recovery} + \frac{\text{unrecovered cost at the beginning of last year}}{\text{cash flow during the last year}}$$

$$\text{payback period A} = 2 + \frac{200}{600} = 2.33 \text{ years}$$

$$\text{payback period B} = 3 + \frac{400}{1200} = 3.33 \text{ years}$$

Because the payback period is a measure of liquidity, for a firm with liquidity concerns, the shorter a project's payback period, the better. However, project decisions should not be made on the basis of their payback periods because of the method's drawbacks.

The main drawbacks of the payback period are that it does not take into account either the time value of money or cash flows beyond the payback period, which means terminal or salvage value wouldn't be considered. These drawbacks mean that the payback period is useless as a measure of profitability.

The main benefit of the payback period is that it is a good measure of project liquidity. Firms with limited access to additional liquidity often impose a maximum payback period and then use a measure of profitability, such as NPV or IRR, to evaluate projects that satisfy this maximum payback period constraint.

Professor's Note: If you have the Professional model of the TI calculator, you can easily calculate the payback period and the discounted payback period (which follows). Once NPV is displayed, use the down arrow to scroll through NFV (net future value), to PB (payback), and DPB (discounted payback). You must use the compute key when "PB=" is displayed. If the annual net cash flows are equal, the payback period is simply project cost divided by the annual cash flow.

Discounted Payback Period

The **discounted payback period** uses the present values of the project's estimated cash flows. It is the number of years it takes a project to recover its initial investment in present value terms and, therefore, must be greater than the payback period without discounting.

Example: Discounted payback method

Compute the discounted payback period for projects A and B described in Table 5. Assume that the firm's cost of capital is 10% and the firm's maximum discounted payback period is four years.

Table 5: Cash Flows for Projects A and B

	Year (t)	0	1	2	3	4
Project A	Net Cash Flow	−2,000	1,000	800	600	200
	Discounted NCF	−2,000	910	661	451	137
	Cumulative DNCF	−2,000	−1,090	−429	22	159
Project B	Net Cash Flow	−2,000	200	600	800	1,200
	Discounted NCF	−2,000	182	496	601	820
	Cumulative DNCF	−2,000	−1,818	−1,322	−721	99

> **Answer:**
>
> $$\text{discounted payback A} = 2 + \frac{429}{451} = 2.95 \text{ years}$$
>
> $$\text{discounted payback B} = 3 + \frac{721}{820} = 3.88 \text{ years}$$

The discounted payback period addresses one of the drawbacks of the payback period by discounting cash flows at the project's required rate of return. However, the discounted payback period still does not consider any cash flows beyond the payback period, which means that it is a poor measure of profitability. Again, its use is primarily as a measure of liquidity.

Profitability Index (PI)

The **profitability index** (PI) is the present value of a project's future cash flows divided by the initial cash outlay:

$$PI = \frac{\text{PV of future cash flows}}{CF_0} = 1 + \frac{NPV}{CF_0}$$

The profitability index is related closely to net present value. The NPV is the difference between the present value of future cash flows and the initial cash outlay, and the PI is the ratio of the present value of future cash flows to the initial cash outlay.

If the NPV of a project is positive, the PI will be greater than one. If the NPV is negative, the PI will be less than one. It follows that the *decision rule* for the PI is:

If PI > 1.0, accept the project.

If PI < 1.0, reject the project.

Example: Profitability index

Going back to our original example, calculate the PI for projects A and B. Note that Table 1 has been reproduced as Table 6.

Table 6: Expected Net After-Tax Cash Flows

Year (t)	Project A	Project B
0	–$2,000	–$2,000
1	1,000	200
2	800	600
3	600	800
4	200	1,200

Answer:

$$\text{PV future cash flows}_A = \frac{1{,}000}{(1.1)^1} + \frac{800}{(1.1)^2} + \frac{600}{(1.1)^3} + \frac{200}{(1.1)^4} = \$2{,}157.64$$

$$PI_A = \frac{\$2{,}157.64}{\$2{,}000} = 1.079$$

$$\text{PV future cash flows}_B = \frac{200}{(1.1)^1} + \frac{600}{(1.1)^2} + \frac{800}{(1.1)^3} + \frac{1{,}200}{(1.1)^4} = \$2{,}098.36$$

$$PI_B = \frac{\$2{,}098.36}{\$2{,}000} = 1.049$$

Decision: If projects A and B are independent, accept both projects because PI > 1 for both projects.

Professor's Note: The accept/reject decision rule here is exactly equivalent to both the NPV and IRR decision rules. That is, if PI > 1, then the NPV must be positive, and the IRR must be greater than the discount rate. Note also that once you have the NPV, you can just add back the initial outlay to get the PV of the cash inflows used here. Recall that the NPV of Project B is $98.36 with an initial cost of $2,000. PI is simply (2,000 + 98.36) / 2000.

LOS 35.e: Explain the NPV profile, compare the NPV and IRR methods when evaluating independent and mutually exclusive projects, and describe the problems associated with each of the evaluation methods.

A project's **NPV profile** is a graph that shows a project's NPV for different discount rates. The NPV profiles for the two projects described in the previous example are presented in Figure 1. The project NPVs are summarized in the table below the graph. The discount rates are on the x-axis of the NPV profile, and the corresponding NPVs are plotted on the y-axis.

Figure 1: NPV Profiles

Discount Rate	NPV_A	NPV_B
0%	600.00	800.00
5%	360.84	413.00
10%	157.64	98.36
15%	(16.66)	(160.28)

Note that the projects' IRRs are the discount rates where the NPV profiles intersect the x-axis, because these are the discount rates for which NPV equals zero. Recall that the IRR is the discount rate that results in an NPV of zero.

Also notice in Figure 1 that the NPV profiles intersect. They intersect at the discount rate for which NPVs of the projects are equal, 7.2%. This rate at which the NPVs are equal is called the **crossover rate**. At discount rates below 7.2% (to the left of the intersection), Project B has the greater NPV, and at discount rates above 7.2%, Project A has a greater NPV. Clearly, the discount rate used in the analysis can determine which one of two mutually exclusive projects will be accepted.

The NPV profiles for projects A and B intersect because of a difference in the timing of the cash flows. Examining the cash flows for the projects (Table 1), we can see that the total cash inflows for Project B are greater ($2,800) than those of Project A ($2,600). Because they both have the same initial cost ($2,000) at a discount rate of zero, Project B has a greater NPV (2,800 − 2,000 = $800) than Project A (2,600 − 2,000 = $600).

We can also see that the cash flows for Project B come later in the project's life. That's why the NPV of Project B falls faster than the NPV of Project A as the discount rate increases, and the NPVs are eventually equal at a discount rate of 7.2%. At discount rates above 7.2%, the fact that the total cash flows of Project B are greater in nominal dollars is overridden by the fact that Project B's cash flows come later in the project's life than those of Project A.

> **Example: Crossover rate**
>
> Two projects have the following cash flows:
>
> | | 20X1 | 20X2 | 20X3 | 20X4 |
> |-----------|------|------|------|------|
> | Project A | −550 | 150 | 300 | 450 |
> | Project B | −300 | 50 | 200 | 300 |
>
> What is the crossover rate for Project A and Project B?
>
> **Answer:**
>
> The crossover rate is the discount rate that makes the NPVs of Projects A and B equal. That is, it makes the NPV of the *differences between* the two projects' cash flows equal zero.
>
> To determine the crossover rate, subtract the cash flows of Project B from those of Project A and calculate the IRR of the differences.
>
> | | 20X1 | 20X2 | 20X3 | 20X4 |
> |-----------------------|------|------|------|------|
> | Project A − Project B | −250 | 100 | 100 | 150 |
>
> CF0 = −250; CF1 = 100; CF2 = 100; CF3 = 150; CPT IRR = 17.5%

The Relative Advantages and Disadvantages of the NPV and IRR Methods

A **key advantage of NPV** is that it is a direct measure of the expected increase in the value of the firm. NPV is theoretically the best method. Its main weakness is that it does not include any consideration of the size of the project. For example, an NPV of $100 is great for a project costing $100 but not so great for a project costing $1 million.

A **key advantage of IRR** is that it measures profitability as a percentage, showing the return on each dollar invested. The IRR provides information on the margin of safety that the NPV does not. From the IRR, we can tell how much below the IRR (estimated return) the actual project return could fall, in percentage terms, before the project becomes uneconomic (has a negative NPV).

The *disadvantages* of the IRR method are (1) the possibility of producing rankings of mutually exclusive projects different from those from NPV analysis and (2) the possibility that a project has multiple IRRs or no IRR.

Conflicting Project Rankings

Consider two projects with an initial investment of €1,000 and a required rate of return of 10%. Project X will generate cash inflows of €500 at the end of each of the next five years. Project Y will generate a single cash flow of €4,000 at the end of the fifth year.

Year	Project X	Project Y
0	–€1,000	–€1,000
1	500	0
2	500	0
3	500	0
4	500	0
5	500	4,000
NPV	€895	€1,484
IRR	41.0%	32.0%

Project X has a higher IRR, but Project Y has a higher NPV. Which is the better project? If Project X is selected, the firm will be worth €895 more because the PV of the expected cash flows is €895 more than the initial cost of the project. Project Y, however, is expected to increase the value of the firm by €1,484. Project Y is the better project. Because NPV measures the expected increase in wealth from undertaking a project, NPV is the only acceptable criterion when ranking projects.

Another reason, besides cash flow timing differences, that NPV and IRR may give conflicting project rankings is differences in project size. Consider two projects, one with an initial outlay of $100,000, and one with an initial outlay of $1 million. The smaller project may have a higher IRR, but the increase in firm value (NPV) may be small compared to the increase in firm value (NPV) of the larger project, even though its IRR is lower.

It is sometimes said that the NPV method implicitly assumes that project cash flows can be reinvested at the discount rate used to calculate NPV. This is a realistic assumption, because it is reasonable to assume that project cash flows could be used to reduce the firm's capital requirements. Any funds that are used to reduce the firm's capital requirements allow the firm to avoid the cost of capital on those funds. Just by reducing its equity capital and debt, the firm could "earn" its cost of capital on funds used to reduce its capital requirements. If we were to rank projects by their IRRs, we would be implicitly assuming that project cash flows could be reinvested at the project's IRR. This is unrealistic and, strictly speaking, if the firm could earn that rate on invested funds, that rate should be the one used to discount project cash flows.

The "Multiple IRR" and "No IRR" Problems

If a project has cash outflows during its life or at the end of its life in addition to its initial cash outflow, the project is said to have an unconventional cash flow pattern. Projects with such cash flows may have more than one IRR (there may be more than one discount rate that will produce an NPV equal to zero).

It is also possible to have a project where there is no discount rate that results in a zero NPV, that is, the project does not have an IRR. A project with no IRR may actually be a profitable project. The lack of an IRR results from the project having unconventional cash flows, where mathematically, no IRR exists. NPV does not have this problem and produces theoretically correct decisions for projects with unconventional cash flow patterns.

Neither of these problems can arise with the NPV method. If a project has non-normal cash flows, the NPV method will give the appropriate accept/reject decision.

LOS 35.f: Describe expected relations among an investment's NPV, company value, and share price.

Because the NPV method is a direct measure of the expected change in firm value from undertaking a capital project, it is also the criterion most related to stock prices. In theory, a positive NPV project should cause a proportionate increase in a company's stock price.

> **Example: Relationship between NPV and stock price**
>
> Presstech is investing $500 million in new printing equipment. The present value of the future after-tax cash flows resulting from the equipment is $750 million. Presstech currently has 100 million shares outstanding, with a current market price of $45 per share. Assuming that this project is new information and is independent of other expectations about the company, calculate the effect of the new equipment on the value of the company and the effect on Presstech's stock price.
>
> **Answer:**
>
> NPV of the new printing equipment project = $750 million − $500 million = $250 million.
>
> Value of company prior to new equipment project = 100 million shares × $45 per share = $4.5 billion.
>
> Value of company after new equipment project = $4.5 billion + $250 million = $4.75 billion.
>
> Price per share after new equipment project = $4.75 billion / 100 million shares = $47.50.
>
> The stock price should increase from $45.00 per share to $47.50 per share as a result of the project.

In reality, the impact of a project on the company's stock price is more complicated than the previous example. A company's stock price is a function of the present value of its expected future earnings stream. As a result, changes in the stock price will result more from changes in *expectations* about a firm's positive NPV projects. If a company announces a project for which managers expect a positive NPV but analysts expect a lower level of profitability from the project than the company does (e.g., an acquisition), the stock price may actually drop on the announcement. As another example, a project announcement may be taken as a signal about other future capital projects, raising expectations and resulting in a stock price increase that is much greater than what the NPV of the announced project would justify.

Key Concepts

LOS 35.a
Capital budgeting is the process of evaluating capital projects, projects with cash flows over more than one year.

The four steps of the capital budgeting process are: (1) Generate investment ideas; (2) Analyze project ideas; (3) Create firm-wide capital budget; and (4) Monitor decisions and conduct a post-audit.

Categories of capital projects include: (1) Replacement projects for maintaining the business or for cost reduction; (2) Expansion projects; (3) New product or market development; (4) Mandatory projects to meet environmental or regulatory requirements; (5) Other projects, such as research and development or pet projects of senior management.

LOS 35.b
Capital budgeting decisions should be based on incremental after-tax cash flows, the expected differences in after-tax cash flows if a project is undertaken. Sunk (already incurred) costs are not considered, but externalities and cash opportunity costs must be included in project cash flows.

LOS 35.c
Acceptable independent projects can all be undertaken, while a firm must choose between or among mutually exclusive projects.

Project sequencing concerns the opportunities for future capital projects that may be created by undertaking a current project.

If a firm cannot undertake all profitable projects because of limited ability to raise capital, the firm should choose that group of fundable positive NPV projects with the highest total NPV.

LOS 35.d
NPV is the sum of the present values of a project's expected cash flows and represents the increase in firm value from undertaking a project. Positive NPV projects should be undertaken, but negative NPV projects are expected to decrease the value of the firm.

The IRR is the discount rate that equates the present values of the project's expected cash inflows and outflows and, thus, is the discount rate for which the NPV of a project is zero. A project for which the IRR is greater (less) than the discount rate will have an NPV that is positive (negative) and should be accepted (not be accepted).

The payback (discounted payback) period is the number of years required to recover the original cost of the project (original cost of the project in present value terms).

The profitability index is the ratio of the present value of a project's future cash flows to its initial cash outlay and is greater than one when a project's NPV is positive.

LOS 35.e

An NPV profile plots a project's NPV as a function of the discount rate, and it intersects the horizontal axis (NPV = 0) at its IRR. If two NPV profiles intersect at some discount rate, that is the crossover rate, and different projects are preferred at discount rates higher and lower than the crossover rate.

For projects with conventional cash flow patterns, the NPV and IRR methods produce the same accept/reject decision, but projects with unconventional cash flow patterns can produce multiple IRRs or no IRR.

Mutually exclusive projects can be ranked based on their NPVs, but rankings based on other methods will not necessarily maximize the value of the firm.

LOS 35.f

The NPV method is a measure of the expected change in company value from undertaking a project. A firm's stock price may be affected to the extent that engaging in a project with that NPV was previously unanticipated by investors.

Study Session 10
Cross-Reference to CFA Institute Assigned Reading #35 – Capital Budgeting

Concept Checkers

1. Which of the following statements concerning the principles underlying the capital budgeting process is *most accurate*?
   A. Cash flows should be based on opportunity costs.
   B. Financing costs should be reflected in a project's incremental cash flows.
   C. The net income for a project is essential for making a correct capital budgeting decision.

2. Which of the following statements about the payback period method is *least accurate*? The payback period:
   A. provides a rough measure of a project's liquidity.
   B. considers all cash flows throughout the entire life of a project.
   C. is the number of years it takes to recover the original cost of the investment.

3. Which of the following statements about NPV and IRR is *least accurate*?
   A. The IRR is the discount rate that equates the present value of the cash inflows with the present value of outflows.
   B. For mutually exclusive projects, if the NPV method and the IRR method give conflicting rankings, the analyst should use the IRRs to select the project.
   C. The NPV method assumes that cash flows will be reinvested at the cost of capital, while IRR rankings implicitly assume that cash flows are reinvested at the IRR.

4. Which of the following statements is *least accurate*? The discounted payback period:
   A. frequently ignores terminal values.
   B. is generally shorter than the regular payback.
   C. is the time it takes for the present value of the project's cash inflows to equal the initial cost of the investment.

5. Which of the following statements about NPV and IRR is *least accurate*?
   A. The IRR can be positive even if the NPV is negative.
   B. When the IRR is equal to the cost of capital, the NPV will be zero.
   C. The NPV will be positive if the IRR is less than the cost of capital.

Use the following data to answer Questions 6 through 10.

A company is considering the purchase of a copier that costs $5,000. Assume a required rate of return of 10% and the following cash flow schedule:

- Year 1: $3,000.
- Year 2: $2,000.
- Year 3: $2,000.

6. What is the project's payback period?
   A. 1.5 years.
   B. 2.0 years.
   C. 2.5 years.

7. The project's discounted payback period is *closest* to:
   A. 1.4 years.
   B. 2.0 years.
   C. 2.4 years.

8. What is the project's NPV?
   A. −$309.
   B. +$883.
   C. +$1,523.

9. The project's IRR is *closest* to:
   A. 10%.
   B. 15%.
   C. 20%.

10. What is the project's profitability index (PI)?
    A. 0.72.
    B. 1.18.
    C. 1.72.

11. An analyst has gathered the following information about a project:
    - Cost $10,000
    - Annual cash inflow $4,000
    - Life   4 years
    - Cost of capital   12%

    Which of the following statements about the project is *least accurate*?
    A. The discounted payback period is 3.5 years.
    B. The IRR of the project is 21.9%; accept the project.
    C. The NPV of the project is +$2,149; accept the project.

Use the following data for Questions 12 and 13.

An analyst has gathered the following data about two projects, each with a 12% required rate of return.

	Project Y	Project Z
Initial cost	$15,000	$20,000
Life	5 years	4 years
Cash inflows	$5,000/year	$7,500/year

12. If the projects are independent, the company should:
    A. accept Project Y and reject Project Z.
    B. reject Project Y and accept Project Z.
    C. accept both projects.

13. If the projects are mutually exclusive, the company should:
    A. reject both projects.
    B. accept Project Y and reject Project Z.
    C. reject Project Y and accept Project Z.

14. The NPV profiles of two projects will intersect:
    A. at their internal rates of return.
    B. if they have different discount rates.
    C. at the discount rate that makes their net present values equal.

15. The post-audit is used to:
    A. improve cash flow forecasts and stimulate management to improve operations and bring results into line with forecasts.
    B. improve cash flow forecasts and eliminate potentially profitable but risky projects.
    C. stimulate management to improve operations, bring results into line with forecasts, and eliminate potentially profitable but risky projects.

16. Fullen Machinery is investing $400 million in new industrial equipment. The present value of the future after-tax cash flows resulting from the equipment is $700 million. Fullen currently has 200 million shares of common stock outstanding, with a current market price of $36 per share. Assuming that this project is new information and is independent of other expectations about the company, what is the theoretical effect of the new equipment on Fullen's stock price? The stock price will:
    A. decrease to $33.50.
    B. increase to $37.50.
    C. increase to $39.50.

For more questions related to this topic review, log in to your Schweser online account and launch SchweserPro™ QBank; and for video instruction covering each LOS in this topic review, log in to your Schweser online account and launch the OnDemand video lectures, if you have purchased these products.

Answers – Concept Checkers

1. **A** Cash flows are based on opportunity costs. Financing costs are recognized in the project's required rate of return. Accounting net income, which includes non-cash expenses, is irrelevant; incremental cash flows are essential for making correct capital budgeting decisions.

2. **B** The payback period ignores cash flows that go beyond the payback period.

3. **B** NPV should always be used if NPV and IRR give conflicting decisions.

4. **B** The discounted payback is longer than the regular payback because cash flows are discounted to their present value.

5. **C** If IRR is less than the cost of capital, the result will be a negative NPV.

6. **B** Cash flow (CF) after year 2 = –5,000 + 3,000 + 2,000 = 0. Cost of copier is paid back in the first two years.

7. **C** Year 1 discounted cash flow = 3,000 / 1.10 = 2,727; year 2 DCF = 2,000 / 1.10^2 = 1,653; year 3 DCF = 2,000 / 1.10^3 = 1,503. CF required after year 2 = –5,000 + 2,727 + 1,653 = –$620, 620 / year 3 DCF = 620 / 1,503 = 0.41, for a discounted payback of 2.4 years.

    Using a financial calculator:
    Year 1: I = 10%; FV = 3,000; N = 1; PMT = 0; CPT → PV = –2,727
    Year 2: N = 2; FV = 2,000; CPT → PV = –1,653
    Year 3: N = 3; CPT → PV = –1,503
    5,000 – (2,727 + 1,653) = 620, 620 / 1,503 = 0.413, so discounted payback = 2 + 0.4 = 2.4.

8. **B** NPV = CF_0 + (discounted cash flows years 0 to 3 calculated in Question 7) = –5,000 + (2,727 + 1,653 + 1,503) = –5,000 + 5,833 = $883.

9. **C** From the information given, you know the NPV is positive, so the IRR must be greater than 10%. You only have two choices, 15% and 20%. Pick one and solve the NPV; if it's not close to zero, you guessed wrong—pick the other one. Alternatively, you can solve directly for the IRR as CF_0 = –5,000, CF_1 = 3,000, CF_2 = 2,000, CF_3 = 2,000. IRR = 20.64%.

10. **B** PI = PV of future cash flows / CF_0 (discounted cash flows years 0 to 3 calculated in Question 7). PI = (2,727 + 1,653 + 1,503) / 5,000 = 1.177.

11. **A** The discounted payback period of 3.15 is calculated as follows:

    $CF_0 = -10{,}000$; $PVCF_1 = \dfrac{4{,}000}{1.12} = 3{,}571$; $PVCF_2 = \dfrac{4{,}000}{1.12^2} = 3{,}189$; $PVCF_3 = \dfrac{4{,}000}{1.12^3} = 2{,}847$;

    and $PVCF_4 = \dfrac{4{,}000}{1.12^4} = 2{,}542$. CF after year 3 = –10,000 + 3,571 + 3,189 + 2,847 = –393

    $\dfrac{393}{\text{year 4 DCF}} = \dfrac{393}{2{,}542} = 0.15$, for a discounted payback period of 3.15 years.

12. **C** Independent projects accept all with positive NPVs or IRRs greater than cost of capital. NPV computation is easy—treat cash flows as an annuity.

    Project Y: N = 5; I = 12; PMT = 5,000; FV = 0; CPT → PV = –18,024
    NPV_A = 18,024 – 15,000 = $3,024

    Project Z: N = 4; I = 12; PMT = 7,500; FV = 0; CPT → PV = –22,780
    NPV_B = 22,780 – 20,000 = $2,780

13. **B** Accept the project with the highest NPV.

14. **C** The crossover rate for the NPV profiles of two projects occurs at the discount rate that results in both projects having equal NPVs.

15. **A** A post-audit identifies what went right and what went wrong. It is used to improve forecasting and operations.

16. **B** The NPV of the new equipment is $700 million – $400 million = $300 million. The value of this project is added to Fullen's current market value. On a per-share basis, the addition is worth $300 million / 200 million shares, for a net addition to the share price of $1.50. $36.00 + $1.50 = $37.50.

The following is a review of the Corporate Finance principles designed to address the learning outcome statements set forth by CFA Institute. Cross-Reference to CFA Institute Assigned Reading #36.

COST OF CAPITAL

Study Session 10

EXAM FOCUS

The firm must decide how to raise the capital to fund its business or finance its growth, dividing it among common equity, debt, and preferred stock. The mix that produces the minimum overall cost of capital will maximize the value of the firm (share price). From this topic review, you must understand weighted average cost of capital and its calculation and be ready to calculate the costs of common equity, preferred stock, and the after-tax cost of debt. Don't worry about choosing among the methods for calculating the cost of common equity; the information given in the question will make it clear which one to use. You must know all these methods and understand why the marginal cost of capital increases as greater amounts of capital are raised over a given period (usually taken to be a year).

LOS 36.a: Calculate and interpret the weighted average cost of capital (WACC) of a company.

LOS 36.b: Describe how taxes affect the cost of capital from different capital sources.

The capital budgeting process involves discounted cash flow analysis. To conduct such analysis, you must know the firm's proper discount rate. This topic review discusses how, as an analyst, you can determine the proper rate at which to discount the cash flows associated with a capital budgeting project. This discount rate is the firm's **weighted average cost of capital** (WACC) and is also referred to as the **marginal cost of capital** (MCC).

Basic definitions. On the right (liability) side of a firm's balance sheet, we have debt, preferred stock, and common equity. These are normally referred to as the *capital components* of the firm. Any increase in a firm's total assets will have to be financed through an increase in at least one of these capital accounts. The cost of each of these components is called the *component cost* of capital.

Throughout this review, we focus on the following capital components and their component costs:

k_d The rate at which the firm can issue new debt. This is the yield to maturity on existing debt. This is also called the before-tax component cost of debt.

$k_d(1-t)$ The after-tax cost of debt. Here, t is the firm's marginal tax rate. The after-tax component cost of debt, $k_d(1-t)$, is used to calculate the WACC.

k_{ps} The cost of preferred stock.

k_{ce} The cost of common equity. It is the required rate of return on common stock and is generally difficult to estimate.

In many countries, the interest paid on corporate debt is tax deductible. Because we are interested in the after-tax cost of capital, we adjust the cost of debt, k_d, for the firm's marginal tax rate, *t*. Because there is typically no tax deduction allowed for payments to common or preferred stockholders, there is no equivalent deduction to k_{ps} or k_{ce}.

How a company raises capital and how it budgets or invests it are considered independently. Most companies have separate departments for the two tasks. The financing department is responsible for keeping costs low and using a balance of funding sources: common equity, preferred stock, and debt. Generally, it is necessary to raise each type of capital in large sums. The large sums may temporarily overweight the most recently issued capital, but in the long run, the firm will adhere to target weights. Because of these and other financing considerations, each investment decision must be made assuming a WACC, which includes each of the different sources of capital and is based on the long-run target weights. A company creates value by producing a return on assets that is higher than the required rate of return on the capital needed to fund those assets.

The WACC, as we have described it, is the cost of financing firm assets. We can view this cost as an opportunity cost. Consider how a company could reduce its costs if it found a way to produce its output using fewer assets, like less working capital. If we need less working capital, we can use the funds freed up to buy back our debt and equity securities in a mix that just matches our target capital structure. Our after-tax savings would be the WACC based on our target capital structure multiplied by the total value of the securities that are no longer outstanding.

For these reasons, any time we are considering a project that requires expenditures, comparing the return on those expenditures to the WACC is the appropriate way to determine whether undertaking that project will increase the value of the firm. This is the essence of the capital budgeting decision. Because a firm's WACC reflects the average risk of the projects that make up the firm, it is not appropriate for evaluating all new projects. It should be adjusted upward for projects with greater-than-average risk and downward for projects with less-than-average risk.

The weights in the calculation of a firm's WACC are the proportions of each source of capital in a firm's capital structure.

Calculating a Company's Weighted Average Cost of Capital

The WACC is given by:

$$\text{WACC} = (w_d)[k_d(1-t)] + (w_{ps})(k_{ps}) + (w_{ce})(k_{ce})$$

where:
w_d = percentage of debt in the capital structure
w_{ps} = percentage of preferred stock in the capital structure
w_{ce} = percentage of common stock in the capital structure

> **Example: Computing WACC**
>
> Suppose Dexter, Inc.'s target capital structure is as follows:
>
> $w_d = 0.45$, $w_{ps} = 0.05$, and $w_{ce} = 0.50$
>
> Its before-tax cost of debt is 8%, its cost of equity is 12%, its cost of preferred stock is 8.4%, and its marginal tax rate is 40%. Calculate Dexter's WACC.
>
> **Answer:**
>
> Dexter's WACC will be:
>
> $$WACC = (w_d)(k_d)(1 - t) + (w_{ps})(k_{ps}) + (w_{ce})(k_{ce})$$
>
> $$WACC = (0.45)(0.08)(0.6) + (0.05)(0.084) + (0.50)(0.12) = 0.0858 \cong 8.6\%$$

LOS 36.c: Describe the use of target capital structure in estimating WACC and how target capital structure weights may be determined.

The weights in the calculation of WACC should be based on the firm's target capital structure; that is, the proportions (based on market values) of debt, preferred stock, and equity that the firm expects to achieve over time. In the absence of any explicit information about a firm's target capital structure from the firm itself, an analyst may simply use the firm's current capital structure (based on market values) as the best indication of its target capital structure. If there has been a noticeable trend in the firm's capital structure, the analyst may want to incorporate this trend into his estimate of the firm's target capital structure. For example, if a firm has been reducing its proportion of debt financing each year for two or three years, the analyst may wish to use a weight on debt that is lower than the firm's current weight on debt in constructing the firm's target capital structure.

Alternatively, an analyst may wish to use the industry average capital structure as the target capital structure for a firm under analysis.

> **Example: Determining target capital structure weights**
>
> The market values of a firm's capital are as follows:
>
> - Debt outstanding: $8 million
> - Preferred stock outstanding: $2 million
> - Common stock outstanding: $10 million
> - Total capital: $20 million
>
> What is the firm's target capital structure based on its existing capital structure?

> **Answer:**
>
> debt 40%, w_d = 0.40
>
> preferred stock 10%, w_{ps} = 0.10
>
> common stock 50%, w_{ce} = 0.50
>
> For the industry average approach, we would simply use the arithmetic average of the current market weights (for each capital source) from a sample of industry firms.

LOS 36.d: Explain how the marginal cost of capital and the investment opportunity schedule are used to determine the optimal capital budget.

A company increases its value and creates wealth for its shareholders by earning more on its investment in assets than is required by those who provide the capital for the firm. A firm's WACC may increase as larger amounts of capital are raised. Thus, its marginal cost of capital, the cost of raising additional capital, can increase as larger amounts are invested in new projects. This is illustrated by the upward-sloping **marginal cost of capital curve** in Figure 1. Given the expected returns (IRRs) on potential projects, we can order the expenditures on additional projects from highest to lowest IRR. This will allow us to construct a downward sloping **investment opportunity schedule**, such as that shown in Figure 1.

Figure 1: The Optimal Capital Budget

The intersection of the investment opportunity schedule with the marginal cost of capital curve identifies the amount of the **optimal capital budget**. The intuition here is that the firm should undertake all those projects with IRRs greater than the cost of funds, the same criterion developed in the capital budgeting topic review. This will maximize the value created. At the same time, no projects with IRRs less than the marginal cost of the additional capital required to fund them should be undertaken, as they will erode the value created by the firm.

LOS 36.e: Explain the marginal cost of capital's role in determining the net present value of a project.

One cautionary note regarding the simple logic behind Figure 1 is in order. All projects do not have the same risk. The WACC is the appropriate discount rate for projects that have approximately the same level of risk as the firm's existing projects. This is because the component costs of capital used to calculate the firm's WACC are based on the existing level of firm risk. To evaluate a project with greater than (the firm's) average risk, a discount rate greater than the firm's existing WACC should be used. Projects with below-average risk should be evaluated using a discount rate less than the firm's WACC.

An additional issue to consider when using a firm's WACC (marginal cost of capital) to evaluate a specific project is that there is an implicit assumption that the capital structure of the firm will remain at the target capital structure over the life of the project.

These complexities aside, we can still conclude that the NPVs of potential projects of firm-average risk should be calculated using the marginal cost of capital for the firm. Projects for which the present value of the after-tax cash inflows is greater than the present value of the after-tax cash outflows should be undertaken by the firm.

LOS 36.f: Calculate and interpret the cost of debt capital using the yield-to-maturity approach and the debt-rating approach.

The **after-tax cost of debt**, $k_d(1-t)$, is used in computing the WACC. It is the interest rate at which firms can issue new debt (k_d) net of the tax savings from the tax deductibility of interest, $k_d(t)$:

after-tax cost of debt = interest rate − tax savings = $k_d - k_d(t) = k_d(1-t)$

after-tax cost of debt = $k_d(1-t)$

> **Example: Cost of debt**
>
> Dexter, Inc., is planning to issue new debt at an interest rate of 8%. Dexter has a 40% marginal federal-plus-state tax rate. What is Dexter's cost of debt capital?
>
> **Answer:**
>
> $k_d(1 - t) = 8\%(1 - 0.4) = 4.8\%$

Professor's Note: It is important that you realize that the cost of debt is the market interest rate (YTM) on new (marginal) debt, not the coupon rate on the firm's existing debt. CFA Institute may provide you with both rates, and you need to select the current market rate.

If a market YTM is not available because the firm's debt is not publicly traded, the analyst may use the rating and maturity of the firm's existing debt to estimate the before-tax cost of debt. If, for example, the firm's debt carries a single-A rating and has an average maturity of 15 years, the analyst can use the yield curve for single-A rated debt to determine the current market rate for debt with a 15-year maturity. This approach is an example of **matrix pricing** or valuing a bond based on the yields of comparable bonds.

If any characteristics of the firm's anticipated debt would affect the yield (e.g., covenants or seniority), the analyst should make the appropriate adjustment to his estimated before-tax cost of debt. For firms that primarily employ floating-rate debt, the analyst should estimate the longer-term cost of the firm's debt using the current yield curve (term structure) for debt of the appropriate rating category.

LOS 36.g: Calculate and interpret the cost of noncallable, nonconvertible preferred stock.

The **cost of preferred stock** (k_{ps}) is:

$$k_{ps} = D_{ps} / P$$

where:
D_{ps} = preferred dividends
P = market price of preferred

> **Example: Cost of preferred stock**
>
> Suppose Dexter, Inc., has preferred stock that pays an $8 dividend per share and sells for $100 per share. What is Dexter's cost of preferred stock?
>
> **Answer:**
>
> $k_{ps} = D_{ps} / P$
>
> $k_{ps} = \$8 / \$100 = 0.08 = 8\%$
>
> Note that the equation $k_{ps} = D_{ps} / P$ is just a rearrangement of the preferred stock valuation model $P = D_{ps} / k_{ps}$, where P is the market price.

LOS 36.h: Calculate and interpret the cost of equity capital using the capital asset pricing model approach, the dividend discount model approach, and the bond-yield-plus-risk-premium approach.

The opportunity **cost of equity capital** (k_{ce}) is the required rate of return on the firm's common stock. The rationale here is that the firm could avoid part of the cost of common stock outstanding by using retained earnings to buy back shares of its own stock. The cost of (i.e., the required return on) common equity can be estimated using one of the following three approaches:

1. **The capital asset pricing model approach.**
   Step 1: Estimate the risk-free rate, R_f. Yields on default risk-free debt such as U.S. Treasury notes are usually used. The most appropriate maturity to choose is one that is close to the useful life of the project.
   Step 2: Estimate the stock's beta, β. This is the stock's risk measure.
   Step 3: Estimate the expected rate of return on the market, $E(R_{mkt})$.
   Step 4: Use the capital asset pricing model (CAPM) equation to estimate the required rate of return:

   $k_{ce} = R_f + \beta[E(R_m) - R_f]$

> **Example: Using CAPM to estimate k_{ce}**
>
> Suppose $R_f = 6\%$, $R_{mkt} = 11\%$, and Dexter has a beta of 1.1. Estimate Dexter's cost of equity.
>
> **Answer:**
>
> The required rate of return for Dexter's stock is:
>
> $k_{ce} = 6\% + 1.1(11\% - 6\%) = 11.5\%$

Professor's Note: If you are unfamiliar with the capital asset pricing model, you can find more detail and the basic elements of its derivation in the Study Session on portfolio management.

2. **The dividend discount model approach.** If dividends are expected to grow at a constant rate, *g*, then the current value of the stock is given by the dividend growth model:

$$P_0 = \frac{D_1}{k_{ce} - g}$$

where:
D_1 = next year's dividend
k_{ce} = required rate of return on common equity
g = firm's expected constant growth rate

Rearranging the terms, you can solve for k_{ce}:

$$k_{ce} = \frac{D_1}{P_0} + g$$

In order to use $k_{ce} = \frac{D_1}{P_0} + g$, you have to estimate the expected growth rate, *g*. This can be done by:

- Using the growth rate as projected by security analysts.
- Using the following equation to estimate a firm's sustainable growth rate:

$$g = (\text{retention rate})(\text{return on equity}) = (1 - \text{payout rate})(\text{ROE})$$

The difficulty with this model is estimating the firm's future growth rate.

Example: Estimating k_{ce} using the dividend discount model

Suppose Dexter's stock sells for $21, next year's dividend is expected to be $1, Dexter's expected ROE is 12%, and Dexter is expected to pay out 40% of its earnings. What is Dexter's cost of equity?

Answer:

g = (ROE)(retention rate)

g = (0.12)(1 − 0.4) = 0.072 = 7.2%

k_{ce} = (1 / 21) + 0.072 = 0.12 or 12%

3. **Bond yield plus risk premium approach.** Analysts often use an ad hoc approach to estimate the required rate of return. They add a risk premium (three to five percentage points) to the market yield on the firm's long-term debt.

   k_{ce} = bond yield + risk premium

> **Example: Estimating k_{ce} with bond yields plus a risk premium**
>
> Dexter's interest rate on long-term debt is 8%. Suppose the risk premium is estimated to be 5%. Estimate Dexter's cost of equity.
>
> **Answer:**
>
> Dexter's estimated cost of equity is:
>
> k_{ce} = 8% + 5% = 13%
>
> Note that the three models gave us three different estimates of k_{ce}. The CAPM estimate was 11.5%, the dividend discount model estimate was 12%, and the bond yield plus risk premium estimate was 13%. Analysts must use their judgment to decide which is most appropriate.

LOS 36.i: Calculate and interpret the beta and cost of capital for a project.

A **project's beta** is a measure of its systematic or market risk. Just as we can use a firm's beta to estimate its required return on equity, we can use a project's beta to adjust for differences between a specific project's risk and the average risk of a firm's projects.

Because a specific project is not represented by a publicly traded security, we typically cannot estimate a project's beta directly. One process that can be used is based on the equity beta of a publicly traded firm that is engaged in a business similar to, and with risk similar to, the project under consideration. This is referred to as the **pure-play method** because we begin with the beta of a company or group of companies that are *purely* engaged in a business similar to that of the project and are therefore comparable to the project. Thus, using the beta of a conglomerate that is engaged in the same business as the project would be inappropriate because its beta depends on its many different lines of business.

The beta of a firm is a function not only of the business risks of its projects (lines of business) but also of its financial structure. For a given set of projects, the greater a firm's reliance on debt financing, the greater its equity beta. For this reason, we must adjust the pure-play beta from a comparable company (or group of companies) for the company's leverage (unlever it) and then adjust it (re-lever it) based on the financial structure of the company evaluating the project. We can then use this equity beta to calculate the cost of equity to be used in evaluating the project.

To get the *asset beta* for a publicly traded firm, we use the following formula:

$$\beta_{ASSET} = \beta_{EQUITY}\left[\frac{1}{1+\left((1-t)\frac{D}{E}\right)}\right]$$

where:
D/E = *comparable company's* debt-to-equity ratio and *t* is its marginal tax rate

To get the equity beta for the project, we use the *subject firm's* tax rate and debt-to-equity ratio:

$$\beta_{PROJECT} = \beta_{ASSET}\left[1+\left((1-t)\frac{D}{E}\right)\right]$$

The following example illustrates this technique.

> **Example: Cost of capital for a project**
>
> Acme, Inc., is considering a project in the food distribution business. It has a D/E ratio of 2, a marginal tax rate of 40%, and its debt currently has a yield of 14%. Balfor, a publicly traded firm that operates only in the food distribution business, has a D/E ratio of 1.5, a marginal tax rate of 30%, and an equity beta of 0.9. The risk-free rate is 5%, and the expected return on the market portfolio is 12%. Calculate Balfor's asset beta, the project's equity beta, and the appropriate WACC to use in evaluating the project.
>
> **Answer:**
>
> Balfor's asset beta:
>
> $$\beta_{ASSET} = 0.9\left[\frac{1}{1+(1-0.3)(1.5)}\right] = 0.439$$
>
> Equity beta for the project:
>
> $$\beta_{PROJECT} = 0.439[1 + (1 - 0.4)(2)] = 0.966$$
>
> Project cost of equity = 5% + 0.966(12% − 5%) = 11.762%
>
> To get the weights of debt and equity, use the D/E ratio and give equity a value of 1. Here, D/E = 2, so if E = 1, D = 2. The weight for debt, D/(D + E), is 2/(2 + 1) = 2/3, and the weight for equity, E/(D + E), is 1/(2 + 1) = 1/3. The appropriate WACC for the project is therefore:
>
> $$\frac{1}{3}(11.762\%) + \frac{2}{3}(14\%)(1-0.4) = 9.52\%$$

While the method is theoretically correct, there are several challenging issues involved in estimating the beta of the comparable (or any) company's equity:

- Beta is estimated using historical returns data. The estimate is sensitive to the length of time used and the frequency (daily, weekly, etc.) of the data.
- The estimate is affected by which index is chosen to represent the market return.
- Betas are believed to revert toward 1 over time, and the estimate may need to be adjusted for this tendency.
- Estimates of beta for small-capitalization firms may need to be adjusted upward to reflect risk inherent in small firms that is not captured by the usual estimation methods.

LOS 36.j: Describe uses of country risk premiums in estimating the cost of equity.

Using the CAPM to estimate the cost of equity is problematic in developing countries because beta does not adequately capture country risk. To reflect the increased risk associated with investing in a developing country, a **country risk premium** is added to the market risk premium when using the CAPM.

The general risk of the developing country is reflected in its **sovereign yield spread**. This is the difference in yields between the developing country's government bonds (denominated in the developed market's currency) and Treasury bonds of a similar maturity. To estimate an equity risk premium for the country, adjust the sovereign yield spread by the ratio of volatility between the country's equity market and its government bond market (for bonds denominated in the developed market's currency). A more volatile equity market increases the country risk premium, other things equal.

The revised CAPM equation is stated as:

$$k_{ce} = R_f + \beta[E(R_{MKT}) - R_f + CRP]$$

where:
CRP = country risk premium

The country risk premium can be calculated as:

$$CRP = \text{sovereign yield spread} \times \left(\frac{\text{annualized standard deviation of equity index of developing country}}{\text{annualized standard deviation of sovereign bond market in terms of the developed market currency}} \right)$$

where:
sovereign yield spread = difference between the yields of government bonds in the developing country and Treasury bonds of similar maturities

> **Example: Country risk premium**
>
> Robert Rodriguez, an analyst with Omni Corporation, is estimating the cost of equity for a project Omni is starting in Venezuela. Rodriguez has compiled the following information for his analysis:
>
> - Project beta = 1.25.
> - Expected market return = 10.4%.
> - Risk-free rate = 4.2%.
> - Country risk premium = 5.53%.
>
> Calculate the cost of equity for Omni's Venezuelan project.
>
> **Answer:**
>
> $$\begin{aligned} k_{ce} &= R_f + \beta\left[E(R_{MKT}) - R_f + CRP\right] \\ &= 0.042 + 1.25\left[0.104 - 0.042 + 0.0553\right] \\ &= 0.042 + 1.25\left[0.1173\right] \\ &= 0.1886, \text{ or } 18.86\% \end{aligned}$$

LOS 36.k: Describe the marginal cost of capital schedule, explain why it may be upward-sloping with respect to additional capital, and calculate and interpret its break-points.

The **marginal cost of capital** (MCC) is the cost of the last new dollar of capital a firm raises. As a firm raises more and more capital, the costs of different sources of financing will increase. For example, as a firm raises additional debt, the cost of debt will rise to account for the additional financial risk. This will occur, for example, if bond covenants in the firm's existing senior debt agreement prohibit the firm from issuing additional debt with the same seniority as the existing debt. Therefore, the company will have to issue more expensive subordinated bonds at a higher cost of debt, which increases the marginal cost of capital.

Also, issuing new equity is more expensive than using retained earnings due to flotation costs (which are discussed in more detail in the next LOS). The bottom line is that raising additional capital results in an increase in the WACC.

The **marginal cost of capital schedule** shows the WACC for different amounts of financing. Typically, the MCC is shown as a graph. Because different sources of financing become more expensive as the firm raises more capital, the MCC schedule typically has an upward slope.

Break points occur any time the cost of one of the components of the company's WACC changes. A break point is calculated as:

$$\text{break point} = \frac{\text{amount of capital at which the component's cost of capital changes}}{\text{weight of the component in the capital structure}}$$

Example: Calculating break points

The Omni Corporation has a target capital structure of 60% equity and 40% debt. The schedule of financing costs for the Omni Corporation is shown in the figure below.

Schedule of Capital Costs for Omni

Amount of New Debt (in millions)	After-Tax Cost of Debt	Amount of New Equity (in millions)	Cost of Equity
$0 to $99	4.2%	$0 to $199	6.5%
$100 to $199	4.6%	$200 to $399	8.0%
$200 to $299	5.0%	$400 to $599	9.5%

Calculate the break points for Omni Corporation and graph the marginal cost of capital schedule.

Answer:

Omni will have a break point each time a component cost of capital changes, for a total of four break points.

$$\text{break point}_{\text{debt} > \$100mm} = \frac{\$100 \text{ million}}{0.4} = \$250 \text{ million}$$

$$\text{break point}_{\text{debt} > \$200mm} = \frac{\$200 \text{ million}}{0.4} = \$500 \text{ million}$$

$$\text{break point}_{\text{equity} > \$200mm} = \frac{\$200 \text{ million}}{0.6} = \$333 \text{ million}$$

$$\text{break point}_{\text{equity} > \$400mm} = \frac{\$400 \text{ million}}{0.6} = \$667 \text{ million}$$

The following figure shows Omni Corporation's WACC for the different break points.

WACC for Alternative Levels of Financing

Capital (in millions)	Equity (60%)	Cost of Equity	Debt (40%)	Cost of Debt	WACC
$50	$30	6.5%	$20	4.2%	5.58%
$250	$150	6.5%	$100	4.6%	5.74%
$333	$200	8.0%	$133	4.6%	6.64%
$500	$300	8.0%	$200	5.0%	6.80%
$667	$400	9.5%	$267	5.0%	7.70%

The following figure is a graph of the marginal cost of capital schedule given in the previous figure. Notice the upward slope of the line due to the increased financing costs as more financing is needed.

Marginal Cost of Capital Schedule for Omni Corporation

WACC (%)

- 5.58% (up to 250)
- 5.74% (250–333)
- 6.64% (333–500)
- 6.80% (500–667)
- 7.70% (above 667)

Capital raised

LOS 36.l: Explain and demonstrate the correct treatment of flotation costs.

Flotation costs are the fees charged by investment bankers when a company raises external equity capital. Flotation costs can be substantial and often amount to between 2% and 7% of the total amount of equity capital raised, depending on the type of offering.

Incorrect Treatment of Flotation Costs

Because the LOS asks for the "correct treatment of flotation costs," that implies that there is an incorrect treatment. Many financial textbooks incorporate flotation costs directly into the cost of capital by increasing the cost of external equity. For example, if a company has a dividend of $1.50 per share, a current price of $30 per share, and an expected growth rate of 6%, the cost of equity without flotation costs would be:

$$r_e = \left(\frac{\$1.50(1+0.06)}{\$30} \right) + 0.06 = 0.1130, \text{ or } 11.30\%$$

Professor's Note: Here we're using the constant growth model, rather than the CAPM, to estimate the cost of equity.

If we incorporate flotation costs of 4.5% directly into the cost of equity computation, the cost of equity increases:

$$r_e = \left[\frac{\$1.50(1+0.06)}{\$30(1-0.045)}\right] + 0.06 = 0.1155, \text{ or } 11.55\%$$

Correct Treatment of Flotation Costs

In the *incorrect* treatment we have just seen, flotation costs effectively increase the WACC by a fixed percentage and will be a factor for the duration of the project because future project cash flows are discounted at this higher WACC to determine project NPV. The problem with this approach is that flotation costs are not an ongoing expense for the firm. Flotation costs are a cash outflow that occurs at the initiation of a project and affect the project NPV by increasing the initial cash outflow. Therefore, *the correct way to account for flotation costs is to adjust the initial project cost*. An analyst should calculate the dollar amount of the flotation cost attributable to the project and increase the initial cash outflow for the project by this amount.

> **Example: Correctly accounting for flotation costs**
>
> Omni Corporation is considering a project that requires a $400,000 cash outlay and is expected to produce cash flows of $150,000 per year for the next four years. Omni's tax rate is 35%, and the before-tax cost of debt is 6.5%. The current share price for Omni's stock is $36 per share, and the expected dividend next year is $2 per share. Omni's expected growth rate is 5%. Assume that Omni finances the project with 50% debt and 50% equity capital and that flotation costs for equity are 4.5%. The appropriate discount rate for the project is the WACC.
>
> Calculate the NPV of the project using the correct treatment of flotation costs and discuss how the result of this method differs from the result obtained from the incorrect treatment of flotation costs.

Answer:

$$\text{after-tax cost of debt} = 6.5\%(1-0.35) = 4.23\%$$

$$\text{cost of equity} = \left(\frac{\$2}{\$36}\right) + 0.05 = 0.1055, \text{ or } 10.55\%$$

$$\text{WACC} = 0.50(0.0423) + 0.50(0.1055) = 7.39\%$$

Because the project is financed with 50% equity, the amount of equity capital raised is 0.50 × $400,000 = $200,000.

Flotation costs are 4.5%, which equates to a dollar cost of $200,000 × 0.045 = $9,000.

$$\text{NPV} = -\$400,000 - \$9,000 + \frac{\$150,000}{1.0739} + \frac{\$150,000}{(1.0739)^2} + \frac{\$150,000}{(1.0739)^3} + \frac{\$150,000}{(1.0739)^4}$$

$$= \$94,640$$

For comparison, if we would have adjusted the cost of equity for flotation costs, the cost of equity would have increased to 10.82% $\left(=\frac{\$2.00}{\$36(1-0.045)} + 0.05\right)$, which would have increased the WACC to 7.53%. Using this method, the NPV of the project would have been:

$$\text{NPV} = -\$400,000 + \frac{\$150,000}{1.0753} + \frac{\$150,000}{(1.0753)^2} + \frac{\$150,000}{(1.0753)^3} + \frac{\$150,000}{(1.0753)^4} = \$102,061$$

The two methods result in significantly different estimates for the project NPV. Adjusting the initial outflow for the dollar amount of the flotation costs is the correct approach because it provides the most accurate assessment of the project's value once all costs are considered.

Note that flotation costs may be tax-deductible for some firms. In that case, the initial cash flow of the project should be adjusted by the after-tax flotation cost. In this example, Omni would have an after-tax flotation cost of $9,000(1 − 0.35) = $5,850 and the project NPV would be $97,790.

Key Concepts

LOS 36.a

$$WACC = (w_d)(k_d)(1-t) + (w_{ps})(k_{ps}) + (w_{ce})(k_{ce})$$

The weighted average cost of capital, or WACC, is calculated using weights based on the market values of each component of a firm's capital structure and is the correct discount rate to use to discount the cash flows of projects with risk equal to the average risk of a firm's projects.

LOS 36.b
Interest expense on a firm's debt is tax deductible, so the pre-tax cost of debt must be reduced by the firm's marginal tax rate to get an after-tax cost of debt capital:

after-tax cost of debt = k_d (1 − firm's marginal tax rate)

The pre-tax and after-tax capital costs are equal for both preferred stock and common equity because dividends paid by the firm are not tax deductible.

LOS 36.c
WACC should be calculated based on a firm's target capital structure weights.

If information on a firm's target capital structure is not available, an analyst can use the firm's current capital structure, based on market values, or the average capital structure in the firm's industry as estimates of the target capital structure.

LOS 36.d
A firm's marginal cost of capital (WACC at each level of capital investment) increases as it needs to raise larger amounts of capital. This is shown by an upward-sloping marginal cost of capital curve.

An investment opportunity schedule shows the IRRs of (in decreasing order), and the initial investment amounts for, a firm's potential projects.

The intersection of a firm's investment opportunity schedule with its marginal cost of capital curve indicates the optimal amount of capital expenditure, the amount of investment required to undertake all positive NPV projects.

LOS 36.e
The marginal cost of capital (the WACC for additional units of capital) should be used as the discount rate when calculating project NPVs for capital budgeting decisions.

Adjustments to the cost of capital are necessary when a project differs in risk from the average risk of a firm's existing projects. The discount rate should be adjusted upward for higher-risk projects and downward for lower-risk projects.

LOS 36.f
The before-tax cost of fixed-rate debt capital, k_d, is the rate at which the firm can issue new debt.
- The yield-to-maturity approach assumes the before-tax cost of debt capital is the YTM on the firm's existing publicly traded debt.
- If a market YTM is not available, the analyst can use the debt rating approach, estimating the before-tax cost of debt capital based on market yields for debt with the same rating and average maturity as the firm's existing debt.

LOS 36.g
The cost (and yield) of noncallable, nonconvertible preferred stock is simply the annual dividend divided by the market price of preferred shares.

LOS 36.h
The cost of equity capital, k_{ce}, is the required rate of return on the firm's common stock.

There are three approaches to estimating k_{ce}:
- CAPM approach: $k_{ce} = R_f + \beta[E(R_{mkt}) - R_f]$.
- Dividend discount model approach: $k_{ce} = (D_1/P_0) + g$.
- Bond yield plus risk premium approach: add a risk premium of 3% to 5% to the market yield on the firm's long-term debt.

LOS 36.i
When a project's risk differs from that of the firm's average project, we can use the beta of a company or group of companies that are exclusively in the same business as the project to calculate the project's required return. This *pure-play method* involves the following steps:

1. Estimate the beta for a comparable company or companies.

2. Unlever the beta to get the asset beta using the marginal tax rate and debt-to-equity ratio for the comparable company:

$$\beta_{ASSET} = \beta_{EQUITY} \left\{ \frac{1}{1 + \left[(1-t)\frac{D}{E}\right]} \right\}$$

3. Re-lever the beta using the marginal tax rate and debt-to-equity ratio for the firm considering the project:

$$\beta_{PROJECT} = \beta_{ASSET} \left\{ 1 + \left[(1-t)\frac{D}{E}\right] \right\}$$

4. Use the CAPM to estimate the required return on equity to use when evaluating the project.

5. Calculate the WACC for the firm using the project's required return on equity.

LOS 36.j
A country risk premium should be added to the market risk premium in the Capital Asset Pricing Model to reflect the added risk associated with investing in a developing market.

LOS 36.k
The marginal cost of capital schedule shows the WACC for successively greater amounts of new capital investment for a period, such as the coming year.

The MCC schedule is typically upward-sloping because raising greater amounts of capital increases the cost of equity and debt financing. Break points (increases) in the marginal cost of capital schedule occur at amounts of total capital raised equal to the amount of each source of capital at which the component cost of capital increases, divided by the target weight for that source of capital.

LOS 36.l
The correct method to account for flotation costs of raising new equity capital is to increase a project's initial cash outflow by the flotation cost attributable to the project when calculating the project's NPV.

Concept Checkers

1. A company has $5 million in debt outstanding with a coupon rate of 12%. Currently, the yield to maturity (YTM) on these bonds is 14%. If the firm's tax rate is 40%, what is the company's after-tax cost of debt?
   A. 5.6%.
   B. 8.4%.
   C. 14.0%.

2. The cost of preferred stock is equal to:
   A. the preferred stock dividend divided by its par value.
   B. [(1 − tax rate) times the preferred stock dividend] divided by price.
   C. the preferred stock dividend divided by its market price.

3. A company's $100, 8% preferred is currently selling for $85. What is the company's cost of preferred equity?
   A. 8.0%.
   B. 9.4%.
   C. 10.8%.

4. The expected dividend is $2.50 for a share of stock priced at $25. What is the cost of equity if the long-term growth in dividends is projected to be 8%?
   A. 15%.
   B. 16%.
   C. 18%.

5. An analyst gathered the following data about a company:

Capital structure	Required rate of return
30% debt	10% for debt
20% preferred stock	11% for preferred stock
50% common stock	18% for common stock

   Assuming a 40% tax rate, what after-tax rate of return must the company earn on its investments?
   A. 13.0%.
   B. 14.2%.
   C. 18.0%.

6. A company is planning a $50 million expansion. The expansion is to be financed by selling $20 million in new debt and $30 million in new common stock. The before-tax required return on debt is 9% and 14% for equity. If the company is in the 40% tax bracket, the company's marginal cost of capital is *closest* to:
   A. 7.2%.
   B. 10.6%.
   C. 12.0%.

Study Session 10
Cross-Reference to CFA Institute Assigned Reading #36 – Cost of Capital

Use the following data to answer Questions 7 through 10.

- A company has a target capital structure of 40% debt and 60% equity.
- The company's bonds with face value of $1,000 pay a 10% coupon (semiannual), mature in 20 years, and sell for $849.54 with a yield to maturity of 12%.
- The company stock beta is 1.2.
- Risk-free rate is 10%, and market risk premium is 5%.
- The company is a constant-growth firm that just paid a dividend of $2, sells for $27 per share, and has a growth rate of 8%.
- The company's marginal tax rate is 40%.

7. The company's after-tax cost of debt is:
   A. 7.2%.
   B. 8.0%.
   C. 9.1%.

8. The company's cost of equity using the capital asset pricing model (CAPM) approach is:
   A. 16.0%.
   B. 16.6%.
   C. 16.9%.

9. The company's cost of equity using the dividend discount model is:
   A. 15.4%.
   B. 16.0%.
   C. 16.6%.

10. The company's weighted average cost of capital (using the cost of equity from CAPM) is *closest* to:
    A. 12.5%.
    B. 13.0%.
    C. 13.5%.

11. What happens to a company's weighted average cost of capital (WACC) if the firm's corporate tax rate increases and if the Federal Reserve causes an increase in the risk-free rate, respectively? (Consider the events independently and assume a beta of less than one.)

Tax rate increase	Increase in risk-free rate
A. Decrease WACC	Increase WACC
B. Decrease WACC	Decrease WACC
C. Increase WACC	Increase WACC

12. Given the following information on a company's capital structure, what is the company's weighted average cost of capital? The marginal tax rate is 40%.

Type of capital	Percent of capital structure	Before-tax component cost
Bonds	40%	7.5%
Preferred stock	5%	11%
Common stock	55%	15%

    A. 10.0%.
    B. 10.6%.
    C. 11.8%.

13. Derek Ramsey is an analyst with Bullseye Corporation, a major U.S.-based discount retailer. Bullseye is considering opening new stores in Brazil and wants to estimate its cost of equity capital for this investment. Ramsey has found that:
    - The appropriate beta to use for the project is 1.3.
    - The market risk premium is 6%.
    - The risk-free interest rate is 4.5%.
    - The country risk premium for Brazil is 3.1%.

    Which of the following is *closest* to the cost of equity that Ramsey should use in his analysis?
    A. 10.5%.
    B. 15.6%.
    C. 16.3%.

14. Manigault Industries currently has assets on its balance sheet of $200 million that are financed with 70% equity and 30% debt. The executive management team at Manigault is considering a major expansion that would require raising additional capital. Rosannna Stallworth, the CFO of Manigault, has put together the following schedule for the costs of debt and equity:

Amount of New Debt (in millions)	After-Tax Cost of Debt	Amount of New Equity (in millions)	Cost of Equity
$0 to $49	4.0%	$0 to $99	7.0%
$50 to $99	4.2%	$100 to $199	8.0%
$100 to $149	4.5%	$200 to $299	9.0%

In a presentation to Manigault's Board of Directors, Stallworth makes the following statements:

Statement 1: If we maintain our target capital structure of 70% equity and 30% debt, the break point at which our cost of equity will increase to 8.0% is $185 million in new capital.

Statement 2: If we want to finance total assets of $450 million, our marginal cost of capital will increase to 7.56%.

Are Stallworth's Statements 1 and 2 *most likely* correct or incorrect?

	Statement 1	Statement 2
A.	Correct	Correct
B.	Incorrect	Correct
C.	Incorrect	Incorrect

15. Black Pearl Yachts is considering a project that requires a $180,000 cash outlay and is expected to produce cash flows of $50,000 per year for the next five years. Black Pearl's tax rate is 25%, and the before-tax cost of debt is 8%. The current share price for Black Pearl's stock is $56 and the expected dividend next year is $2.80 per share. Black Pearl's expected growth rate is 5%. Assume that Black Pearl finances the project with 60% equity and 40% debt, and the flotation cost for equity is 4.0%. The appropriate discount rate is the weighted average cost of capital (WACC). Which of the following choices is *closest* to the dollar amount of the flotation costs and the NPV for the project, assuming that flotation costs are accounted for properly?

	Dollar amount of flotation costs	NPV of project
A.	$4,320	$17,548
B.	$4,320	$13,228
C.	$7,200	$17,548

16. Jay Company has a debt-to-equity ratio of 2.0. Jay is evaluating the cost of equity for a project in the same line of business as Cass Company and will use the pure-play method with Cass as the comparable firm. Cass has a beta of 1.2 and a debt-to-equity ratio of 1.6. The project beta *most likely*:
    A. will be less than Jay Company's beta.
    B. will be greater than Jay Company's beta.
    C. could be greater than or less than Jay Company's beta.

For more questions related to this topic review, log in to your Schweser online account and launch SchweserPro™ QBank; and for video instruction covering each LOS in this topic review, log in to your Schweser online account and launch the OnDemand video lectures, if you have purchased these products.

Answers – Concept Checkers

1. **B** $k_d(1 - t) = (0.14)(1 - 0.4) = 8.4\%$

2. **C** Cost of preferred stock = $k_{ps} = D_{ps} / P$

3. **B** $k_{ps} = D_{ps} / P_{ps}$, $D_{ps} = \$100 \times 8\% = \$8$, $k_{ps} = 8 / 85 = 9.4\%$

4. **C** Using the dividend yield plus growth rate approach: $k_{ce} = (D_1 / P_0) + g = (2.50 / 25.00) + 8\% = 18\%$.

5. **A** WACC = $(w_d)(k_d)(1 - t) + (w_{ps})(k_{ps}) + (w_{ce})(k_{ce}) = (0.3)(0.1)(1 - 0.4) + (0.2)(0.11) + (0.5)(0.18) = 13\%$

6. **B** $w_d = 20 / (20 + 30) = 0.4$, $w_{ce} = 30 / (20 + 30) = 0.6$

    WACC = $(w_d)(k_d)(1 - t) + (w_{ce})(k_{ce}) = (0.4)(9)(1 - 0.4) + (0.6)(14) = 10.56\% = $ MCC

7. **A** $k_d(1 - t) = 12(1 - 0.4) = 7.2\%$

8. **A** Using the CAPM formula, $k_{ce} = R_f + \beta[E(R_{mkt}) - R_f] = 10 + 1.2(5) = 16\%$.

9. **B** $D_1 = D_0(1 + g) = 2(1.08) = 2.16$; $k_{ce} = (D_1 / P_0) + g = (2.16 / 27) + 0.08 = 16\%$

10. **A** WACC = $(w_d)(k_d)(1 - t) + (w_{ce})(k_{ce}) = (0.4)(7.2) + (0.6)(16) = 12.48\%$

11. **A** An increase in the corporate tax rate will reduce the after-tax cost of debt, causing the WACC to fall. More specifically, because the after-tax cost of debt = $(k_d)(1 - t)$, the term $(1 - t)$ decreases, decreasing the after-tax cost of debt. If the risk-free rate were to increase, the costs of debt and equity would both increase, thus causing the firm's cost of capital to increase.

12. **B** WACC = $(w_d)(k_d)(1 - t) + (w_{ps})(k_{ps}) + (w_{ce})(k_{ce}) = (0.4)(7.5)(1 - 0.4) + (0.05)(11) + (0.55)(15) = 10.6\%$

13. **C** $k_e = R_f + \beta[E(R_{MKT}) - R_f + CRP]$
    $= 0.045 + 1.3[0.06 + 0.031]$
    $= 0.163$, or 16.3%

    Note that the "market risk premium" refers to the quantity $[E(R_{MKT}) - R_f]$.

14. **C** Statement 1 is incorrect. The break point at which the cost of equity changes to 8.0% is:

    $$\text{break point} = \frac{\text{amount of capital at which the component's cost of capital changes}}{\text{weight of the component in the WACC}}$$

    $$= \frac{\$100 \text{ million}}{0.70} = \$142.86 \text{ million}$$

    Statement 2 is also incorrect. If Manigault wants to finance $450 million of total assets, that means that the firm will need to raise $450 – $200 = $250 million in additional capital. Using the target capital structure of 70% equity, 30% debt, the firm will need to raise 0.70 × $250 = $175 million in new equity and 0.30 × $250 = $75 in new debt. Looking at the capital schedule, the cost associated with $75 million in new debt is

4.2%, and the cost associated with $175 million in new equity is 8.0%. The marginal cost of capital at that point will be (0.3 × 4.2%) + (0.7 × 8.0%) = 6.86%.

15. **B** Because the project is financed with 60% equity, the amount of equity capital raised is 0.60 × $180,000 = $108,000.

    Flotation costs are 4.0%, which equates to a dollar cost of $108,000 × 0.04 = $4,320.

    After-tax cost of debt = 8.0% (1 − 0.25) = 6.0%

    Cost of equity = $\left(\dfrac{\$2.80}{\$56.00}\right) + 0.05 = 0.10$, or 10.0%

    WACC = 0.60(0.10) + 0.40(0.06) = 8.4%

    NPV =
    $-\$180{,}000 - \$4{,}320 + \dfrac{\$50{,}000}{1.084} + \dfrac{\$50{,}000}{(1.084)^2} + \dfrac{\$50{,}000}{(1.084)^3} + \dfrac{\$50{,}000}{(1.084)^4} + \dfrac{\$50{,}000}{(1.084)^5} = \$13{,}228$

16. **C** The project beta calculated using the pure-play method is not necessarily related in a predictable way to the beta of the firm that is performing the project.

The following is a review of the Corporate Finance principles designed to address the learning outcome statements set forth by CFA Institute. Cross-Reference to CFA Institute Assigned Reading #37.

MEASURES OF LEVERAGE

Study Session 11

EXAM FOCUS

Here we define and calculate various measures of leverage and the firm characteristics that affect the levels of operating and financial leverage. Operating leverage magnifies the effect of changes in sales on operating earnings. Financial leverage magnifies the effect of changes in operating earnings on net income (earnings per share). The breakeven quantity of sales is that quantity of sales for which total revenue just covers total costs. The operating breakeven quantity of sales is the quantity of sales for which total revenue just covers total operating costs. Be sure you understand how a firm's decisions regarding its operating structure and scale and its decisions regarding the use of debt and equity financing (its capital structure) affect its breakeven levels of sales and the uncertainty regarding its operating earnings and net income.

LOS 37.a: Define and explain leverage, business risk, sales risk, operating risk, and financial risk and classify a risk.

Leverage, in the sense we use it here, refers to the amount of fixed costs a firm has. These fixed costs may be fixed operating expenses, such as building or equipment leases, or fixed financing costs, such as interest payments on debt. Greater leverage leads to greater variability of the firm's after-tax operating earnings and net income. A given change in sales will lead to a greater change in operating earnings when the firm employs operating leverage; a given change in operating earnings will lead to a greater change in net income when the firm employs financial leverage.

Professor's Note: The British refer to leverage as "gearing."

Business risk refers to the risk associated with a firm's operating income and is the result of uncertainty about a firm's revenues and the expenditures necessary to produce those revenues. Business risk is the combination of sales risk and operating risk.

- **Sales risk** is the uncertainty about the firm's sales.
- **Operating risk** refers to the additional uncertainty about operating earnings caused by fixed operating costs. The greater the proportion of fixed costs to variable costs, the greater a firm's operating risk.

Financial risk refers to the additional risk that the firm's common stockholders must bear when a firm uses fixed cost (debt) financing. When a company finances its operations with debt, it takes on fixed expenses in the form of interest payments. The greater the proportion of debt in a firm's capital structure, the greater the firm's financial risk.

LOS 37.b: Calculate and interpret the degree of operating leverage, the degree of financial leverage, and the degree of total leverage.

The **degree of operating leverage** (DOL) is defined as the percentage change in operating income (EBIT) that results from a given percentage change in sales:

$$\text{DOL} = \frac{\text{percentage change in EBIT}}{\text{percentage change in sales}} = \frac{\frac{\Delta \text{EBIT}}{\text{EBIT}}}{\frac{\Delta Q}{Q}}$$

To calculate a firm's DOL for a particular level of unit sales, Q, DOL is:

$$\text{DOL} = \frac{Q(P-V)}{Q(P-V)-F}$$

where:
Q = quantity of units sold
P = price per unit
V = variable cost per unit
F = fixed costs

Multiplying, we have:

$$\text{DOL} = \frac{S-TVC}{S-TVC-F}$$

where:
S = sales
TVC = total variable costs
F = fixed costs

Note that in this form, the denominator is operating earnings (EBIT).

> **Example: Degree of operating leverage**
>
> Consider the costs for the projects presented in the following table. Assuming that 100,000 units are produced for each firm, calculate the DOL for Atom Company and Beta Company.
>
> **Operating Costs for Atom Company and Beta Company**
>
> | | Atom Company | Beta Company |
> |---|---|---|
> | Price | $4.00 | $4.00 |
> | Variable costs | $3.00 | $2.00 |
> | Fixed costs | $40,000 | $120,000 |
> | Revenue | $400,000 | $400,000 |
>
> **Answer:**
>
> For Atom Company:
>
> $$DOL(Atom) = \frac{Q(P-V)}{[Q(P-V)-F]} = \frac{100,000(4-3)}{[100,000(4-3)-40,000]}$$
>
> $$DOL(Atom) = \frac{100,000}{60,000} = 1.67$$
>
> For Beta Company:
>
> $$DOL(Beta) = \frac{Q(P-V)}{[Q(P-V)-F]} = \frac{100,000(4-2)}{[100,000(4-2)-120,000]}$$
>
> $$DOL(Beta) = \frac{200,000}{80,000} = 2.50$$
>
> The results indicate that if Beta Company has a 10% increase in sales, its EBIT will increase by 2.50 × 10% = 25%, while for Atom Company, the increase in EBIT will be 1.67 × 10% = 16.7%.

It is important to note that the degree of operating leverage for a company depends on the level of sales. For example, if Atom Company sells 300,000 units, the DOL is decreased:

$$DOL(Atom) = \frac{Q(P-V)}{[Q(P-V)-F]} = \frac{300,000(4-3)}{[300,000(4-3)-40,000]} = \frac{300,000}{260,000} = 1.15$$

DOL is highest at low levels of sales and declines at higher levels of sales.

The **degree of financial leverage** (DFL) is interpreted as the ratio of the percentage change in net income (or EPS) to the percentage change in EBIT:

$$DFL = \frac{\text{percentage change in EPS}}{\text{percentage change in EBIT}}$$

For a particular level of operating earnings, DFL is calculated as:

$$DFL = \frac{EBIT}{EBIT - \text{interest}}$$

Professor's Note: The terms "earnings per share" (EPS) and "net income" are used interchangeably in this topic review.

Example: Degree of financial leverage

From the previous example, Atom Company's operating income for selling 100,000 units is $60,000. Assume that Atom Company has annual interest expense of $18,000. If Atom's EBIT increases by 10%, by how much will its earnings per share increase?

Answer:

$$DFL = \frac{EBIT}{EBIT - I} = \frac{\$60,000}{\$60,000 - \$18,000} = 1.43$$

$$\%\Delta EPS = DFL \times \%\Delta EBIT = 1.43 \times 10\% = 14.3\%$$

Hence, earnings per share will increase by 14.3%.

Professor's Note: Look back at the formulas for DOL and DFL and convince yourself that if there are no fixed costs, DOL is equal to one, and that if there are no interest costs, DFL is equal to one. Values of one mean no leverage. No fixed costs, no operating leverage. No interest costs, no financial leverage. This should help tie these formulas to the concepts and help you know when you have the formulas right (or wrong). If you plug in zero for fixed costs, DOL should be one, and if you plug in zero for interest, DFL should be one.

The **degree of total leverage** (DTL) combines the degree of operating leverage and financial leverage. DTL measures the sensitivity of EPS to change in sales. DTL is computed as:

$$DTL = DOL \times DFL$$

$$DTL = \frac{\%\Delta EBIT}{\%\Delta sales} \times \frac{\%\Delta EPS}{\%\Delta EBIT} = \frac{\%\Delta EPS}{\%\Delta sales}$$

$$DTL = \frac{Q(P-V)}{Q(P-V) - F - I}$$

$$DTL = \frac{S - TVC}{S - TVC - F - I}$$

Example: Degree of total leverage

Continuing with our previous example, how much will Atom's EPS increase if Atom increases its sales by 10%?

Answer:

From the previous examples:

$DOL_{Atom} = 1.67$

$DFL_{Atom} = 1.43$

$DTL = DOL \times DFL = 1.67 \times 1.43 = 2.39$

Professor's Note: There is some rounding here. If we use 1.6666 for DOL and 1.42857 for DFL, we obtain the DTL of 2.38.

Note that we also could have calculated the DTL the long way. From the previous example, the current value of Atom's dollar sales is $4 × 100,000 = $400,000.

$$DTL = \frac{S - TVC}{S - TVC - F - I} = \frac{\$400,000 - \$300,000}{\$400,000 - \$300,000 - \$40,000 - \$18,000} = 2.38$$

$\%\Delta EPS = DTL \times \%\Delta sales = 2.38 \times 10\% = 23.8\%$

EPS will increase by 23.8%.

LOS 37.c: Analyze the effect of financial leverage on a company's net income and return on equity.

The use of financial leverage significantly increases the risk and potential reward to common stockholders. The following examples involving Beta Company illustrate how financial leverage affects net income and shareholders' return on equity (ROE).

Example 1: Beta Company financed with 100% equity

Assume that the Beta Company has $500,000 in assets that are financed with 100% equity. Fixed costs are $120,000. Beta is expected to sell 100,000 units, resulting in operating income of [100,000 ($4 − $2)] − $120,000 = $80,000. Beta's tax rate is 40%. Calculate Beta's net income and return on equity if its EBIT increases or decreases by 10%.

Answer:

Beta's Return on Equity With 100% Equity Financing

	EBIT Less 10%	Expected EBIT	EBIT Plus 10%
EBIT	$72,000	$80,000	$88,000
Interest expense	0	0	0
Income before taxes	$72,000	$80,000	$88,000
Taxes at 40%	28,800	32,000	35,200
Net income	$43,200	$48,000	$52,800
Shareholders' equity	$500,000	$500,000	$500,000
Return on equity (ROE)	8.64%	9.60%	10.56%

Example 2: Beta Company financed with 50% equity and 50% debt

Continuing the previous example, assume that Beta Company is financed with 50% equity and 50% debt. The interest rate on the debt is 6%. Calculate Beta's net income and return on equity if its EBIT increases or decreases by 10%. Beta's tax rate is 40%.

Answer:

Beta's Return on Equity with 50% Equity Financing

	EBIT Less 10%	Expected EBIT	EBIT Plus 10%
EBIT	$72,000	$80,000	$88,000
Interest expense at 6%	15,000	15,000	15,000
Income before taxes	$57,000	$65,000	$73,000
Taxes at 40%	22,800	26,000	29,200
Net income	$34,200	$39,000	$43,800
Shareholders' equity	$250,000	$250,000	$250,000
Return on equity (ROE)	13.68%	15.60%	17.52%

The interest expense associated with using debt represents a fixed cost that reduces net income. However, the lower net income value is spread over a smaller base of shareholders' equity, serving to magnify the ROE. In all three of the scenarios shown in the two examples, ROE is higher using leverage than it is without leverage.

Further analyzing the differences between the examples, we can see that the use of financial leverage not only increases the *level* of ROE, it also increases the *rate of change* for ROE. In the unleveraged scenario, ROE varies directly with the change in EBIT. For an increase in EBIT of 10%, the ROE increases from 9.60% to 10.56%, for a rate of change of 10%. In the leveraged scenario, ROE is more volatile. For an increase in EBIT of 10%, the ROE increases from 15.60% to 17.52%, for a rate of change of 12.3%.

The use of financial leverage increases the risk of default but also increases the potential return for equity holders.

Professor's Note: Recall how this relationship is reflected in the DuPont formula used to analyze ROE. One of the components of the DuPont formula is the equity multiplier (assets/equity), which captures the effect of financial leverage on ROE.

LOS 37.d: Calculate the breakeven quantity of sales and determine the company's net income at various sales levels.

LOS 37.e: Calculate and interpret the operating breakeven quantity of sales.

The level of sales that a firm must generate to cover all of its fixed and variable costs is called the breakeven quantity. The **breakeven quantity of sales** is the quantity of sales for which revenues equal total costs, so that net income is zero. We can calculate the breakeven quantity by simply determining how many units must be sold to just cover total fixed costs.

For each unit sold, the **contribution margin**, which is the difference between price and variable cost per unit, is available to help cover fixed costs. We can thus describe the breakeven quantity of sales, Q_{BE}, as:

$$Q_{BE} = \frac{\text{fixed operating costs} + \text{fixed financing costs}}{\text{price} - \text{variable cost per unit}}$$

> **Example: Breakeven quantity of sales**
>
> Consider the prices and costs for Atom Company and Beta Company shown in the following table. Compute and illustrate the breakeven quantity of sales for each company.
>
> **Operating Costs for Atom Company and Beta Company**
>
> | | Atom Company | Beta Company |
> |---|---|---|
> | Price | $4.00 | $4.00 |
> | Variable costs | $3.00 | $2.00 |
> | Fixed operating costs | $10,000 | $80,000 |
> | Fixed financing costs | $30,000 | $40,000 |
>
> **Answer:**
>
> For Atom Company, the breakeven quantity is:
>
> $$Q_{BE}(\text{Atom}) = \frac{\$10,000 + \$30,000}{\$4.00 - \$3.00} = 40,000 \text{ units}$$
>
> Similarly, for Beta Company, the breakeven quantity is:
>
> $$Q_{BE}(\text{Beta}) = \frac{\$80,000 + \$40,000}{\$4.00 - \$2.00} = 60,000 \text{ units}$$

The breakeven quantity and the relationship between sales revenue, total costs, net income, and net loss are illustrated in Figures 1 and 2.

Figure 1: Breakeven Analysis for Atom Company

For Atom Company: $Q_{BE} = (\$30,000 + \$10,000) / (\$4.00 - \$3.00) = 40,000$ units

Figure 2: Breakeven Analysis for Beta Company

For Beta Company: Q_{BE} = ($80,000 + $40,000) / ($4.00 − $2.00) = 60,000 units

We can also calculate an **operating breakeven quantity of sales**. In this case, we consider only fixed operating costs and ignore fixed financing costs. The calculation is simply:

$$Q_{OBE} = \frac{\text{fixed operating costs}}{\text{price} - \text{variable cost per unit}}$$

> **Example: Operating breakeven quantity of sales**
>
> Calculate the operating breakeven quantity of sales for Atom and Beta, using the same data from the previous example.
>
> **Answer:**
>
> For Atom, the operating breakeven quantity of sales is:
>
> $10,000 / ($4.00 − $3.00) = 10,000 units
>
> For Beta, the operating breakeven quantity of sales is:
>
> $80,000 / ($4.00 − $2.00) = 40,000 units

We can summarize the effects of leverage on net income through an examination of Figures 1 and 2. Other things equal, a firm that chooses operating and financial structures that result in greater total fixed costs will have a higher breakeven quantity of sales. Leverage of either type magnifies the effects of changes in sales on net income. The further a firm's sales are from its breakeven level of sales, the greater the magnifying effects of leverage on net income.

Study Session 11
Cross-Reference to CFA Institute Assigned Reading #37 – Measures of Leverage

These same conclusions apply to operating leverage and the operating breakeven quantity of sales. One company may choose a larger scale of operations (larger factory), resulting in a greater operating breakeven quantity of sales and greater leverage, other things equal.

Note that the degree of total leverage is calculated for a particular level of sales. The slope of the net income line in Figures 1 and 2 is related to total leverage but is not the same thing. The degree of total leverage is different for every level of sales.

KEY CONCEPTS

LOS 37.a
Leverage increases the risk and potential return of a firm's earnings and cash flows.

Operating leverage increases with fixed operating costs.

Financial leverage increases with fixed financing costs.

Sales risk is uncertainty about the firm's sales.

Business risk refers to the uncertainty about operating earnings (EBIT) and results from variability in sales and expenses. Business risk is magnified by operating leverage.

Financial risk refers to the additional variability of EPS compared to EBIT. Financial risk increases with greater use of fixed cost financing (debt) in a company's capital structure.

LOS 37.b
The degree of operating leverage (DOL) is calculated as $\dfrac{Q(P-V)}{Q(P-V)-F}$ and is interpreted as $\dfrac{\%\Delta EBIT}{\%\Delta sales}$.

The degree of financial leverage (DFL) is calculated as $\dfrac{EBIT}{EBIT-I}$ and is interpreted as $\dfrac{\%\Delta EPS}{\%\Delta EBIT}$.

The degree of total leverage (DTL) is the combination of operating and financial leverage and is calculated as DOL × DFL and interpreted as $\dfrac{\%\Delta EPS}{\%\Delta sales}$.

LOS 37.c
Using more debt and less equity in a firm's capital structure reduces net income through added interest expense but also reduces net equity. The net effect can be to either increase or decrease ROE.

LOS 37.d
The breakeven quantity of sales is the amount of sales necessary to produce a net income of zero (total revenue just covers total costs) and can be calculated as:

$$\dfrac{\text{fixed operating costs} + \text{fixed financing costs}}{\text{price} - \text{variable cost per unit}}$$

Net income at various sales levels can be calculated as total revenue (i.e., price × quantity sold) minus total costs (i.e., total fixed costs plus total variable costs).

LOS 37.e
The operating breakeven quantity of sales is the amount of sales necessary to produce an operating income of zero (total revenue just covers total operating costs) and can be calculated as:

$$\dfrac{\text{fixed operating costs}}{\text{price} - \text{variable cost per unit}}$$

Study Session 11
Cross-Reference to CFA Institute Assigned Reading #37 – Measures of Leverage

CONCEPT CHECKERS

1. Business risk is the combination of:
   A. operating risk and financial risk.
   B. sales risk and financial risk.
   C. operating risk and sales risk.

2. Which of the following is a key determinant of operating leverage?
   A. Level and cost of debt.
   B. The competitive nature of the business.
   C. The trade-off between fixed and variable costs.

3. Which of the following statements about capital structure and leverage is *most accurate*?
   A. Financial leverage is directly related to operating leverage.
   B. Increasing the corporate tax rate will not affect capital structure decisions.
   C. A firm with low operating leverage has a small proportion of its total costs in fixed costs.

4. Jayco, Inc., sells blue ink for $4 a bottle. The ink's variable cost per bottle is $2. Ink has fixed operating costs of $4,000 and fixed financing costs of $6,000. What is Jayco's breakeven quantity of sales, in units?
   A. 2,000.
   B. 3,000.
   C. 5,000.

5. Jayco, Inc., sells blue ink for $4 a bottle. The ink's variable cost per bottle is $2. Ink has fixed operating costs of $4,000 and fixed financing costs of $6,000. What is Jayco's operating breakeven quantity of sales, in units?
   A. 2,000.
   B. 3,000.
   C. 5,000.

6. If Jayco's sales increase by 10%, Jayco's EBIT increases by 15%. If Jayco's EBIT increases by 10%, Jayco's EPS increases by 12%. Jayco's degree of operating leverage (DOL) and degree of total leverage (DTL) are *closest* to:
   A. 1.2 DOL and 1.5 DTL.
   B. 1.2 DOL and 2.7 DTL.
   C. 1.5 DOL and 1.8 DTL.

Use the following data to answer Questions 7 and 8.

Jayco, Inc., sells 10,000 units at a price of $5 per unit. Jayco's fixed costs are $8,000, interest expense is $2,000, variable costs are $3 per unit, and EBIT is $12,000.

7. Jayco's degree of operating leverage (DOL) and degree of financial leverage (DFL) are *closest* to:
   A. 2.50 DOL and 1.00 DFL.
   B. 1.67 DOL and 2.00 DFL.
   C. 1.67 DOL and 1.20 DFL.

8. Jayco's degree of total leverage (DTL) is *closest* to:
    A. 2.00.
    B. 1.75.
    C. 1.50.

9. Vischer Concrete has $1.2 million in assets that are currently financed with 100% equity. Vischer's EBIT is $300,000, and its tax rate is 30%. If Vischer changes its capital structure (recapitalizes) to include 40% debt, what is Vischer's ROE before and after the change? Assume that the interest rate on debt is 5%.

	ROE at 100% equity	ROE at 60% equity
A.	17.5%	26.8%
B.	25.0%	26.8%
C.	25.0%	37.5%

For more questions related to this topic review, log in to your Schweser online account and launch SchweserPro™ QBank; and for video instruction covering each LOS in this topic review, log in to your Schweser online account and launch the OnDemand video lectures, if you have purchased these products.

Answers – Concept Checkers

1. **C** Business risk refers to the risk associated with a firm's operating income and is the result of uncertainty about a firm's revenues and the expenditures necessary to produce those revenues. Business risk is the combination of sales risk (the uncertainty associated with the price and quantity of goods and services sold) and operating risk (the leverage created by the use of fixed costs in the firm's operations).

2. **C** The extent to which costs are fixed determines operating leverage.

3. **C** If fixed costs are a small percentage of total costs, operating leverage is low. Operating leverage is separate from financial leverage, which depends on the amount of debt in the capital structure. Increasing the tax rate would make the after-tax cost of debt cheaper.

4. **C** $Q_{BE} = \dfrac{\$4,000 + \$6,000}{\$4.00 - \$2.00} = 5,000$ units

5. **A** $Q_{OBE} = \dfrac{\$4,000}{\$4.00 - \$2.00} = 2,000$ units

6. **C** $DOL = \dfrac{15\%}{10\%} = 1.5$

    $DFL = \dfrac{12\%}{10\%} = 1.2$

    $DTL = DOL \times DFL = 1.5 \times 1.2 = 1.8$

7. **C** $DOL = \dfrac{Q(P-V)}{[Q(P-V)-F]} = \dfrac{10,000(5-3)}{[10,000(5-3)-8,000]} = 1.67$

    $DFL = \dfrac{EBIT}{EBIT-I} = \dfrac{12,000}{12,000-2,000} = 1.2$

8. **A** $DTL = \dfrac{Q(P-V)}{[Q(P-V)-F-I]} = \dfrac{10,000(5-3)}{[10,000(5-3)-8,000-2,000]} = 2$, or because we

    calculated the components in Question 7, DTL = DOL × DFL = 1.67 × 1.2 = 2.0

9. **A** With 100% equity:

EBIT	$300,000
Interest expense	0
Income before taxes	$300,000
Taxes at 30%	90,000
Net income	$210,000
Shareholder's equity	$1,200,000
ROE = NI/equity	17.5%

With 60% equity:

EBIT	$300,000
Interest expense ($480,000 at 5%)	24,000
Income before taxes	$276,000
Taxes at 30%	82,800
Net income	$193,200
Shareholders' equity	$720,000
ROE = NI/equity	26.8%

The following is a review of the Corporate Finance principles designed to address the learning outcome statements set forth by CFA Institute. Cross-Reference to CFA Institute Assigned Reading #38.

DIVIDENDS AND SHARE REPURCHASES: BASICS

Study Session 11

EXAM FOCUS

Dividends have been a large component of the total returns that stocks have provided over time. Cash dividends and share repurchases are two ways that firms can pay out earnings to current shareholders. In this topic review, you will learn the terminology and mechanics of dividend payments. You should also get comfortable with calculating the EPS and book value of a firm after a share repurchase, given the relevant information about the firm and the source of the funds.

LOS 38.a: Describe regular cash dividends, extra dividends, liquidating dividends, stock dividends, stock splits, and reverse stock splits, including their expected effect on shareholders' wealth and a company's financial ratios.

Cash dividends, as the name implies, are payments made to shareholders in cash. They come in three forms:

1. **Regular dividends** occur when a company pays out a portion of profits on a consistent schedule (e.g., quarterly). A long-term record of stable or increasing dividends is widely viewed by investors as a sign of a company's financial stability.

2. **Special dividends** are used when favorable circumstances allow the firm to make a one-time cash payment to shareholders, in addition to any regular dividends the firm pays. Many cyclical firms (e.g., automakers) will use a special dividend to share profits with shareholders when times are good but maintain the flexibility to conserve cash when profits are down. Other names for special dividends include *extra dividends* and *irregular dividends*.

3. **Liquidating dividends** occur when a company goes out of business and distributes the proceeds to shareholders. For tax purposes, a liquidating dividend is treated as a return of capital and amounts over the investor's tax basis are taxed as capital gains.

No matter which form cash dividends take, their net effect is to transfer cash from the company to its shareholders. The payment of a cash dividend reduces a company's assets and the market value of its equity. This means that immediately after a dividend is paid, the price of the stock should drop by the amount of the dividend. For example, if a company's stock price is $25 per share and the company pays $1 per share as a dividend, the price of the stock should immediately drop to $24 per share to account for the lower asset and equity values of the firm.

Stock dividends are dividends paid out in new shares of stock rather than cash. In this case, there will be more shares outstanding, but each one will be worth less. Stock dividends are commonly expressed as a percentage. A 20% stock dividend means every shareholder gets 20% more stock. On the firm's balance sheet, issuing a stock dividend decreases retained earnings and increases contributed capital by the same amount. Total shareholders' equity remains unchanged.

> **Example: Stock dividend**
>
> Dwight Craver owns 100 shares of Carson Construction Company at a current price of $30 per share. Carson has 1,000,000 shares of stock outstanding, and its earnings per share (EPS) for the last year were $1.50. Carson declares a 20% stock dividend to all shareholders of record as of June 30.
>
> What is the effect of the stock dividend on the market price of the stock, and what is the impact of the dividend on Craver's ownership position in the company?
>
> **Answer:**
>
> **Impact of 20% Stock Dividend on Shareholders**
>
> | | Before Stock Dividend | After Stock Dividend |
> |---|---|---|
> | Shares outstanding | 1,000,000 | 1,000,000 × 1.20 = 1,200,000 |
> | Earnings per share | $1.50 | $1.50 / 1.20 = $1.25 |
> | Stock price | $30.00 | $30.00 / 1.20 = $25.00 |
> | Total market value | 1,000,000 × $30 = $30,000,000 | 1,200,000 × $25 = $30,000,000 |
> | Shares owned | 100 | 100 × 1.20 = 120 |
> | Ownership value | 100 × $30 = $3,000 | 120 × $25 = $3,000 |
> | Ownership stake | 100 / 1,000,000 = 0.01% | 120 / 1,200,000 = 0.01% |
>
> The effect of the stock dividend is to increase the number of shares outstanding by 20%. However, because company earnings stay the same, EPS decline and the price of the firm's stock drops from $30 to $25. Craver's receipt of more shares is exactly offset by the drop in stock price, and his wealth and ownership position in the company are unchanged.

Stock splits divide each existing share into multiple shares, thus creating more shares. There are now more shares, but the price of each share will drop correspondingly to the number of shares created, so there is no change in the owner's wealth. Splits are expressed as a ratio. In a 3-for-1 stock split, each old share is split into three new shares. Stock splits are more common today than stock dividends.

> **Example: Stock split**
>
> Carson Construction Company declares a 3-for-2 stock split. The current stock price is $30, earnings for last year were $1.50, dividends were $0.60 per share, and there are 1 million shares outstanding. What is the impact on Carson's shares outstanding, stock price, EPS, dividends per share, dividend yield, P/E, and market value?
>
> **Answer:**
>
> **Impact of a 3-for-2 Stock Split on Shareholders**
>
> | | Before Stock Split | After Stock Split |
> |---|---|---|
> | Shares outstanding | 1,000,000 | 1,000,000 × (3/2) = 1,500,000 |
> | Stock price | $30.00 | $30.00 / (3/2) = $20.00 |
> | Earnings per share | $1.50 | $1.50 / (3/2) = $1.00 |
> | Dividends per share | $0.60 | $0.60 / (3/2) = $0.40 |
> | Dividend yield | $0.60 / $30.00 = 2.0% | $0.40 / $20.00 = 2.0% |
> | P/E ratio | $30.00 / $1.50 = 20 | $20.00 / $1.00 = 20 |
> | Total market value | 1,000,000 × $30 = $30,000,000 | 1,500,000 × $20 = $30,000,000 |
>
> The number of shares outstanding increases, but the stock price, EPS, and dividends per share decrease by a proportional amount. The dividend yield, P/E ratio, and total market value of the firm remain the same. As in our prior example, the effect on the firm's shareholders also remains the same. The number of shares would increase (100 × 3 / 2 = 150), but the ownership value and stake are unchanged.

The bottom line for stock splits and stock dividends is that they increase the total number of shares outstanding, but because the stock price and earnings per share are adjusted proportionally, the value of a shareholder's total shares is unchanged.

Some firms use stock splits and stock dividends to keep stock prices within a perceived optimal trading range of $20 to $80 per share. What does academic research have to say about this?

- Stock prices tend to rise after a split or stock dividend.
- Price increases appear to occur because stock splits are taken as a positive signal from management about future earnings.
- If a report of good earnings does not follow a stock split, prices tend to revert to their original (split-adjusted) levels.
- Stock splits and dividends tend to reduce liquidity due to higher percentage brokerage fees on lower-priced stocks.

The conclusion is that stock splits and stock dividends create more shares but don't increase shareholder value.

Reverse stock splits are the opposite of stock splits. After a reverse split, there are fewer shares outstanding but a higher stock price. Because these factors offset one another, shareholder wealth is unchanged. The logic behind a reverse stock split is that the perceived optimal stock price range is $20 to $80 per share, and most investors consider a stock with a price less than $5 per share less than investment grade. Exchanges may impose a minimum stock price and delist those that fall below that price. A company in financial distress whose stock has fallen dramatically may declare a reverse stock split to increase the stock price.

Effects on Financial Ratios

Paying a cash dividend decreases assets (cash) and shareholders' equity (retained earnings). Other things equal, the decrease in cash will decrease a company's liquidity ratios and increase its debt-to-assets ratio, while the decrease in shareholders' equity will increase its debt-to-equity ratio.

Stock dividends, stock splits, and reverse stock splits have no effect on a company's leverage ratios or liquidity ratios. These transactions do not change the value of a company's assets or shareholders' equity; they merely change the number of equity shares.

LOS 38.b: Describe dividend payment chronology, including the significance of declaration, holder-of-record, ex-dividend, and payment dates.

An example of a typical dividend payment schedule is shown in Figure 1.

Figure 1: Dividend Payment Chronology

Declaration date	Ex-dividend date	Holder-of-record date	Payment date
August 25	September 15	September 17	September 30

- **Declaration date.** The date the board of directors approves payment of the dividend.
- **Ex-dividend date.** The first day a share of stock trades without the dividend. The ex-dividend date is also the cutoff date for receiving the dividend and occurs two business days before the holder-of-record date. If you buy the share on or after the ex-dividend date, you will not receive the dividend.
- **Holder-of-record date.** The date on which the shareholders of record are designated to receive the dividend.
- **Payment date.** The date the dividend checks are mailed out or when the payment is electronically transferred to shareholder accounts.

Stocks are traded ex-dividend on and after the ex-dividend date, so stock prices should fall by the amount of the dividend on the ex-dividend date. Because of taxes, however, the drop in price may be closer to the after-tax value of dividends.

> *Professor's Note: The reason that the holder-of-record date is two business days after the ex-dividend date has to do with the fact that the settlement date for stocks is three business days after the trade date (t + 3). If an investor buys a stock the day before the ex-dividend date, the trade will settle three business days later on the holder-of-record date, and the investor will receive the dividend.*

LOS 38.c: Compare share repurchase methods.

A **share repurchase** is a transaction in which a company buys back shares of its own common stock. Companies use three methods to repurchase shares:

1. **Buy in the open market.** Companies may repurchase stock in the open market at the prevailing market price. A share repurchase is authorized by the board of directors for a certain number of shares. Buying in the open market gives the company the flexibility to choose the timing of the transaction.

2. **Buy a fixed number of shares at a fixed price.** A company may repurchase stock by making a **tender offer** to repurchase a specific number of shares at a price that is usually at a premium to the current market price. Shareholders may tender their shares according to the terms of the offer. If shareholders try to tender more shares than the total repurchase, the company will typically buy back a pro rata amount from each shareholder. The company may select a tender offer price or use a **Dutch auction** (described in the Economics prerequisite readings) to determine the lowest price at which it can repurchase the number of shares desired.

3. **Repurchase by direct negotiation.** Companies may negotiate directly with a large shareholder to buy back a block of shares, usually at a premium to the market price. A company may engage in direct negotiation in order to keep a large block of shares from coming into the market and reducing the stock price or to repurchase shares from a potential acquirer after an unsuccessful takeover attempt. If the firm pays more than market value for the shares, the result is an increase in wealth for the seller and an equal decrease in wealth for remaining firm shareholders.

LOS 38.d: Calculate and compare the effect of a share repurchase on earnings per share when 1) the repurchase is financed with the company's excess cash and 2) the company uses debt to finance the repurchase.

A share repurchase will reduce the number of shares outstanding, which will tend to increase earnings per share. On the other hand, purchasing shares with company funds will reduce interest income and earnings, and purchasing shares with borrowed funds incurs interest costs, which will reduce earnings directly by the after-tax cost of the borrowed funds. The relation of the percentage decrease in earnings and the percentage decrease in the number of shares used to calculate EPS will determine whether the effect of a stock repurchase on EPS will be positive or negative.

Before we look at the calculations involved in determining the effect of a share repurchase on EPS, consider the following intuitive approach. The earnings yield for a share of stock is simply EPS divided by the share price. A $20 stock with EPS of $1 has an earnings yield of 5%. If the after-tax yield on company funds used to repurchase shares, or the after-tax cost of borrowed funds used to repurchase shares, is greater than 5%, EPS will fall as a result of the repurchase. If the after-tax yield on company funds used to repurchase shares, or the after-tax cost of borrowed funds used to repurchase shares, is less than 5%, EPS will rise as a result of the repurchase.

> **Example: Share repurchase when after-tax cost of debt is less than earnings yield**
>
> Spencer Pharmaceuticals, Inc., (SPI) plans to borrow $30 million that it will use to repurchase shares. SPI's chief financial officer has compiled the following information:
>
> - Share price at the time of buyback = $50.
> - Shares outstanding before buyback = 20,000,000.
> - EPS before buyback = $5.00.
> - Earnings yield = $5.00 / $50 = 10%.
> - After-tax cost of borrowing = 8%.
> - Planned buyback = 600,000 shares.
>
> Calculate the EPS after the buyback.
>
> **Answer:**
>
> total earnings = $5.00 × 20,000,000 = $100,000,000
>
> $$\text{EPS after buyback} = \frac{\text{total earnings} - \text{after-tax cost of funds}}{\text{shares outstanding after buyback}}$$
>
> $$= \frac{\$100,000,000 - (600,000 \text{ shares} \times \$50 \times 0.08)}{(20,000,000 - 600,000) \text{ shares}}$$
>
> $$= \frac{\$100,000,000 - \$2,400,000}{19,400,000 \text{ shares}}$$
>
> $$= \frac{\$97,600,000}{19,400,000 \text{ shares}}$$
>
> $$= \$5.03$$
>
> Because the 8% after-tax cost of borrowing is less than the 10% earnings yield (E/P) of the shares, the share repurchase will increase the company's EPS.

Study Session 11
Cross-Reference to CFA Institute Assigned Reading #38 – Dividends and Share Repurchases: Basics

> **Example: Share repurchase when after-tax cost of debt is greater than earnings yield**
>
> Spencer Pharmaceuticals, Inc., (SPI) plans to borrow $30 million that it will use to repurchase shares. Creditors perceive the company to be a significant credit risk, and the after-tax cost of borrowing is 15%. Using the other information from the previous example, calculate the EPS after the buyback.
>
> **Answer:**
>
> $$\text{EPS after buyback} = \frac{\text{total earnings} - \text{after-tax cost of funds}}{\text{shares outstanding after buyback}}$$
>
> $$= \frac{\$100{,}000{,}000 - (600{,}000 \text{ shares} \times \$50 \times 0.15)}{(20{,}000{,}000 - 600{,}000) \text{ shares}}$$
>
> $$= \frac{\$100{,}000{,}000 - \$4{,}500{,}000}{19{,}400{,}000 \text{ shares}}$$
>
> $$= \frac{\$95{,}500{,}000}{19{,}400{,}000 \text{ shares}}$$
>
> $$= \$4.92$$
>
> Because the after-tax cost of borrowing of 15% exceeds the earnings yield of 10%, the added interest paid reduces EPS after the buyback.

The conclusion is that a share repurchase using borrowed funds will increase EPS if the after-tax cost of debt used to buy back shares is less than the earnings yield of the shares before the repurchase. It will decrease EPS if the cost of debt is greater than the earnings yield, and it will not change EPS if the two are equal.

LOS 38.e: Calculate the effect of a share repurchase on book value per share.

Share repurchases may also have an impact on the book value of a share of stock.

> **Example: Effect of a share repurchase on book value per share**
>
> The share prices of Blue, Inc., and Red Company are both $25 per share, and each company has 20 million shares outstanding. Both companies have announced a $10 million stock buyback. Blue, Inc., has a book value of $300 million, while Red Company has a book value of $700 million.
>
> Calculate the book value per share (BVPS) of each company after the share repurchase.
>
> **Answer:**
>
> Share buyback for both companies = $10 million / $25 per share = 400,000 shares.
>
> Remaining shares for both companies = 20 million – 400,000 = 19.6 million.
>
> Blue, Inc.'s current BVPS = $300 million / 20 million = $15.
> The market price per share of $25 is greater than the BVPS of $15.
>
> >Book value after repurchase: $300 million – $10 million = $290 million
> >BVPS = $290 million / 19.6 million = $14.80
> >BVPS decreased by $0.20
>
> Red Company's current BVPS = $700 million / 20 million = $35.
> The market price per share of $25 is less than the BVPS of $35.
>
> >Book value after repurchase: $700 million – $10 million = $690 million
> >BVPS = $690 million / 19.6 million = $35.20
> >BVPS increased by $0.20

The conclusion is that BVPS will decrease if the repurchase price is greater than the original BVPS and increase if the repurchase price is less than the original BVPS.

LOS 38.f: Explain why a cash dividend and a share repurchase of the same amount are equivalent in terms of the effect on shareholders' wealth, all else being equal.

Because shares are repurchased using a company's own cash, a share repurchase can be considered an alternative to a cash dividend as a way of distributing earnings to shareholders.

Assuming the tax treatment of the two alternatives is the same, a share repurchase has the same impact on shareholder wealth as a cash dividend payment of an equal amount.

> **Example: Impact of share repurchase and cash dividend of equal amounts**
>
> Spencer Pharmaceuticals, Inc., (SPI) has 20,000,000 shares outstanding with a current market value of $50 per share. SPI made $100 million in profits for the recent quarter, and because only 70% of these profits will be reinvested back into the company, SPI's Board of Directors is considering two alternatives for distributing the remaining 30% to shareholders:
>
> - Pay a cash dividend of $30,000,000 / 20,000,000 shares = $1.50 per share.
> - Repurchase $30,000,000 worth of common stock.
>
> Assume that dividends are received when the shares go ex-dividend, the stock can be repurchased at the market price of $50 per share, and there are no differences in tax treatment between the two alternatives. How would the wealth of an SPI shareholder be affected by the board's decision on the method of distribution?
>
> **Answer:**
>
> **(1) Cash dividend**
>
> After the shares go ex-dividend, a shareholder of a single share would have $1.50 in cash and a share worth $50 − $1.50 = $48.50.
>
> The ex-dividend value of $48.50 can also be calculated as the market value of equity after the distribution of the $30 million, divided by the number of shares outstanding after the dividend payment:
>
> $$\frac{(20{,}000{,}000)(\$50) - \$30{,}000{,}000}{20{,}000{,}000} = \$48.50$$
>
> total wealth from the ownership of one share = $48.50 + $1.50 = $50
>
> **(2) Share repurchase**
>
> With $30,000,000, SPI could repurchase $30,000,000 / $50 = 600,000 shares of common stock. The share price after the repurchase is calculated as the market value of equity after the $30,000,000 repurchase divided by the shares outstanding after the repurchase:
>
> $$\frac{(20{,}000{,}000)(\$50) - \$30{,}000{,}000}{20{,}000{,}000 - 600{,}000} = \frac{\$970{,}000{,}000}{19{,}400{,}000} = \$50$$
>
> total wealth from the ownership of one share = $50

KEY CONCEPTS

LOS 38.a
Cash dividends are a payment from a company to a shareholder that reduces both the value of the company's assets and the market value of equity. They can come in the forms of regular, special, or liquidating dividends.

Stock dividends are distributions of new shares rather than cash. Stock splits divide each existing share into multiple shares. Both create more shares, but there is a proportionate drop in the price per share, so there is no effect on the total value of each shareholder's shares.

Other things equal, paying a cash dividend decreases liquidity ratios and increases leverage ratios. Stock dividends and stock splits do not affect liquidity or leverage ratios.

LOS 38.b
The chronology of a dividend payout is:
- Declaration date.
- Ex-dividend date.
- Holder-of-record date.
- Payment date.

Stocks purchased on or after the ex-dividend date will not receive the dividend. The ex-dividend date is two business days prior to the holder-of-record date.

LOS 38.c
Companies can repurchase shares of their own stock by buying shares in the open market, buying back a fixed number of shares at a fixed price through a tender offer, or directly negotiating to buy a large block of shares from a large shareholder.

LOS 38.d
The effect of share repurchases using borrowed funds on EPS is:
- If the company's E/P is equal to the after-tax cost of borrowing, there will be no effect on EPS.
- If the company's E/P is greater than the after-tax cost of borrowing, EPS will increase.
- If the company's E/P is less than the after-tax cost of borrowing, EPS will decrease.

LOS 38.e
The effect of a share repurchase on book value per share is:
- An increase if the share price is less than the original BVPS.
- A decrease if the share price is greater than the original BVPS.

LOS 38.f
A share repurchase is economically equivalent to a cash dividend of an equal amount, assuming the tax treatment of the two alternatives is the same.

Study Session 11
Cross-Reference to CFA Institute Assigned Reading #38 – Dividends and Share Repurchases: Basics

CONCEPT CHECKERS

1. Which of the following is *most likely* to increase shareholders' wealth?
   A. A stock dividend.
   B. A stock split.
   C. A special dividend.

2. Which of the following is *most accurate*? The first date on which the purchaser of a stock will not receive a dividend that has been declared is the:
   A. declaration date.
   B. ex-dividend date.
   C. holder-of-record date.

3. A share repurchase that begins with a company communicating to shareholders a specific number of shares and a range of acceptable prices is *most likely* to be a(n):
   A. open market repurchase.
   B. fixed price tender offer.
   C. Dutch auction.

4. If a company's after-tax borrowing rate is greater than the company's earning yield when the company repurchases stock with borrowed money, going forward, the earnings per share is *most likely* to:
   A. increase.
   B. decrease.
   C. remain unchanged.

5. After a share repurchase, book value per share is *most likely* to increase if, pre-purchase, BVPS was:
   A. greater than the market price per share.
   B. less than the market price per share.
   C. negative.

6. A company is considering either an open market share repurchase or a cash dividend of an equal amount. Compared to the open market share repurchase, the cash dividend is *most likely* to:
   A. increase a shareholder's wealth by a greater amount.
   B. increase a shareholder's wealth by a lesser amount.
   C. have a relative impact that depends on the tax treatment of the two alternatives.

7. Studdard Controls recently declared a quarterly dividend of $1.25 payable on Thursday, April 25, to holders of record on Friday, April 12. What is the last day an investor could purchase Studdard stock and still receive the quarterly dividend?
   A. April 9.
   B. April 10.
   C. April 12.

8. Arizona Seafood, Inc., plans $45 million in new borrowing to repurchase 3,600,000 shares at their market price of $12.50. The yield on the new debt will be 12%. The company has 36 million shares outstanding and EPS of $0.60 before the repurchase. The company's tax rate is 40%. The company's EPS after the share repurchase will be *closest* to:
   A. $0.50.
   B. $0.57.
   C. $0.67.

9. Northern Financial Co. has a BVPS of $5. The company has announced a $15 million share buyback. The share price is $60 and the company has 40 million shares outstanding. After the share repurchase, the company's BVPS will be *closest* to:
   A. $4.65.
   B. $4.90.
   C. $5.03.

For more questions related to this topic review, log in to your Schweser online account and launch SchweserPro™ QBank; and for video instruction covering each LOS in this topic review, log in to your Schweser online account and launch the OnDemand video lectures, if you have purchased these products.

Answers – Concept Checkers

1. **C** "Special" dividends (also known as "extra" or "irregular" dividends) are likely to be associated with increased shareholder wealth because they are usually used to distribute excess profits to shareholders after a period of unusually high earnings. Stock dividends and stock splits create more shares; however, there is a proportionate drop in the price per share, so there is no effect on shareholder wealth.

2. **B** The chronology of a dividend payout is declaration date, ex-dividend date, holder-of-record date, and payment date. The ex-dividend date is the cutoff date for receiving the dividend: stocks purchased on or after the ex-dividend date will not receive the dividend.

3. **C** Dutch auctions begin with the company communicating to shareholders a specific number of shares and a range of acceptable prices. When companies repurchase shares in the open market, they buy at market prices and in quantities as conditions warrant. In a fixed price tender offer, the company announces a fixed number of shares to be repurchased and a fixed price.

4. **B** Earnings per share is expected to decrease after a share repurchase if the company's after-tax borrowing rate is greater than the company's earning yield.

5. **A** Book value per share will increase after a share repurchase if book value per share was greater than market price per share. BVPS will decrease after a share repurchase if BVPS was less than market price.

6. **C** A share repurchase is economically equivalent to a cash dividend of an equal amount, assuming the tax treatment of the two alternatives is the same.

7. **A** If an investor purchases shares of stock on or after the ex-dividend date, she will NOT receive the dividend. Therefore, to receive the dividend, the investor must purchase stock the day before the ex-dividend date. The ex-dividend day is always two business days before the holder-of-record date. Two days before April 12 is April 10; therefore, the last day the investor can purchase shares and still receive the dividend is April 9.

8. **B** Total earnings are $0.60 \times 36{,}000{,}000 = \$21{,}600{,}000$.

    After-tax cost of debt is $12\% \times (1 - 0.40) = 7.2\%$.

    $$\text{EPS after buyback} = \frac{\text{total earnings} - \text{after-tax cost of funds}}{\text{shares outstanding after buyback}}$$

    $$= \frac{\$21{,}600{,}000 - (3{,}600{,}000 \text{ shares} \times \$12.50 \times 0.072)}{36{,}000{,}000 \text{ shares} - 3{,}600{,}000 \text{ shares}}$$

    $$= \frac{\$21{,}600{,}000 - \$3{,}240{,}000}{32{,}400{,}000 \text{ shares}} = \frac{\$18{,}360{,}000}{32{,}400{,}000 \text{ shares}}$$

    EPS = $0.57

9. **A** Shares to be repurchased are $15 million / $60 = 250,000 shares.

Remaining shares after the repurchase will be 40,000,000 − 250,000 = 39,750,000 shares.

Book value before the repurchase is 40,000,000 × $5.00 = $200,000,000.

Book value after the repurchase will be $200,000,000 − $15,000,000 = $185,000,000.

BVPS = $185,000,000 / 39,750,000 = $4.654 per share.

The following is a review of the Corporate Finance principles designed to address the learning outcome statements set forth by CFA Institute. Cross-Reference to CFA Institute Assigned Reading #39.

Working Capital Management

Study Session 11

Exam Focus

Firm liquidity is an important concern for an analyst, including how a firm manages its working capital, its short-term financing policy, and its sources of short-term financing for liquidity needs. A good portion of this topic review repeats material on ratios and yield calculations from previous topic areas and introduces types of debt securities that will also be covered in the topic reviews for fixed income investments.

New concepts introduced here are the management of current assets and liabilities, types of short-term bank financing, and the receivables aging schedule. Understand well why the management of inventory, receivables, and payables is important to a firm's overall profitability and value. The general guidelines for establishing and evaluating a firm's short-term investment policies and for evaluating short-term funding strategy and policy should be sufficient here. Focus on the overall objectives and how they can be met.

LOS 39.a: Describe primary and secondary sources of liquidity and factors that influence a company's liquidity position.

A company's **primary sources of liquidity** are the sources of cash it uses in its normal day-to-day operations. The company's *cash balances* result from selling goods and services, collecting receivables, and generating cash from other sources such as short-term investments. Typical sources of *short-term funding* include trade credit from vendors and lines of credit from banks. Effective *cash flow management* of a firm's collections and payments can also be a source of liquidity for a company.

Secondary sources of liquidity include liquidating short-term or long-lived assets, negotiating debt agreements (i.e., renegotiating), or filing for bankruptcy and reorganizing the company. While using its primary sources of liquidity is unlikely to change the company's normal operations, resorting to secondary sources of liquidity such as these can change the company's financial structure and operations significantly and may indicate that its financial position is deteriorating.

Factors That Influence a Company's Liquidity Position

In general, a company's liquidity position improves if it can get cash to flow in more quickly and flow out more slowly. Factors that weaken a company's liquidity position are called *drags and pulls* on liquidity.

Drags on liquidity delay or reduce cash inflows, or increase borrowing costs. Examples include uncollected receivables and bad debts, obsolete inventory (takes longer to sell and can require sharp price discounts), and tight short-term credit due to economic conditions.

Pulls on liquidity accelerate cash outflows. Examples include paying vendors sooner than is optimal and changes in credit terms that require repayment of outstanding balances.

LOS 39.b: Compare a company's liquidity measures with those of peer companies.

Some companies tend to have chronically weak liquidity positions, often due to specific factors that affect the company or its industry. These companies typically need to borrow against their long-lived assets to acquire working capital.

Liquidity ratios are employed by analysts to determine the firm's ability to pay its short-term liabilities.

- The *current ratio* is the best-known measure of liquidity:

$$\text{current ratio} = \frac{\text{current assets}}{\text{current liabilities}}$$

The higher the current ratio, the more likely it is that the company will be able to pay its short-term bills. A current ratio of less than one means that the company has negative working capital and is probably facing a liquidity crisis. Working capital equals current assets minus current liabilities.

- The *quick ratio* or *acid-test ratio* is a more stringent measure of liquidity because it does not include inventories and other assets that might not be very liquid:

$$\text{quick ratio} = \frac{\text{cash + short-term marketable securities + receivables}}{\text{current liabilities}}$$

The higher the quick ratio, the more likely it is that the company will be able to pay its short-term bills.

The current and quick ratios differ only in the assumed liquidity of the current assets that the analyst projects will be used to pay off current liabilities.

- A measure of accounts receivable liquidity is the *receivables turnover*:

$$\text{receivables turnover} = \frac{\text{credit sales}}{\text{average receivables}}$$

It is considered desirable to have a receivables turnover figure close to the industry norm.

Professor's Note: This formula for the receivables turnover ratio uses credit sales in the numerator, rather than total sales as shown in the earlier topic review on ratio analysis. While an analyst within a company will know what proportion of sales are credit or cash sales, an external analyst will likely not have this information but may be able to estimate it based on standard industry practice.

In most cases when a ratio compares a balance sheet account (such as receivables) with an income or cash flow item (such as sales), the balance sheet item will be the average of the account instead of simply the end-of-year balance. Averages are calculated by adding the beginning-of-year account value and the end-of-year account value, then dividing the sum by two.

- The inverse of the receivables turnover multiplied by 365 is the *number of days of receivables* (also called *average days' sales outstanding*), which is the average number of days it takes for the company's customers to pay their bills:

$$\text{number of days of receivables} = \frac{365}{\text{receivables turnover}} = \frac{\text{average receivables}}{\text{average day's credit sales}}$$

It is considered desirable to have a collection period (and receivables turnover) close to the industry norm. The firm's credit terms are another important benchmark used to interpret this ratio. A collection period that is too high might mean that customers are too slow in paying their bills, which means too much capital is tied up in assets. A collection period that is too low might indicate that the firm's credit policy is too rigorous, which might be hampering sales.

- A measure of a firm's efficiency with respect to its processing and inventory management is the *inventory turnover*:

$$\text{inventory turnover} = \frac{\text{cost of goods sold}}{\text{average inventory}}$$

Professor's Note: Pay careful attention to the numerator in the turnover ratios. For inventory turnover, be sure to use cost of goods sold, not sales.

- The inverse of the inventory turnover multiplied by 365 is the *average inventory processing period* or *number of days of inventory*:

$$\text{number of days of inventory} = \frac{365}{\text{inventory turnover}} = \frac{\text{average inventory}}{\text{average day's COGS}}$$

As is the case with accounts receivable, it is considered desirable to have an inventory processing period (and inventory turnover) close to the industry norm. A processing period that is too high might mean that too much capital is tied up in inventory and could mean that the inventory is obsolete. A processing period that is too low might indicate that the firm has inadequate stock on hand, which could hurt sales.

- A measure of the use of trade credit by the firm is the *payables turnover ratio*:

$$\text{payables turnover ratio} = \frac{\text{purchases}}{\text{average trade payables}}$$

- The inverse of the payables turnover ratio multiplied by 365 is the *payables payment period* or *number of days of payables*, which is the average amount of time it takes the company to pay its bills:

$$\text{number of days of payables} = \frac{365}{\text{payables turnover ratio}} = \frac{\text{average payables}}{\text{average day's purchases}}$$

LOS 39.c: Evaluate working capital effectiveness of a company based on its operating and cash conversion cycles and compare the company's effectiveness with that of peer companies.

- The **operating cycle**, the average number of days that it takes to turn raw materials into cash proceeds from sales, is:

   operating cycle = days of inventory + days of receivables

- The *cash conversion cycle* or *net operating cycle* is the length of time it takes to turn the firm's cash investment in inventory back into cash, in the form of collections from the sales of that inventory. The cash conversion cycle is computed from the average receivables collection period, average inventory processing period, and the payables payment period:

$$\text{cash conversion cycle} = \binom{\text{average days}}{\text{of receivables}} + \binom{\text{average days}}{\text{of inventory}} - \binom{\text{average days}}{\text{of payables}}$$

High cash conversion cycles are considered undesirable. A conversion cycle that is too high implies that the company has an excessive amount of investment in working capital.

LOS 39.d: Describe how different types of cash flows affect a company's net daily cash position.

Daily cash position refers to uninvested cash balances a firm has available to make routine purchases and pay expenses as they come due. The purpose of managing a firm's daily cash position is to have sufficient cash on hand (that is, make sure the firm's net daily cash position never becomes negative) but to avoid keeping excess cash because of the interest income foregone by not investing the cash.

Typical cash inflows for a firm include its cash from sales and collections of receivables; cash received from subsidiaries; dividends, interest, and principal received from investments in securities; tax refunds; and borrowing. Typical cash outflows include payments to employees and vendors; cash transferred to subsidiaries; payments of interest and principal on debt; investments in securities; taxes paid; and dividends paid.

To manage its cash position effectively, a firm should analyze its typical cash inflows and outflows by category and prepare forecasts over short-term (daily or weekly balances for the next several weeks), medium-term (monthly balances for the next year), and long-term time horizons. A firm can use these forecasts to identify periods when its cash balance may become low enough to require short-term borrowing, or high enough to invest excess cash in short-term securities.

LOS 39.e: Calculate and interpret comparable yields on various securities, compare portfolio returns against a standard benchmark, and evaluate a company's short-term investment policy guidelines.

Short-term securities in which a firm can invest cash include:

- U.S. Treasury bills.
- Short-term federal agency securities.
- Bank certificates of deposit.
- Banker's acceptances.
- Time deposits.
- Repurchase agreements.
- Commercial paper.
- Money market mutual funds.
- Adjustable-rate preferred stock.

Adjustable-rate preferred stock has a dividend rate that is reset quarterly to current market yields and offers corporate holders a tax advantage because a percentage of the dividends received are exempt from federal tax. The other securities listed are all described in more detail in the topic reviews on fixed income securities.

We covered the yield calculations for short-term discount securities in the "Discounted Cash Flow Applications" topic review in Quantitative Methods.

The percentage discount from face value is:

$$\% \text{ discount} = \left(\frac{\text{face value} - \text{price}}{\text{face value}} \right)$$

The discount-basis yield (bank discount yield or BDY) is:

$$\text{discount-basis yield} = \left(\frac{\text{face value} - \text{price}}{\text{face value}}\right)\left(\frac{360}{\text{days}}\right) = \%\text{ discount} \times \left(\frac{360}{\text{days}}\right)$$

The money market yield is:

$$\text{money market yield} = \left(\frac{\text{face value} - \text{price}}{\text{price}}\right)\left(\frac{360}{\text{days}}\right) = \text{holding period yield} \times \left(\frac{360}{\text{days}}\right)$$

where:
"days" = days to maturity
"price" = purchase price of the security

The bond equivalent yield measure for short-term discount securities is calculated as:

$$\text{bond equivalent yield} = \left(\frac{\text{face value} - \text{price}}{\text{price}}\right)\left(\frac{365}{\text{days to maturity}}\right)$$

$$= \text{holding period yield} \times \left(\frac{365}{\text{days}}\right)$$

Professor's Note: In Quantitative Methods, the bond equivalent yield was defined differently as two times the effective semiannual yield.

Returns on the firm's short-term securities investments should be stated as bond equivalent yields. The return on the portfolio should be expressed as a weighted average of these yields.

Cash Management Investment Policy

Typically, the objective of cash management is to earn a market return without taking on much risk, either liquidity risk or default risk. Firms invest cash that may be needed in the short term in securities of relatively high credit quality and relatively short maturities to minimize these risks.

It is advisable to have a written investment policy statement. An investment policy statement typically begins with a statement of the purpose and objective of the investment portfolio, some general guidelines about the strategy to be employed to achieve those objectives, and the types of securities that will be used. The investment policy statement will also include specific information on who is allowed to purchase securities, who is responsible for complying with company guidelines, and what steps will be taken if the investment guidelines are not followed. Finally, the investment policy statement will include limitations on the specific types of securities permitted for investment of short-term funds, limitations on the credit ratings of portfolio securities, and limitations on the proportions of the total short-term securities portfolio that can be invested in the various types of permitted securities.

An investment policy statement should be evaluated on how well the policy can be expected to satisfy the goals and purpose of short-term investments, generating yield without taking on excessive credit or liquidity risk. The policy should not be overly restrictive in the context of meeting the goals of safety and liquidity.

LOS 39.f: Evaluate a company's management of accounts receivable, inventory, and accounts payable over time and compared to peer companies.

The management of accounts receivable begins with calculating the average days of receivables and comparing this ratio to the firm's historical performance or to the average ratios for a group of comparable companies. More detail about the accounts receivable performance can be gained by using an **aging schedule** such as that presented in Figure 1.

Figure 1: Receivables Aging (thousands of dollars)

Days Outstanding	March	April	May
< 31 days	200	212	195
31–60 days	150	165	140
61–90 days	100	90	92
> 90 days	50	70	66

In March, $200,000 of accounts receivable were current—that is, had been outstanding less than 31 days; $50,000 of the receivables at the end of March had been outstanding for more than 90 days.

Presenting this data as percentages of total outstanding receivables can facilitate analysis of how the aging schedule for receivables is changing over time. An example is presented in Figure 2.

Figure 2: Receivables Aging (% of totals)

Days Outstanding	March	April	May
< 31 days	40%	39%	40%
31–60 days	30%	31%	28%
61–90 days	20%	17%	19%
> 90 days	10%	13%	13%

Another useful metric for monitoring the accounts receivable performance is the *weighted average collection period*, which indicates the average days outstanding per dollar of receivables. As illustrated in Figure 3, the weights are the percentage of total receivables in each category, and these are multiplied by the average days to collect accounts within each aging category.

Figure 3: Weighted Average Collection Period—March

Days Outstanding	Average Collection Days	% Weight	Days × Weight
< 31 days	22	40%	8.8
31–60 days	44	30%	13.2
61–90 days	74	20%	14.8
> 90 days	135	10%	13.5
Weighted Average Collection Period			50.3 days

The information necessary to compare a firm's aging schedule and weighted average collection period to other firms is not available. However, analysis of the historical trends and significant changes in a firm's aging schedule and weighted average collection days can give a clearer picture of what is driving changes in the simpler metric of average days of receivables. The company must always evaluate the trade-off between stricter credit terms (and borrower creditworthiness) and the ability to make sales. Terms that are too strict will lead to less-than-optimal sales. Terms that are too lenient will increase sales at the cost of longer average days of receivables, which must be funded at some cost, and will increase bad accounts, directly affecting profitability.

Inventory Management

Inventory management involves a trade-off as well. Inventory levels that are too low will result in lost sales due to stock-outs, while inventory that is too large will have carrying costs because the firm's capital is tied up in inventory. Reducing inventory will free up cash that can be invested in interest-bearing securities or used to reduce debt or equity funding. Increasing average days' inventory or a decreasing inventory turnover ratio can both indicate that inventory is too large. A large inventory can lead to greater losses from obsolete items and can also indicate that obsolete items that no longer sell well are included in inventory.

Comparing average days of inventory and inventory turnover ratios between industries, or even between two firms that have different business strategies, can be misleading. The grocery business typically has high inventory turnover, while an art gallery's inventory turnover will typically be low. An auto parts firm that stocks hard-to-find parts for antique cars will likely have a low inventory turnover (and charge premium prices) compared to a chain auto parts store that does most of its business in standard items like oil filters, brake parts, and antifreeze. In any business, inventory management is an important component of effective overall financial management.

Accounts Payable Management

Just as a company must manage its receivables because they require working capital (and therefore have a funding cost), payables must be managed well because they represent a source of working capital to the firm. If the firm pays its payables prior to their due dates, cash is used unnecessarily and interest on it is sacrificed. If a firm pays its payables late, it can damage relationships with suppliers and lead to more restrictive credit terms or even the requirement that purchases be made for cash. Late payment can also result in interest charges that are high compared to other sources of short-term financing.

Typical terms on payables (trade credit) contain a discount available to those who pay quickly as well as a due date. Terms of "2/10 net 60" mean that if the invoice is paid within ten days, the company gets a 2% discount on the invoiced amount and that if the company does not take advantage of the discount, the net amount is due 60 days from the date of the invoice.

The cost to the company of not taking the discount for early payment can be evaluated as an annualized rate:

$$\text{cost of trade credit} = \left(1 + \frac{\%\ \text{discount}}{1 - \%\ \text{discount}}\right)^{\frac{365}{\text{days past discount}}} - 1$$

where:
days past discount = number of days after the end of the discount period

Professor's Note: You should recognize this from Quantitative Methods as the formula for converting a short-term rate to an effective annual rate. The term [% discount / (1 − % discount)] is the holding period return to the firm of taking advantage of a discount, in the same way that the holding period return on a pure discount security is [discount / (face − discount)].

Trade credit can be a source of liquidity for a company. However, when the cost of trade credit is greater than the company's cost of short-term liquidity from other sources, the company is better off paying the invoice within (ideally at the end of) the discount period.

Example: Cost of trade credit

Calculate and interpret the annualized cost of trade credit for invoice terms of 2/10 net 60, when the invoice is paid on the 40th, 50th, or 60th day.

> **Answer:**
>
> The discount is 2%. The annualized cost of not taking the discount can be calculated when the invoice is paid on:
>
> Day 40: $\left(1+\dfrac{0.02}{1-0.02}\right)^{\frac{365}{40-10}} - 1 = 27.9\%$
>
> Day 50: $\left(1+\dfrac{0.02}{1-0.02}\right)^{\frac{365}{50-10}} - 1 = 20.2\%$
>
> Day 60: $\left(1+\dfrac{0.02}{1-0.02}\right)^{\frac{365}{60-10}} - 1 = 15.9\%$
>
> The annualized cost of trade credit decreases as the payment period increases. If the company does not take the 2% discount within the first ten days, it should wait until the due date (day 60) to pay the invoice.

Our primary quantitative measure of payables management is average days of payables outstanding, which can also be calculated as:

$$\text{number of days of payables} = \frac{\text{accounts payable}}{\text{average day's purchases}}$$

where:

$$\text{average day's purchases} = \frac{\text{annual purchases}}{365}$$

A company with a short payables period (high payables turnover) may simply be taking advantage of discounts for paying early because it has good low-cost funds available to finance its working capital needs. A company with a long payables period may be such an important buyer that it can effectively utilize accounts payable as a source of short-term funding with relatively little cost (because suppliers will put up with it). Monitoring the changes in days' payables outstanding over time for a single firm will, however, aid the analyst. An extension of days' payables may serve as an early warning of deteriorating short-term liquidity.

LOS 39.g: Evaluate the choices of short-term funding available to a company and recommend a financing method.

There are several sources of short-term funding available to a company, from both bank and non-bank sources. We list the most important of these here.

Sources of Short-Term Funding From Banks

Lines of credit are used primarily by large, financially sound companies.

- *Uncommitted line of credit.* A bank extends an offer of credit for a certain amount but may refuse to lend if circumstances change.
- *Committed (regular) line of credit.* A bank extends an offer of credit that it "commits to" for some period of time. The fact that the bank has committed to extend credit in amounts up to the credit line makes this a more reliable source of short-term funding than an uncommitted line of credit. Banks charge a fee for making such a commitment. Loans under the agreement are typically for periods of less than a year, and interest charges are stated in terms of a short-term reference rate, such as LIBOR or the U.S. prime rate, plus a margin to compensate for the credit risk of the loan. Outside the United States, similar arrangements are referred to as *overdraft lines of credit.*
- *Revolving line of credit.* An even more reliable source of short-term financing than a committed line of credit, revolving lines of credit are typically for longer terms, sometimes as long as years. Along with committed lines of credit, revolving credit lines can be verified and can be listed on a firm's financial statements in the footnotes as a source of liquidity.

Companies with weaker credit may have to pledge assets as collateral for bank borrowings. Fixed assets, inventory, and accounts receivable may all serve as collateral for loans. Short-term financing is typically collateralized by receivables or inventory and longer-term loans are secured with a claim to fixed (longer-term) assets. The bank may also have a *blanket lien* which gives it a claim to all current and future firm assets as collateral in case the primary collateral is insufficient and the borrowing firm defaults. When a firm assigns its receivables to the bank making a loan, the company still services the receivables and remains responsible for any receivables that are not paid.

Banker's acceptances are used by firms that export goods. A banker's acceptance is a guarantee from the bank of the firm that has ordered the goods stating that a payment will be made upon receipt of the goods. The exporting company can then sell this acceptance at a discount in order to generate immediate funds.

Factoring refers to the actual sale of receivables at a discount from their face values. The size of the discount will depend on how long it is until the receivables are due, the creditworthiness of the firm's credit customers, and the firm's collection history on its receivables. The "factor" (the buyer of the receivables) takes on the responsibility for collecting receivables and the credit risk of the receivables portfolio.

Non-Bank Sources of Short-Term Funding

Smaller firms and firms with poor credit may use nonbank *finance companies* for short-term funding. The cost of such funding is higher than other sources and is used by firms for which normal bank sources of short-term funding are not available.

Large, creditworthy companies can issue short-term debt securities called **commercial paper**. Whether the firm sells the paper directly to investors (direct placement) or sells it through dealers (dealer-placed paper), the interest costs are typically slightly less than the rate they could get from a bank.

In managing its short-term financing, a firm should focus on the objectives of having sufficient sources of funding for current, as well as future foreseeable, cash needs and should seek the most cost-effective rates available given its needs, assets, and creditworthiness. The firm should have the ability to prepay short-term borrowings when cash flow permits and have the flexibility to structure its short-term financing so that the debt matures without peaks and can be matched to expected cash flows. For large borrowers, it is important that the firm has alternative sources of short-term funding and even alternative lenders for a particular type of financing. It is often worth having slightly higher overall short-term funding costs in order to have flexibility and redundant sources of financing.

Key Concepts

LOS 39.a
Primary sources of liquidity are the sources of cash a company uses in its normal operations. If its primary sources are inadequate, a company can use secondary sources of liquidity such as asset sales, debt renegotiation, and bankruptcy reorganization.

A company's liquidity position depends on the effectiveness of its cash flow management and is influenced by drags on its cash inflows (e.g., uncollected receivables, obsolete inventory) and pulls on its cash outflows (e.g., early payments to vendors, reductions in credit limits).

LOS 39.b
Measures of a company's short-term liquidity include:
- Current ratio = current assets / current liabilities.
- Quick ratio = (cash + marketable securities + receivables) / current liabilities.

Measures of how well a company is managing its working capital include:
- Receivables turnover = credit sales / average receivables.
- Number of days of receivables = 365 / receivables turnover.
- Inventory turnover = cost of goods sold / average inventory.
- Number of days of inventory = 365 / inventory turnover.
- Payables turnover = purchases / average trade payables.
- Number of days of payables = 365 / payables turnover.

LOS 39.c
The operating cycle and the cash conversion cycle are summary measures of the effectiveness of a company's working capital management.
- Operating cycle = days of inventory + days of receivables.
- Cash conversion cycle = days of inventory + days of receivables − days of payables.

Operating and cash conversion cycles that are high relative to a company's peers suggest the company has too much cash tied up in working capital.

LOS 39.d
To manage its net daily cash position, a firm needs to forecast its cash inflows and outflows and identify periods when its cash balance may be lower than needed or higher than desired. Cash inflows include operating receipts, cash from subsidiaries, cash received from securities investments, tax refunds, and borrowing. Cash outflows include purchases, payroll, cash transfers to subsidiaries, interest and principal paid on debt, investments in securities, taxes paid, and dividends paid.

LOS 39.e

Commonly used annualized yields for short-term pure discount securities are based on the days to maturity (days) of the securities and include:
- Discount-basis yields = % discount from face value × (360/days).
- Money market yields = HPY × (360/days).
- Bond-equivalent yields = HPY × (365/days).

The overall objective of short-term cash management is to earn a reasonable return while taking on only very limited credit and liquidity risk. Returns on the firm's short-term securities investments should be stated as bond equivalent yields. The return on the portfolio should be expressed as a weighted average of these yields.

An investment policy statement should include the objectives of the cash management program, details of who is authorized to purchase securities, authorization for the purchase of specific types of securities, limitations on portfolio proportions of each type, and procedures in the event that guidelines are violated.

LOS 39.f

A firm's inventory, receivables, and payables management can be evaluated by comparing days of inventory, days of receivables, and days of payables for the firm over time and by comparing them to industry averages or averages for a group of peer companies.

A receivables aging schedule and a schedule of weighted average days of receivables can each provide additional detail for evaluating receivables management.

LOS 39.g

There are many choices for short-term borrowing. The firm should keep costs down while also allowing for future flexibility and alternative sources.

The choice of short-term funding sources depends on a firm's size and creditworthiness. Sources available, in order of decreasing firm creditworthiness and increasing cost, include:
- Commercial paper.
- Bank lines of credit.
- Collateralized borrowing.
- Nonbank financing.
- Factoring.

Concept Checkers

1. Firm A and Firm B have the same quick ratio, but Firm A has a greater current ratio than Firm B. Compared to Firm B, it is *most likely* that Firm A has:
   A. greater inventory.
   B. greater payables.
   C. a higher receivables turnover ratio.

2. An increase in Rowley Corp's cash conversion cycle and a decrease in Rowley's operating cycle could result from:

Cash conversion cycle ↑	Operating cycle ↓
A. Decreased receivables turnover	Increased payables turnover
B. Decreased receivables turnover	Decrease in days of inventory
C. Increased inventory turnover	Increased payables turnover

3. An example of a primary source of liquidity is:
   A. liquidating assets.
   B. negotiating debt contracts.
   C. short-term investment portfolios.

4. Which of the following statements *most accurately* describes a key aspect of managing a firm's net daily cash position?
   A. Analyze cash inflows and outflows to forecast future needs for cash.
   B. Maximize the firm's cash inflows and minimize its cash outflows.
   C. Minimize uninvested cash balances because they earn a return of zero.

5. Boyle, Inc., just purchased a banker's acceptance for $25,400. It will mature in 80 days for $26,500. The discount-basis yield and the bond equivalent yield for this security are *closest* to:

Discount-basis	Bond equivalent
A. 18.7%	18.7%
B. 18.7%	19.8%
C. 4.2%	19.8%

6. Chapmin Corp. is a large domestic services firm with a good credit rating. The source of short-term financing it would *most likely* use is:
   A. factoring of receivables.
   B. issuing commercial paper.
   C. issuing bankers' acceptances.

For more questions related to this topic review, log in to your Schweser online account and launch SchweserPro™ QBank; and for video instruction covering each LOS in this topic review, log in to your Schweser online account and launch the OnDemand video lectures, if you have purchased these products.

Answers – Concept Checkers

1. **A** Inventory is in the numerator of the current ratio but not in the quick ratio. Greater inventory for Firm A is consistent with a greater current ratio for Firm A.

2. **B** A decrease in receivables turnover would increase days of receivables and increase the cash conversion cycle. A decrease in days of inventory would decrease the operating cycle.

3. **C** Primary sources of liquidity include ready cash balances, short-term funds (e.g., short-term investment portfolios), and cash flow management. Secondary sources of liquidity include negotiating debt contracts, liquidating assets, and filing for bankruptcy protection and reorganization.

4. **A** The goal of managing the net daily cash position is to ensure that adequate cash is available to prevent the firm from having to arrange financing on short notice (and thus at high cost), while earning a return on cash balances when they are temporarily high by investing in short-term securities. A firm can meet this goal by forecasting its cash inflows and outflows to identify periods when its cash balance is expected to be lower or higher than needed. "Minimizing uninvested cash balances" is inaccurate because a firm should maintain some target amount of available cash.

5. **B** The actual discount on the acceptance is (26,500 − 25,400) / 26,500 = 4.151%. The annualized discount, or discount-basis yield, is 4.151(360/80) = 18.68%.

   The holding period yield is (26,500 − 25,400) / 25,400 = 4.331%. The bond equivalent yield is 4.331(365/80) = 19.76%.

6. **B** Large firms with good credit have access to the commercial paper market and can get lower financing costs with commercial paper than they can with bank borrowing. Bankers' acceptances are used by companies involved in international trade. Factoring of receivables is a higher-cost source of funds and is used more by smaller firms that do not have particularly strong credit.

Self-Test: Corporate Finance

You have now finished the Corporate Finance topic section. To get immediate feedback on how effective your study has been for this material, log in to your Schweser online account and take the self-test for this topic area. The number of questions on this test is equal to the number of questions for the topic on one-half of the actual Level I CFA exam. Questions are more exam-like than typical Concept Checkers or QBank questions; a score of less than 70% indicates that your study likely needs improvement. These tests are timed and allow 1.5 minutes per question.

The following is a review of the Portfolio Management principles designed to address the learning outcome statements set forth by CFA Institute. Cross-Reference to CFA Institute Assigned Reading #40.

PORTFOLIO MANAGEMENT: AN OVERVIEW

Study Session 12

EXAM FOCUS

Here, we introduce the portfolio management process and the investment policy statement. In this topic review, you will learn the investment needs of different types of investors, as well as the different kinds of pooled investments. Later, our topic review of "Basics of Portfolio Planning and Construction" will provide more detail on investment policy statements and investor objectives and constraints.

LOS 40.a: Describe the portfolio approach to investing.

The **portfolio perspective** refers to evaluating individual investments by their contribution to the risk and return of an investor's portfolio. The alternative to taking a portfolio perspective is to examine the risk and return of individual investments in isolation. An investor who holds all his wealth in a single stock because he believes it to be the best stock available is not taking the portfolio perspective—his portfolio is very risky compared to holding a diversified portfolio of stocks. Modern portfolio theory concludes that the extra risk from holding only a single security is not rewarded with higher expected investment returns. Conversely, diversification allows an investor to reduce portfolio risk without necessarily reducing the portfolio's expected return.

In the early 1950s, the research of Professor Harry Markowitz provided a framework for measuring the risk-reduction benefits of diversification. Using the standard deviation of returns as the measure of investment risk, he investigated how combining risky securities into a portfolio affected the portfolio's risk and expected return. One important conclusion of his model is that unless the returns of the risky assets are perfectly positively correlated, risk is reduced by diversifying across assets.

In the 1960s, professors Treynor, Sharpe, Mossin, and Lintner independently extended this work into what has become known as modern portfolio theory (MPT). MPT results in equilibrium expected returns for securities and portfolios that are a linear function of each security's or portfolio's market risk (the risk that cannot be reduced by diversification).

One measure of the benefits of diversification is the **diversification ratio**. It is calculated as the ratio of the risk of an equally weighted portfolio of n securities (measured by its standard deviation of returns) to the risk of a single security selected at random from the n securities. Note that the expected return of an equal-weighted portfolio is also the expected return from selecting one of the n portfolio securities at random (the simple average of expected security returns in both instances). If the average standard deviation of returns for the *n* stocks is 25%, and the standard deviation of returns for an equally weighted portfolio of the *n* stocks is 18%, the diversification ratio is 18 / 25 = 0.72.

While the diversification ratio provides a quick measure of the potential benefits of diversification, an equal-weighted portfolio is not necessarily the portfolio that provides the greatest reduction in risk. Computer optimization can calculate the portfolio weights that will produce the lowest portfolio risk (standard deviation of returns) for a given group of securities.

Portfolio diversification works best when financial markets are operating normally; diversification provides less reduction of risk during market turmoil, such as the credit contagion of 2008. During periods of financial crisis, correlations tend to increase, which reduces the benefits of diversification.

LOS 40.b: Describe types of investors and distinctive characteristics and needs of each.

Individual investors save and invest for a variety of reasons, including purchasing a house or educating their children. In many countries, special accounts allow citizens to invest for retirement and to defer any taxes on investment income and gains until the funds are withdrawn. Defined contribution pension plans are popular vehicles for these investments. Pension plans are described later in this topic review.

Many types of **institutions** have large investment portfolios. An **endowment** is a fund that is dedicated to providing financial support on an ongoing basis for a specific purpose. For example, in the United States, many universities have large endowment funds to support their programs. A **foundation** is a fund established for charitable purposes to support specific types of activities or to fund research related to a particular disease. A typical foundation's investment objective is to fund the activity or research on a continuing basis without decreasing the real (inflation adjusted) value of the portfolio assets. Foundations and endowments typically have long investment horizons, high risk tolerance, and, aside from their planned spending needs, little need for additional liquidity.

The investment objective of a **bank**, simply put, is to earn more on the bank's loans and investments than the bank pays for deposits of various types. Banks seek to keep risk low and need adequate liquidity to meet investor withdrawals as they occur.

Insurance companies invest customer premiums with the objective of funding customer claims as they occur. Life insurance companies have a relatively long-term investment horizon, while property and casualty (P&C) insurers have a shorter investment horizon because claims are expected to arise sooner than for life insurers.

Investment companies manage the pooled funds of many investors. **Mutual funds** manage these pooled funds in particular styles (e.g., index investing, growth investing, bond investing) and restrict their investments to particular subcategories of investments (e.g., large-firm stocks, energy stocks, speculative bonds) or particular regions (emerging market stocks, international bonds, Asian-firm stocks).

Sovereign wealth funds refer to pools of assets owned by a government. For example, the Abu Dhabi Investment Authority, a sovereign wealth fund in the United Arab Emirates funded by Abu Dhabi government surpluses, has an estimated US$627 billion in assets.[1]

Figure 1 provides a summary of the risk tolerance, investment horizon, liquidity needs, and income objectives for different types of investors.

Figure 1: Characteristics of Different Types of Investors

Investor	Risk Tolerance	Investment Horizon	Liquidity Needs	Income Needs
Individuals	Depends on individual	Depends on individual	Depends on individual	Depends on individual
Banks	Low	Short	High	Pay interest
Endowments	High	Long	Low	Spending level
Insurance	Low	Long—life Short—P&C	High	Low
Mutual funds	Depends on fund	Depends on fund	High	Depends on fund
Defined benefit pensions	High	Long	Low	Depends on age

LOS 40.c: Describe defined contribution and defined benefit pension plans.

A **defined contribution pension plan** is a retirement plan in which the firm contributes a sum each period to the employee's retirement account. The firm's contribution can be based on any number of factors, including years of service, the employee's age, compensation, profitability, or even a percentage of the employee's contribution. In any event, the firm makes no promise to the employee regarding the future value of the plan assets. The investment decisions are left to the employee, who assumes all of the investment risk.

In a **defined benefit pension plan**, the firm promises to make periodic payments to employees after retirement. The benefit is usually based on the employee's years of service and the employee's compensation at, or near, retirement. For example, an employee might earn a retirement benefit of 2% of her final salary for each year of service. Consequently, an employee with 20 years of service and a final salary of $100,000, would receive $40,000 ($100,000 final salary × 2% × 20 years of service) each year upon retirement until death. Because the employee's future benefit is defined, the employer assumes the investment risk. The employer makes contributions to a fund

---

[1]. Source: SWF Institute (*www.swfinstitute.org/fund-rankings*).

established to provide the promised future benefits. Poor investment performance will increase the amount of required employer contributions to the fund.

LOS 40.d: Describe the steps in the portfolio management process.

There are three major steps in the portfolio management process:

Step 1: The **planning step** begins with an analysis of the investor's risk tolerance, return objectives, time horizon, tax exposure, liquidity needs, income needs, and any unique circumstances or investor preferences.

This analysis results in an **investment policy statement** (IPS) that details the investor's investment objectives and constraints. It should also specify an objective benchmark (such as an index return) against which the success of the portfolio management process will be measured. The IPS should be updated at least every few years and any time the investor's objectives or constraints change significantly.

Step 2: The **execution step** involves an analysis of the risk and return characteristics of various asset classes to determine how funds will be allocated to the various asset types. Often, in what is referred to as a *top-down* analysis, a portfolio manager will examine current economic conditions and forecasts of such macroeconomic variables as GDP growth, inflation, and interest rates, in order to identify the asset classes that are most attractive. The resulting portfolio is typically diversified across such asset classes as cash, fixed-income securities, publicly traded equities, hedge funds, private equity, and real estate, as well as commodities and other real assets.

Once the asset class allocations are determined, portfolio managers may attempt to identify the most attractive securities within the asset class. Security analysts use model valuations for securities to identify those that appear undervalued in what is termed *bottom-up* security analysis.

Step 3: The **feedback step** is the final step. Over time, investor circumstances will change, risk and return characteristics of asset classes will change, and the actual weights of the assets in the portfolio will change with asset prices. The portfolio manager must monitor these changes and **rebalance** the portfolio periodically in response, adjusting the allocations to the various asset classes back to their desired percentages. The manager must also measure portfolio performance and evaluate it relative to the return on the benchmark portfolio identified in the IPS.

LOS 40.e: Describe mutual funds and compare them with other pooled investment products.

Mutual funds are one form of **pooled investments** (i.e., a single portfolio that contains investment funds from multiple investors). Each investor owns shares representing ownership of a portion of the overall portfolio. The total net value of the assets in the fund (pool) divided by the number of such shares issued is referred to as the **net asset value** (NAV) of each share.

With an **open-end fund**, investors can buy newly issued shares at the NAV. Newly invested cash is invested by the mutual fund managers in additional portfolio securities. Investors can **redeem** their shares (sell them back to the fund) at NAV as well. All mutual funds charge a fee for the ongoing management of the portfolio assets, which is expressed as a percentage of the net asset value of the fund. **No-load funds** do not charge additional fees for purchasing shares (up-front fees) or for redeeming shares (redemption fees). **Load funds** charge either up-front fees, redemption fees, or both.

Closed-end funds are professionally managed pools of investor money that do not take new investments into the fund or redeem investor shares. The shares of a closed-end fund trade like equity shares (on exchanges or over-the-counter). As with open-end funds, the portfolio management firm charges ongoing management fees.

Types of Mutual Funds

Money market funds invest in short-term debt securities and provide interest income with very low risk of changes in share value. Fund NAVs are typically set to one currency unit, but there have been instances over recent years in which the NAV of some funds declined when the securities they held dropped dramatically in value. Funds are differentiated by the types of money market securities they purchase and their average maturities.

Bond mutual funds invest in fixed-income securities. They are differentiated by bond maturities, credit ratings, issuers, and types. Examples include government bond funds, tax-exempt bond funds, high-yield (lower rated corporate) bond funds, and global bond funds.

A great variety of **stock mutual funds** are available to investors. **Index funds** are **passively managed**; that is, the portfolio is constructed to match the performance of a particular index, such as the Standard & Poor's 500 Index. **Actively managed** funds refer to funds where the management selects individual securities with the goal of producing returns greater than those of their benchmark indexes. Annual management fees are higher for actively managed funds, and actively managed funds have higher turnover of portfolio securities (the percentage of investments that are changed during the year). This leads to greater tax liabilities compared to passively managed index funds.

Other Forms of Pooled Investments

Exchange-traded funds (ETFs) are similar to closed-end funds in that purchases and sales are made in the market rather than with the fund itself. There are important differences, however. While closed-end funds are often actively managed, ETFs are most often invested to match a particular index (passively managed). With closed-end funds, the market price of shares can differ significantly from their NAV due to imbalances between investor supply and demand for shares at any point in time. Special redemption provisions for ETFs are designed to keep their market prices very close to their NAVs.

ETFs can be sold short, purchased on margin, and traded at intraday prices, whereas open-end funds are typically sold and redeemed only daily, based on the share NAV calculated with closing asset prices. Investors in ETFs must pay brokerage commissions when they trade, and there is a spread between the bid price at which market makers will buy shares and the ask price at which market makers will sell shares. With most ETFs, investors receive any dividend income on portfolio stocks in cash, while open-end funds offer the alternative of reinvesting dividends in additional fund shares. One final difference is that ETFs may produce less capital gains liability compared to open-end index funds. This is because investor sales of ETF shares do not require the fund to sell any securities. If an open-end fund has significant redemptions that cause it to sell appreciated portfolio shares, shareholders incur a capital gains tax liability.

A **separately managed account** is a portfolio that is owned by a single investor and managed according to that investor's needs and preferences. No shares are issued, as the single investor owns the entire account.

Hedge funds are pools of investor funds that are not regulated to the extent that mutual funds are. Hedge funds are limited in the number of investors who can invest in the fund and are often sold only to qualified investors who have a minimum amount of overall portfolio wealth. Minimum investments can be quite high, often between $250,000 and $1 million.

There is a great variety of hedge fund strategies, and major hedge fund categories are based on the investment strategy that the funds pursue:

- **Long/short funds** buy securities that are expected to outperform the overall market and sell securities short that are expected to underperform the overall market.
- **Equity market-neutral funds** are long/short funds with long stock positions that are just offset in value by stocks sold short. These funds are designed to be neutral with respect to overall market movements so that they can be profitable in both up and down markets as long as their longs outperform their shorts.
- An equity hedge fund with a **bias** is a long/short fund dedicated to a larger long position relative to short sales (a **long bias**) or to a greater short position relative to long positions (a **short bias**).
- **Event-driven funds** invest in response to one-time corporate events, such as mergers and acquisitions.
- **Fixed-income arbitrage funds** take long and short positions in debt securities, attempting to profit from minor mispricings while minimizing the effects of interest rate changes on portfolio values.
- **Convertible bond arbitrage funds** take long and short positions in convertible bonds and the equity shares they can be converted into in order to profit from a relative mispricing between the two.
- **Global macro funds** speculate on changes in international interest rates and currency exchange rates, often using derivative securities and a great amount of leverage.

Buyout funds (private equity funds) typically buy entire public companies and take them private (their shares no longer trade). The purchase of the companies is often funded with a significant increase in the firm's debt (a leveraged buyout). The fund attempts to reorganize the firm to increase its cash flow, pay down its debt, increase the value of its equity, and then sell the restructured firm or its parts in a public offering or to another company over a fairly short time horizon of three to five years.

Venture capital funds typically invest in companies in their start-up phase, with the intent to grow them into valuable companies that can be sold publicly via an IPO or sold to an established firm. Both buyout funds and venture capital funds are very involved in the management of their portfolio companies and often have expertise in the industries on which they focus.

Key Concepts

LOS 40.a
A diversified portfolio produces reduced risk for a given level of expected return, compared to investing in an individual security. Modern portfolio theory concludes that investors that do not take a portfolio perspective bear risk that is not rewarded with greater expected return.

LOS 40.b
Types of investment management clients and their characteristics:

Investor Type	Risk Tolerance	Investment Horizon	Liquidity Needs	Income Needs
Individuals	Depends on individual	Depends on individual	Depends on individual	Depends on individual
Banks	Low	Short	High	Pay interest
Endowments	High	Long	Low	Spending level
Insurance	Low	Long—life Short—P&C	High	Low
Mutual funds	Depends on fund	Depends on fund	High	Depends on fund
Defined benefit pension	High	Long	Low	Depends on age

LOS 40.c
In a defined contribution plan, the employer contributes a certain sum each period to the employee's retirement account. The employer makes no promise regarding the future value of the plan assets; thus, the employee assumes all of the investment risk.

In a defined benefit plan, the employer promises to make periodic payments to the employee after retirement. Because the employee's future benefit is defined, the employer assumes the investment risk.

Study Session 12
Cross-Reference to CFA Institute Assigned Reading #40 – Portfolio Management: An Overview

LOS 40.d
The three steps in the portfolio management process are:

1. **Planning:** Determine client needs and circumstances, including the client's return objectives, risk tolerance, constraints, and preferences. Create, and then periodically review and update, an investment policy statement (IPS) that spells out these needs and circumstances.

2. **Execution:** Construct the client portfolio by determining suitable allocations to various asset classes based on the IPS and on expectations about macroeconomic variables such as inflation, interest rates, and GDP growth (top-down analysis). Identify attractively priced securities within an asset class for client portfolios based on valuation estimates from security analysts (bottom-up analysis).

3. **Feedback:** Monitor and rebalance the portfolio to adjust asset class allocations and securities holdings in response to market performance. Measure and report performance relative to the performance benchmark specified in the IPS.

LOS 40.e
Mutual funds combine funds from many investors into a single portfolio that is invested in a specified class of securities or to match a specific index. Many varieties exist, including money market funds, bond funds, stock funds, and balanced (hybrid) funds. Open-ended shares can be bought or sold at the net asset value. Closed-ended funds have a fixed number of shares that trade at a price determined by the market.

Exchange-traded funds are similar to mutual funds, but investors can buy and sell ETF shares in the same way as shares of stock. Management fees are generally low, though trading ETFs results in brokerage costs.

Separately managed accounts are portfolios managed for individual investors who have substantial assets. In return for an annual fee based on assets, the investor receives personalized investment advice.

Hedge funds are available only to accredited investors and are exempt from most reporting requirements. Many different hedge fund strategies exist. A typical annual fee structure is 20% of excess performance plus 2% of assets under management.

Buyout funds involve taking a company private by buying all available shares, usually funded by issuing debt. The company is then restructured to increase cash flow. Investors typically exit the investment within three to five years.

Venture capital funds are similar to buyout funds, except that the companies purchased are in the start-up phase. Venture capital funds, like buyout funds, also provide advice and expertise to the start-ups.

CONCEPT CHECKERS

1. Compared to investing in a single security, diversification provides investors a way to:
   A. increase the expected rate of return.
   B. decrease the volatility of returns.
   C. increase the probability of high returns.

2. Portfolio diversification is *least likely* to protect against losses:
   A. during severe market turmoil.
   B. when markets are operating normally.
   C. when the portfolio securities have low return correlation.

3. In a defined contribution pension plan:
   A. the employee accepts the investment risk.
   B. the plan sponsor promises a predetermined retirement income to participants.
   C. the plan manager attempts to match the fund's assets to its liabilities.

4. In a defined benefit pension plan:
   A. the employee assumes the investment risk.
   B. the employer contributes to the employee's retirement account each period.
   C. the plan sponsor promises a predetermined retirement income to participants.

5. Low risk tolerance and high liquidity requirements *best* describe the typical investment needs of a(n):
   A. defined-benefit pension plan.
   B. foundation.
   C. insurance company.

6. A long time horizon and low liquidity requirements *best* describe the investment needs of a(n):
   A. endowment.
   B. insurance company.
   C. bank.

7. Which of the following is *least likely* to be considered an appropriate schedule for reviewing and updating an investment policy statement?
   A. At regular intervals (e.g., every year).
   B. When there is a major change in the client's constraints.
   C. Frequently, based on the recent performance of the portfolio.

8. A top-down security analysis begins by:
   A. analyzing a firm's business prospects and quality of management.
   B. identifying the most attractive companies within each industry.
   C. examining economic conditions.

9. Compared to exchange-traded funds (ETFs), open-end mutual funds are typically associated with lower:
   A. brokerage costs.
   B. minimum investment amounts.
   C. management fees.

10. Both buyout funds and venture capital funds:
    A. expect that only a small percentage of investments will pay off.
    B. play an active role in the management of companies.
    C. restructure companies to increase cash flow.

11. Hedge funds *most likely*:
    A. have stricter reporting requirements than a typical investment firm because of their use of leverage and derivatives.
    B. hold equal values of long and short securities.
    C. are not offered for sale to the general public.

For more questions related to this topic review, log in to your Schweser online account and launch SchweserPro™ QBank; and for video instruction covering each LOS in this topic review, log in to your Schweser online account and launch the OnDemand video lectures, if you have purchased these products.

Study Session 12
Cross-Reference to CFA Institute Assigned Reading #40 – Portfolio Management: An Overview

ANSWERS – CONCEPT CHECKERS

1. **B** Diversification provides an investor reduced risk. However, the expected return is generally similar or less than that expected from investing in a single risky security. Very high or very low returns become less likely.

2. **A** Portfolio diversification has been shown to be relatively ineffective during severe market turmoil. Portfolio diversification is most effective when the securities have low correlation and the markets are operating normally.

3. **A** In a defined contribution pension plan, the employee accepts the investment risk. The plan sponsor and manager neither promise a specific level of retirement income to participants nor make investment decisions. These are features of a defined benefit plan.

4. **C** In a defined benefit plan, the employer promises a specific level of benefits to employees when they retire. Thus, the employer bears the investment risk.

5. **C** Insurance companies need to be able to pay claims as they arise, which leads to insurance firms having low risk tolerance and high liquidity needs. Defined benefit pension plans and foundations both typically have high risk tolerance and low liquidity needs.

6. **A** An endowment has a long time horizon and low liquidity needs, as an endowment generally intends to fund its causes perpetually. Both insurance companies and banks require high liquidity.

7. **C** An IPS should be updated at regular intervals and whenever there is a major change in the client's objectives or constraints. Updating an IPS based on portfolio performance is not recommended.

8. **C** A top-down analysis begins with an analysis of broad economic trends. After an industry that is expected to perform well is chosen, the most attractive companies within that industry are identified. A bottom-up analysis begins with criteria such as firms' business prospects and quality of management.

9. **A** Open-end mutual funds do not have brokerage costs, as the shares are purchased from and redeemed with the fund company. Minimum investment amounts and management fees are typically higher for mutual funds.

10. **B** Both buyout funds and venture capital funds play an active role in the management of companies. Unlike venture capital funds, buyout funds expect that the majority of investments will pay off. Venture capital funds do not typically restructure companies.

11. **C** Hedge funds may not be offered for sale to the general public; they can be sold only to qualified investors who meet certain criteria. Hedge funds that hold equal values of long and short securities today make up only a small percentage of funds; many other kinds of hedge funds exist that make no attempt to be market neutral. Hedge funds have reporting requirements that are less strict than those of a typical investment firm.

The following is a review of the Portfolio Management principles designed to address the learning outcome statements set forth by CFA Institute. Cross-Reference to CFA Institute Assigned Reading #41.

Risk Management: An Introduction

Study Session 12

Exam Focus

Here we present a framework for risk management that is broad enough to be applied to corporations in general, financial firms, and individuals, as well as to the management of securities portfolios in any context. The main idea is that organizations should estimate the various risks they face and then reduce some risks and accept or increase other risks. The result should be a bundle of risks that simultaneously matches the risk tolerance of the organization and provides the greatest benefits in terms of reaching the organization's goals. Note that risk is not minimized though this process. The concept of risk budgeting, the categorization of types of risks, and the various methods of risk mitigation all offer testable material.

LOS 41.a: Define risk management.

The **risk management** process seeks to 1) identify the risk tolerance of the organization, 2) identify and measure the risks that the organization faces, and 3) modify and monitor these risks.

The process does not seek to minimize or eliminate all of these risks. The organization may increase its exposure to risks it decides to take because it is better able to manage and respond to them. The organization may decrease its exposure to risks that it is less well able to manage and respond to by making organizational changes, purchasing insurance, or entering into hedging transactions. Through these choices the firm aligns the risks it takes with its risk tolerances for these various types of risk.

Risk (uncertainty) is not something to be avoided by an organization or in an investment portfolio. Returns above the risk-free rate are earned by taking on risk. While returns for any period are not under the control of managers, the specific risks and overall level of risk the organization takes are under their control. We can think of risk management as determining organizational risks, determining the optimal bundle of risks for the organization, and implementing risk mitigation strategies to achieve that bundle of risks.

We describe the principles of risk management here in a framework that can be applied broadly, not only to firms or organizations in general, but also to the management of investment portfolios and financial firms, and even to individuals deciding how much risk and which specific risks they will take. Individuals follow a similar approach, selecting a bundle of risks that is optimal for maximizing their expected utility (rather than returns or profit).

LOS 41.b: Describe features of a risk management framework.

An overall **risk management framework** encompasses several activities, including:

- Establishing processes and policies for risk governance.
- Determining the organization's risk tolerance.
- Identifying and measuring existing risks.
- Managing and mitigating risks to achieve the optimal bundle of risks.
- Monitoring risk exposures over time.
- Communicating across the organization.
- Performing strategic risk analysis.

This framework is general, but all of these elements should be addressed in any comprehensive risk management framework. Only by understanding the risks the organization faces, and having the processes and procedures in place to effectively manage and monitor these risks, can an organization align its risk exposures to the goals of the organization.

LOS 41.c: Define risk governance and describe elements of effective risk governance.

Risk governance refers to senior management's determination of the risk tolerance of the organization, the elements of its optimal risk exposure strategy, and the framework for oversight of the risk management function. Risk governance seeks to manage risk in a way that supports the overall goals of the organization so it can achieve the best business outcome consistent with the organization's overall risk tolerance. Risk governance provides organization-wide guidance on the risks that should be pursued in an efficient manner, risks that should be subject to limits, and risks that should be reduced or avoided.

A risk management committee can provide a way for various parts of the organization to bring up issues of risk measurement, integration of risks, and the best ways to mitigate undesirable risks.

LOS 41.d: Explain how risk tolerance affects risk management.

Determining an organization's **risk tolerance** involves setting the overall risk exposure the organization will take by identifying the risks the firm can effectively take and the risks that the organization should reduce or avoid. Some of the factors that determine an organization's risk tolerance are its expertise in its lines of business, its skill at responding to negative outside events, its regulatory environment, and its financial strength and ability to withstand losses.

When analyzing risk tolerance, management should examine risks that may exist within the organization as well as those that may arise from outside. The various risks the firm is exposed to must each be considered and weighted against the expected benefits of bearing those risks and how these fit the overall goals of the organization.

LOS 41.e: Describe risk budgeting and its role in risk governance.

Risk budgeting is the process of allocating firm resources to assets (or investments) by considering their various risk characteristics and how they combine to meet the organization's risk tolerance. The goal is to allocate the overall amount of acceptable risk to the mix of assets or investments that have the greatest expected returns over time.

The risk budget may be a single metric, such as portfolio beta, value at risk, portfolio duration, or returns variance. A risk budget may be constructed based on categories of investments, such as domestic equities, domestic debt securities, international equities, and international debt securities. Another way to allocate a risk budget is to identify specific risk factors that comprise the overall risk of the portfolio or organization. In this case, specific risk factors that affect asset classes to varying degrees, such as interest rate risk, equity market risk, and foreign exchange rate risk, are estimated and aggregated to determine whether they match the overall risk tolerance of the organization.

LOS 41.f: Identify financial and non-financial sources of risk and describe how they may interact.

Financial risks are those that arise from exposure to financial markets. Examples are:

- **Credit risk.** This is the uncertainty about whether the counterparty to a transaction will fulfill its contractual obligations.
- **Liquidity risk.** This is the risk of loss when selling an asset at a time when market conditions make the sales price less than the underlying fair value of the asset.
- **Market risk.** This is the uncertainty about market prices of assets (stocks, commodities, and currencies) and interest rates.

Non-financial risks arise from the operations of the organization and from sources external to the organization. Examples are:

- **Operational risk.** This is the risk that human error or faulty organizational processes will result in losses.
- **Solvency risk.** This is the risk that the organization will be unable to continue to operate because it has run out of cash.
- **Regulatory risk.** This is the risk that the regulatory environment will change, imposing costs on the firm or restricting its activities.
- **Governmental or political risk** (including **tax risk**). This is the risk that political actions outside a specific regulatory framework, such as increases in tax rates, will impose significant costs on an organization.

- **Legal risk.** This is the uncertainty about the organization's exposure to future legal action.
- **Model risk.** This is the risk that asset valuations based on the organization's analytical models are incorrect.
- **Tail risk.** This is the risk that extreme events (those in the tails of the distribution of outcomes) are more likely than the organization's analysis indicates, especially from incorrectly concluding that the distribution of outcomes is normal.
- **Accounting risk.** This is the risk that the organization's accounting policies and estimates are judged to be incorrect.

For individuals, risks, such as risk of death (**mortality risk**) prior to providing for their families' future needs and the risk of living longer than anticipated (**longevity risk**) so that assets run out, are very important in financial planning. Mortality risk is most often addressed with life insurance, and longevity risk can be reduced by purchasing a lifetime annuity. Risk of health care expenses is addressed with health insurance. Although the risks for an individual are in some ways different from those of organizations, the overall approach is the same, choosing which risks to bear (self-insure), which risks to prevent or avoid, and which risks to take in order to maximize the expected outcome in terms of personal utility or satisfaction.

The various risks an organization faces are not independent; they interact in many ways. Consider a firm with market risk that it reduces with option contracts. If markets decline significantly, the firm is owed a payment from the firm on the other side of the option trade, so now there is significant counterparty or credit risk. There also may be legal risks if the counterparty seeks to avoid the payment through loopholes in the contract. Credit losses and legal losses may result in greater liquidity risk as positions must be sold. Additional losses from selling in a declining or less liquid market may increase solvency risk because of the negative impact on the firm's cash position.

Interactions among risks must be considered because such interactions are many and frequent. They can be especially important during periods of stress in financial markets, when risk management is most important to the health and possibly the survival of the organization.

LOS 41.g: Describe methods for measuring and modifying risk exposures and factors to consider in choosing among the methods.

Measures of risk for specific asset types include standard deviation, beta, and duration.

- **Standard deviation** is a measure of the volatility of asset prices and interest rates. Standard deviation may not be the appropriate measure of risk for non-normal probability distributions, especially those with negative skew or positive excess kurtosis (fat tails).
- **Beta** measures the market risk of equity securities and portfolios of equity securities. This measure considers the risk reduction benefits of diversification and is appropriate for securities held in a well-diversified portfolio, whereas standard deviation is a measure of risk on a stand-alone basis.
- **Duration** is a measure of the price sensitivity of debt securities to changes in interest rates.

Professor's Note: We describe and calculate standard deviation in Quantitative Methods; duration in Fixed Income; and beta in the current topic area, Portfolio Management.

Derivatives risks (sometimes referred to as "the Greeks") include:

- **Delta.** This is the sensitivity of derivatives values to the price of the underlying asset.
- **Gamma.** This is the sensitivity of delta to changes in the price of the underlying asset.
- **Vega.** This is the sensitivity of derivatives values to the volatility of the price of the underlying asset.
- **Rho.** This is the sensitivity of derivatives values to changes in the risk-free rate.

Tail risk is the uncertainty about the probability of extreme (negative) outcomes. Commonly used measures of tail risk (sometimes referred to as **downside risk**) include Value at Risk and Conditional VaR.

Value at risk (VaR) is the minimum loss over a period that will occur with a specific probability. Consider a bank that has a one-week VaR of 200 million euros with a probability of 3%. That means that a one-week loss of at least 200 million euros is expected to occur 3% of the time. Note that this is not the maximum one-week loss the bank will experience; it is the minimum loss that will occur 3% of the time. VaR does not provide a maximum loss for a period. VaR has become accepted as a risk measure for banks and is used in establishing minimum capital requirements.

There are various methods of calculating VaR, and both the inputs and models used will affect the calculated value, perhaps significantly. As is always the case with estimates of risk, incorrect inputs or inappropriate distribution assumptions will lead to misleading results. Given these limitations, VaR should be used in conjunction with other risk measures.

Conditional VaR (CVaR) is the expected value of a loss, *given* that the loss exceeds a minimum amount. Relating this to the VaR measure presented above, the CVaR would be the expected loss, given that the loss was at least 200 million euros. It is calculated as the probability-weighted average loss for all losses expected to be at least 200 million euros. CVaR is similar to the measure of loss given default that is used in estimating risk for debt securities.

Subjective and Market-Based Estimates of Risk

Two methods of risk assessment that are used to supplement measures such as VaR and CVaR are stress testing and scenario analysis. **Stress testing** examines the effects of a specific (usually extreme) change in a key variable such as an interest rate or exchange rate. **Scenario analysis** refers to a similar what-if analysis of expected loss but incorporates changes in multiple inputs. A given scenario might combine an interest rate change with a significant change in oil prices or exchange rates.

Quantifying the risk to an organization of very infrequent events is quite difficult. The risk of the bankruptcy of a firm that has never experienced significant financial distress is often a subjective estimate rather than a data-driven estimate. Estimates of risk can also be based on the market prices of insurance, derivatives, or other securities that can be used to hedge those risks. These hedging costs provide information on market participants' aggregate estimate of the expected loss of specific risks.

Operational risks are difficult to quantify for a single organization because they are very difficult to predict and may result in very large costs to the organization. One way to approach this problem is to examine a large sample of firms in order to determine an overall probability of significant losses due to operational risks and the average loss of firms that have experienced such losses.

Unexpected changes in tax laws or the regulatory environment can impose large costs on an organization. The political nature of such changes makes them quite difficult to predict. Subjective estimates, rather than data-driven quantitative estimates, are necessary. As is often the case, even a subjective, non-quantitative estimate of risk probabilities and magnitudes is better than not addressing the risk factor at all.

Modifying Risk Exposures

Risk management does not seek to eliminate all risks. The goal is to retain the optimal mix of risks for the organization. This may mean taking on more of some risks, decreasing others, and eliminating some altogether. Once the risk management team has estimated various risks, management may decide to prevent or avoid a risk, accept a risk, transfer a risk, or shift a risk.

One way to avoid a risk is to not engage in the activity with the uncertain outcome. If political risks in a country are to be avoided, simply not investing in securities of firms based in that country or not expanding a business enterprise to that country would avoid those risks. A decision to avoid certain risks typically would come from top management as a part of establishing the risk tolerance of the organization and would be instituted because the risks are judged to outweigh the potential benefits of specific activities.

Some risks can be prevented. The risk of a data breach can be prevented with a greater level of security for the data and stronger processes. In this case, the benefits of reducing or eliminating the risk are judged to be greater than the cost of doing so.

For risks that management has decided to bear, the organization will seek to bear them efficiently. **Diversification** may offer a way to more efficiently bear a specific risk.

> *Professor's Note: We explain how diversification can reduce risk in our review of "Portfolio Risk and Return: Part I."*

Sometimes the term **self-insurance** is used to describe a situation where an organization has decided to bear a risk. Note, however, that this simply means that it will bear any associated losses from this risk factor. It is possible that this represents inaction rather than the result of analysis and strategic decision making. In some cases, the firm will establish a reserve account to cover losses as a way of mitigating the impact of losses on the organization.

For a risk an organization has decided not to bear, risk transfer or risk shifting can be employed. With a **risk transfer**, another party takes on the risk. Insurance is a type of risk transfer. The risk of fire destroying a warehouse complex is shifted to an insurance company by buying an insurance policy and paying the policy premiums. Insurance companies diversify across many risks so the premiums of some insured parties pay the losses of others. Ideally, the various risks the insurance company insures are not highly correlated, as that can reduce or eliminate any diversification benefits. An insurance company with highly correlated risks (or a single very large risk) may itself shift some of the resulting risk by buying reinsurance from another company.

With a **surety bond**, an insurance company has agreed to make a payment if a third party fails to perform under the terms of a contract or agreement with the organization. For example, a company may be exposed to losses if a key supplier does not deliver on time, slowing a project and resulting in penalty payments by the company. Insurers also issue **fidelity bonds**, which will pay for losses that result from employee theft or misconduct. Managements that purchase insurance, surety bonds, or fidelity bonds have determined that the benefits of risk reduction are greater than the cost of the insurance.

Risk shifting is a way to change the distribution of possible outcomes and is accomplished primarily with derivative contracts. For example, financial firms that do not want to bear currency risk on some foreign currency denominated debt securities can use forward currency contracts, futures contracts, or swaps to reduce or eliminate that risk. A firm with a large position in a specific stock can buy put options that provide a minimum sale price for the securities, altering the distribution of possible outcomes (in this case providing a floor value for the securities). On the other hand, a firm could sell call options on a specific stock, altering the distribution of possible outcomes by giving up some of the upside potential of the stock but decreasing its downside risk by the amount of the premiums received from the sale of the call options.

Choosing Among Risk Modification Methods

Organizations may use multiple methods of risk modification to reduce a single risk. The criterion is always a comparison of the costs and benefits of risk modification. Some risks may be mitigated by diversification, some shifted by insurance where it is available and economical, some shifted though the use of derivatives, and some simply borne or self-insured. The end result is a risk profile that matches the risk tolerance established for the organization and includes the risks that top management has determined match the goals of the organization in terms of cost versus potential returns.

Key Concepts

LOS 41.a
Risk management is the process of identifying and measuring the risks an organization (or portfolio manager or individual) faces, determining an acceptable level of overall risk (establishing risk tolerance), deciding which risks should be taken and which risks should be reduced or avoided, and putting the structure in place to maintain the bundle of risks that is expected to best achieve the goals of the organization.

LOS 41.b
An overall risk management framework should address the following activities:
- Identifying and measuring existing risks.
- Determining the organization's overall risk tolerance.
- Establishing the processes and policies for risk governance.
- Managing and mitigating risks to achieve the optimal bundle of risks.
- Monitoring risk exposures over time.
- Communicating across the organization.
- Performing strategic risk analysis.

LOS 41.c
Risk governance refers to senior management's determination of the risk tolerance of the organization, the elements of its optimal risk exposure strategy, and the framework for oversight of the risk management function.

LOS 41.d
The risk tolerance for an organization is the overall amount of risk it will take in pursuing its goals and is determined by top management.

LOS 41.e
Risk budgeting is the process of allocating the total risk the firm will take (risk tolerance) to assets or investments by considering the risk characteristics of each and how they can be combined to best meet the organization's goals. The budget can be a single risk measure or the sum of various risk factors.

LOS 41.f
Financial risks are those that arise from exposure to financial markets, including credit risk, liquidity risk, and market risk. Non-financial risks are the risks from the operation of the organization and from sources external to the organization. Individuals face mortality and longevity risk, in addition to financial risks.

Interactions among risks are frequent and can be especially significant during periods of stress in financial markets.

LOS 41.g
Risk of assets is measured by standard deviation, beta, or duration. Derivatives risk measures include delta, gamma, vega, and rho. Tail risk is measured with value at risk (VaR) or Conditional VaR. Some risks must be measured subjectively.

An organization may decide to bear a risk (self-insurance), avoid or take steps to prevent a risk, efficiently manage a risk through diversification, transfer a risk with insurance or a surety bond, or shift a risk (change the distribution of uncertain outcomes) with derivatives.

Organizations may use multiple methods of risk modification after considering the costs and benefits of the various methods. The end result is a risk profile that matches the organization's risk tolerance and includes the risks that top management has determined match the organization's goals.

CONCEPT CHECKERS

1. An investor has the *most* control over her portfolio's:
   A. risk.
   B. relative returns.
   C. risk-adjusted returns.

2. Effective risk management would *most likely* attempt to:
   A. maximize expected return for a given level of risk.
   B. minimize risk for a given level of expected return.
   C. reduce any significant risks the firm is exposed to.

3. Risk budgeting can *best* be described as:
   A. setting an annual limit on risk taken.
   B. selecting assets by their risk characteristics.
   C. establishing a maximum amount of risk to be taken.

4. Risk governance should *most appropriately* be addressed within an organization at the:
   A. enterprise level.
   B. business unit level.
   C. individual employee level.

5. Risk shifting is *most likely* achieved by:
   A. risk mitigation.
   B. using derivative securities.
   C. transferring risk to an insurance company.

6. Which of the following is *most appropriately* termed a financial risk?
   A. Credit risk.
   B. Solvency risk.
   C. Settlement risk.

7. A risk management framework *least likely* includes:
   A. risk governance, risk mitigation, and strategic risk analysis.
   B. identifying and measuring risks, risk policies and processes, and risk governance.
   C. risk mitigation, tracking the organization's risk profile, and establishing position limits.

For more questions related to this topic review, log in to your Schweser online account and launch SchweserPro™ QBank; and for video instruction covering each LOS in this topic review, log in to your Schweser online account and launch the OnDemand video lectures, if you have purchased these products.

Answers – Concept Checkers

1. **A** An investor can select securities to achieve a given level of portfolio risk. Returns cannot be controlled.

2. **A** Risk management requires establishment of a risk tolerance (maximum acceptable level of risk) for the organization and will attempt to maximize expected returns for that level of risk. Some significant risks the firm is exposed to may be borne by the firm or even increased as a result of risk management.

3. **B** Risk budgeting refers to selecting assets or securities by their risk characteristics up to the maximum allowable amount of risk. The maximum amount of risk to be taken is established through risk governance.

4. **A** Risk governance should be approached from an enterprise view, with senior management determining risk tolerance and a risk management strategy on an organization-wide level.

5. **B** Risk shifting changes the distribution of possible outcomes, typically through the use of derivative securities. Risk shifting is one technique for mitigating risk. Transferring risk to an insurance company is termed risk transfer.

6. **A** The main sources of financial risk are market risk, credit risk, and liquidity risk. Solvency risk and settlement risk are classified as non-financial risks.

7. **C** A risk management framework includes the procedures, analytical tools, and infrastructure to conduct the risk governance process. It includes all of the items listed with the exception of establishing position limits, which is an example of the operational implementation of a system of risk management.

The following is a review of the Portfolio Management principles designed to address the learning outcome statements set forth by CFA Institute. Cross-Reference to CFA Institute Assigned Reading #42.

Portfolio Risk and Return: Part I

Study Session 12

Exam Focus

This topic review makes use of many of the statistical and returns measures we covered in Quantitative Methods. You should understand the historical return and risk rankings of the major asset classes and how the correlation (covariance) of returns between assets and between various asset classes affects the risk of portfolios. Risk aversion describes an investor's preferences related to the tradeoff between risk and return. These preferences, along with the risk and return characteristics of available portfolios, can be used to illustrate the selection of an optimal portfolio for a given investor, that is, the portfolio that maximizes the investor's expected utility.

LOS 42.a: Calculate and interpret major return measures and describe their appropriate uses.

Holding period return (HPR) is simply the percentage increase in the value of an investment over a given time period:

$$\text{holding period return} = \frac{\text{end-of-period value}}{\text{beginning-of-period value}} - 1 = \frac{P_t + \text{Div}_t}{P_0} - 1 = \frac{P_t - P_0 + \text{Div}_t}{P_0}$$

If a stock is valued at €20 at the beginning of the period, pays €1 in dividends over the period, and at the end of the period is valued at €22, the HPR is:

HPR = (22 + 1) / 20 − 1 = 0.15 = 15%

Average Returns

The **arithmetic mean return** is the simple average of a series of periodic returns. It has the statistical property of being an unbiased estimator of the true mean of the underlying distribution of returns:

$$\text{arithmetic mean return} = \frac{(R_1 + R_2 + R_3 + ... + R_n)}{n}$$

The **geometric mean return** is a compound annual rate. When periodic rates of return vary from period to period, the geometric mean return will have a value less than the arithmetic mean return:

$$\text{geometric mean return} = \sqrt[n]{(1+R_1)\times(1+R_2)\times(1+R_3)\times\ldots\times(1+R_n)} - 1$$

For example, for returns R_t over three annual periods, the geometric mean return is calculated as follows:

> **Example: Return measures**
>
> An investor purchased $1,000 of a mutual fund's shares. The fund had the following total returns over a 3-year period: +5%, –8%, +12%. Calculate the value at the end of the 3-year period, the holding period return, the mean annual return, and the geometric mean annual return.
>
> **Answer:**
>
> Ending value = (1,000)(1.05)(0.92)(1.12) = $1,081.92.
>
> Holding period return = (1.05)(0.92)(1.12) − 1 = 0.08192 = 8.192%, which can also be calculated as 1,081.92 / 1,000 − 1 = 8.192%.
>
> Arithmetic mean return = (5% − 8% + 12%) / 3 = 3%.
>
> Geometric mean return = $\sqrt[3]{(1.05)(0.92)(1.12)} - 1 = 0.02659 = 2.66\%$, which can also be calculated as geometric mean return = $\sqrt[3]{1+\text{HPR}} - 1 = \sqrt[3]{1.08192} - 1 = 2.66\%$.

The **money-weighted rate of return** is the internal rate of return on a portfolio based on all of its cash inflows and outflows. To calculate a money-weighted rate of return, consider the beginning value and additional deposits of cash by the investor to be inflows and consider withdrawals of cash, interest, and dividends (which are additional cash available to be withdrawn) and the ending value to be outflows.

> **Example: Money-weighted rate of return**
>
> Assume an investor buys a share of stock for $80 at t = 0 and at the end of the next year (t = 1), she buys an additional share for $70. At the end of Year 2, the investor sells both shares for $85 each. At the end of each year in the holding period, the stock paid a $1.50 per share dividend. What is the money-weighted rate of return?
>
> **Answer:**
>
> *Step 1:* Determine the timing of each cash flow and whether the cash flow is an inflow (+), into the account, or an outflow (−), available from the account.
>
> | | | | |
> |---|---|---|---|
> | t = 0: | purchase of first share | = | +$80.00 inflow to account |
> | t = 1: | purchase of second share | = | +$70.00 |
> | | dividend from first share | = | −$1.50 |
> | | Subtotal, t = 1 | | +$68.50 inflow to account |
> | t = 2: | dividend from two shares | = | −$3.00 |
> | | proceeds from selling shares | = | −$170.00 |
> | | Subtotal, t = 2 | | −$173.00 outflow from account |
>
> *Step 2:* Net the cash flows for each time period and set the PV of cash inflows equal to the present value of cash outflows.
>
> $$PV_{inflows} = PV_{outflows}$$
>
> $$\$80 + \frac{\$68.50}{(1+r)} = \frac{\$173.00}{(1+r)^2}$$
>
> *Step 3:* Solve for r to find the money-weighted rate of return.
>
> Net cash flows: CF_0 = +80; CF_1 = +68.5; CF_2 = −173
>
> The money-weighted rate of return is 10.35%.

In the previous example, the cash flows in and out of the account occur at 1-year intervals so that we solved for an annual money-weighted rate of return. More generally, we must use the shortest period between significant cash flows into or out of the account when setting up the internal rate of return calculation. For example, if we use one month as our period (zero cash flow for months with no cash flows), the internal rate of return calculation will yield a monthly rate of return. In that case, we would need to compound the monthly money-weighted return for 12 months to translate it into an effective annual rate.

Other Return Measures

Gross return refers to the total return on a security portfolio before deducting fees for the management and administration of the investment account. **Net return** refers to the return after these fees have been deducted. Note that commissions on trades and other costs that are necessary to generate the investment returns are deducted in both gross and net return measures.

Pretax nominal return refers to the return prior to paying taxes. Dividend income, interest income, short-term capital gains, and long-term capital gains may all be taxed at different rates.

After-tax nominal return refers to the return after the tax liability is deducted.

Real return is nominal return adjusted for inflation. Consider an investor who earns a nominal return of 7% over a year when inflation is 2%. The investor's approximate real return is simply 7 − 2 = 5%. The investor's exact real return is slightly lower, 1.07 / 1.02 − 1 = 0.049 = 4.9%.

Real return measures the increase in an investor's purchasing power: how much more goods she can purchase at the end of one year due to the increase in the value of her investments. If she invests $1,000 and earns a nominal return of 7%, she will have $1,070 at the end of the year. If the price of the goods she consumes has gone up 2%, from $1.00 to $1.02, she will be able to consume 1,070 / 1.02 = 1,049 units. She has given up consuming 1,000 units today but instead is able to purchase 1,049 units at the end of one year. Her purchasing power has gone up 4.9%; this is her real return.

A **leveraged return** refers to a return to an investor that is a multiple of the return on the underlying asset. The leveraged return is calculated as the gain or loss on the investment as a percentage of an investor's cash investment. An investment in a derivative security, such as a futures contract, produces a leveraged return because the cash deposited is only a fraction of the value of the assets underlying the futures contract. Leveraged investments in real estate are very common: investors pay for only part of the cost of the property with their own cash, and the rest of the amount is paid for with borrowed money.

LOS 42.b: Describe characteristics of the major asset classes that investors consider in forming portfolios.

An examination of the returns and standard deviation of returns for the major investable asset classes supports the idea of a tradeoff between risk and return. Using U.S. data over the period 1926–2008 as an example, shown in Figure 1, small-capitalization stocks have had the greatest average returns and greatest risk over the period. T-bills had the lowest average returns and the lowest standard deviation of returns.

Figure 1: Risk and Return of Major Asset Classes in the United States (1926–2008)[1]

Assets Class	Average Annual Return (Geometric Mean)	Standard Deviation (Annualized Monthly)
Small-cap stocks	11.7%	33.0%
Large-cap stocks	9.6%	20.9%
Long-term corporate bonds	5.9%	8.4%
Long-term Treasury bonds	5.7%	9.4%
Treasury bills	3.7%	3.1%
Inflation	3.0%	4.2%

Results for other markets around the world are similar: asset classes with the greatest average returns also have the highest standard deviations of returns.

The annual nominal return on U.S. equities has varied greatly from year to year, ranging from losses greater than 40% to gains of more than 50%. We can approximate the real returns over the period by subtracting inflation. The asset class with the least risk, T-bills, had a real return of only approximately 0.7% over the period, while the approximate real return on U.S. large-cap stocks was 6.6%. Because annual inflation fluctuated greatly over the period, real returns have been much more stable than nominal returns.

Evaluating investments using expected return and variance of returns is a simplification because returns do not follow a normal distribution; distributions are negatively skewed, with greater kurtosis (fatter tails) than a normal distribution. The negative skew reflects a tendency towards large downside deviations, while the positive excess kurtosis reflects frequent extreme deviations on both the upside and downside. These non-normal characteristics of skewness ($\neq 0$) and kurtosis ($\neq 3$) should be taken into account when analyzing investments.

Liquidity is an additional characteristic to consider when choosing investments because liquidity can affect the price and, therefore, the expected return of a security. Liquidity can be a major concern in emerging markets and for securities that trade infrequently, such as low-quality corporate bonds.

LOS 42.c: Calculate and interpret the mean, variance, and covariance (or correlation) of asset returns based on historical data.

Variance (Standard Deviation) of Returns for an Individual Security

In finance, the variance and standard deviation of returns are common measures of investment risk. Both of these are measures of the variability of a distribution of returns about its mean or expected value.

---

1. 2009 Ibbotson SBBI Classic Yearbook.

We can calculate the population variance, σ^2, when we know the return R_t for each period, the total number periods (T), and the mean or expected value of the population's distribution (μ), as follows:

$$\sigma^2 = \frac{\sum_{t=1}^{T}(R_t - \mu)^2}{T}$$

In the world of finance, we are typically analyzing only a sample of returns data, rather than the entire population. To calculate sample variance, s^2, using a sample of T historical returns and the mean, $\overline{R}$, of the observations, we use the following formula:

$$s^2 = \frac{\sum_{t=1}^{T}(R_t - \overline{R})^2}{T-1}$$

Covariance and Correlation of Returns for Two Securities

Covariance measures the extent to which two variables move together over time. A positive covariance means that the variables (e.g., rates of return on two stocks) tend to move together. Negative covariance means that the two variables tend to move in opposite directions. A covariance of zero means there is no linear relationship between the two variables. To put it another way, if the covariance of returns between two assets is zero, knowing the return for the next period on one of the assets tells you nothing about the return of the other asset for the period.

Here we will focus on the calculation of the covariance between two assets' returns using **historical data**. The calculation of the sample covariance is based on the following formula:

$$\text{Cov}_{1,2} = \frac{\sum_{t=1}^{n}\{[R_{t,1} - \overline{R}_1][R_{t,2} - \overline{R}_2]\}}{n-1}$$

where:
$R_{t,1}$ = return on Asset 1 in period t
$R_{t,2}$ = return on Asset 2 in period t
$\overline{R}_1$ = mean return on Asset 1
$\overline{R}_2$ = mean return on Asset 2
n = number of periods

The magnitude of the covariance depends on the magnitude of the individual stocks' standard deviations and the relationship between their co-movements. Covariance is an absolute measure and is measured in return units squared.

The covariance of the returns of two securities can be standardized by dividing by the product of the standard deviations of the two securities. This standardized measure of co-movement is called **correlation** and is computed as:

$$\rho_{1,2} = \frac{Cov_{1,2}}{\sigma_1 \sigma_2}$$

The relation can also be written as:

$$Cov_{1,2} = \rho_{1,2} \sigma_1 \sigma_2$$

The term $\rho_{1,2}$ is called the *correlation coefficient* between the returns of securities 1 and 2. The correlation coefficient has no units. It is a pure measure of the co-movement of the two stocks' returns and is bounded by –1 and +1.

How should you interpret the correlation coefficient?

- A correlation coefficient of +1 means that deviations from the mean or expected return are always proportional in the same direction. That is, they are perfectly positively correlated.
- A correlation coefficient of –1 means that deviations from the mean or expected return are always proportional in opposite directions. That is, they are perfectly negatively correlated.
- A correlation coefficient of zero means that there is no linear relationship between the two stocks' returns. They are uncorrelated. One way to interpret a correlation (or covariance) of zero is that, in any period, knowing the actual value of one variable tells you nothing about the value of the other.

> **Example: Calculating mean return, returns variance, returns covariance, and correlation**
>
> Given the six years of percentage returns for Stocks 1 and 2 in the following table, calculate the mean return, sample variance, sample covariance, and correlation for the two returns series.
>
> | Year | Stock 1 Return | Stock 2 Return | $(R_t - \bar{R}_1)$ | $(R_t - \bar{R}_2)$ | $(R_t - \bar{R}_1)(R_t - \bar{R}_2)$ |
> |---|---|---|---|---|---|
> | 20X4 | +0.10 | +0.20 | +0.05 | +0.10 | +0.005 |
> | 20X5 | –0.15 | –0.20 | –0.20 | –0.30 | +0.060 |
> | 20X6 | +0.20 | –0.10 | +0.15 | –0.20 | –0.030 |
> | 20X7 | +0.25 | +0.30 | +0.20 | +0.20 | +0.040 |
> | 20X8 | –0.30 | –0.20 | –0.35 | –0.30 | +0.105 |
> | 20X9 | +0.20 | +0.60 | +0.15 | +0.50 | +0.075 |
> | | $\sum R_1 = 0.30$ | $\sum R_2 = 0.60$ | | | $\Sigma = 0.255$ |
> | | $\bar{R}_1 = 0.05$ | $\bar{R}_2 = 0.10$ | | | |

Answer:

To calculate the mean returns for the samples, we sum the returns for each stock and divide by the number of years. The mean returns are $\overline{R}_1 = 30 / 6 = 5\%$ for Stock 1 and $\overline{R}_2 = 60 / 6 = 10\%$ for Stock 2.

Using the deviations of each year's returns from the mean return for Stock 1, we can calculate the sample variance as follows:

$$s_1^2 = \frac{(0.05)^2 + (-0.20)^2 + (0.15)^2 + (0.20)^2 + (-0.35)^2 + (0.15)^2}{6-1} = 0.05$$

Using the deviations of each year's returns from the mean return for Stock 2, we can calculate the sample variance as follows:

$$s_2^2 = \frac{(0.10)^2 + (-0.30)^2 + (-0.20)^2 + (0.20)^2 + (-0.30)^2 + (0.50)^2}{6-1} = 0.104$$

In the right-hand column of the table, we have summed the products of the deviations of Stocks 1 and 2 from their means to get 0.255.

The sample covariance is calculated as $0.255 / (6 - 1) = 0.051$.

To convert the covariance into correlation, we use the sample standard deviations of returns for the two stocks:

$$s_1 = \sqrt{0.05} = 0.2236 = 22.36\%$$

$$s_2 = \sqrt{0.104} = 0.3225 = 32.25\%$$

Finally, we can calculate the correlation coefficient for the two stocks' returns as follows:

$$\rho_{1,2} = \text{sample correlation } (r_{1,2}) = \frac{\text{Cov}_{1,2}}{s_1 s_2} = \frac{0.0510}{0.2236 \times 0.3225} = 0.7072$$

LOS 42.d: Explain risk aversion and its implications for portfolio selection.

A **risk-averse** investor is simply one that dislikes risk (i.e., prefers less risk to more risk). Given two investments that have equal expected returns, a risk-averse investor will choose the one with less risk (standard deviation, σ).

A **risk-seeking** (risk-loving) investor actually prefers more risk to less and, given equal expected returns, will choose the more risky investment. A **risk-neutral** investor has no preference regarding risk and would be indifferent between two such investments.

Consider this gamble: A coin will be flipped; if it comes up heads, you receive $100; if it comes up tails, you receive nothing. The expected payoff is 0.5($100) + 0.5($0) = $50. A risk-averse investor would choose a payment of $50 (a certain outcome) over the gamble. A risk-seeking investor would prefer the gamble to a certain payment of $50. A risk-neutral investor would be indifferent between the gamble and a certain payment of $50.

If expected returns are identical, a risk-averse investor will always choose the investment with the least risk. However, an investor may select a very risky portfolio despite being risk averse; a risk-averse investor will hold very risky assets if he feels that the extra return he expects to earn is adequate compensation for the additional risk.

LOS 42.e: Calculate and interpret portfolio standard deviation.

The variance of returns for a portfolio of two risky assets is calculated as follows:

$$Var_{portfolio} = w_1^2 \sigma_1^2 + w_2^2 \sigma_2^2 + 2 w_1 w_2 Cov_{12}$$

where w_1 is the proportion of the portfolio invested in Asset 1, and w_2 is the proportion of the portfolio invested in Asset 2. w_2 must equal $(1 - w_1)$.

Previously, we established that the correlation of returns for two assets is calculated as:

$\rho_{12} = \dfrac{Cov_{12}}{\sigma_1 \sigma_2}$, so that we can also write $Cov_{12} = \rho_{12} \sigma_1 \sigma_2$.

Substituting this term for Cov_{12} in the formula for the variance of returns for a portfolio of two risky assets, we have the following:

$$Var_{portfolio} = w_1^2 \sigma_1^2 + w_2^2 \sigma_2^2 + 2 w_1 w_2 \rho_{12} \sigma_1 \sigma_2$$

Because $Var_{portfolio} = \sigma^2_{portfolio}$:

$$\sigma_{portfolio} = \sqrt{w_1^2 \sigma_1^2 + w_2^2 \sigma_2^2 + 2 w_1 w_2 \rho_{12} \sigma_1 \sigma_2}$$

Writing the formula in this form allows us to easily see the effect of the correlation of returns between the two assets on portfolio risk.

LOS 42.f: Describe the effect on a portfolio's risk of investing in assets that are less than perfectly correlated.

If two risky asset returns are perfectly positively correlated, $\rho_{12} = +1$, then the square root of portfolio variance (the portfolio standard deviation of returns) is equal to:

$$\sigma_{portfolio} = \sqrt{Var_{portfolio}} = \sqrt{w_1^2\sigma_1^2 + w_2^2\sigma_2^2 + 2w_1w_2\sigma_1\sigma_2(1)} = w_1\sigma_1 + w_2\sigma_2$$

Professor's Note: This might be easier to see by examining the algebra in reverse. If $w_1\sigma_1 + w_2\sigma_2$ equals the square root of the term under the radical in this special case, then $(w_1\sigma_1 + w_2\sigma_2)^2$ should equal the term under the radical. If we expand $(w_1\sigma_1 + w_2\sigma_2)^2$, we get:

$$(w_1\sigma_1 + w_2\sigma_2)^2 = (w_1\sigma_1)^2 + (w_1\sigma_1)(w_2\sigma_2) + (w_2\sigma_2)(w_1\sigma_1) + (w_2\sigma_2)^2$$

$$= (w_1\sigma_1)^2 + (w_2\sigma_2)^2 + 2(w_1\sigma_1)(w_2\sigma_2)$$

$$= w_1^2\sigma_1^2 + w_2^2\sigma_2^2 + 2w_1\sigma_1w_2\sigma_2$$

In this unique case, with $\rho_{12} = 1$, the portfolio standard deviation is simply a weighted average of the standard deviations of the individual asset returns. A portfolio 25% invested in Asset 1 and 75% invested in Asset 2 will have a standard deviation of returns equal to 25% of the standard deviation (σ_1) of Asset 1's return, plus 75% of the standard deviation (σ_2) of Asset 2's return.

Focusing on returns correlation, we can see that the greatest portfolio risk results when the correlation between asset returns is +1. For any value of correlation less than +1, portfolio variance is reduced. Note that for a correlation of zero, the entire third term in the portfolio variance equation is zero. For negative values of correlation ρ_{12}, the third term becomes negative and further reduces portfolio variance and standard deviation.

We will illustrate this property with an example.

> **Example: Portfolio risk as correlation varies**
>
> Consider two risky assets that have returns variances of 0.0625 and 0.0324, respectively. The assets' standard deviations of returns are then 25% and 18%, respectively. Calculate the variances and standard deviations of portfolio returns for an equal-weighted portfolio of the two assets when their correlation of returns is 1, 0.5, 0, and –0.5.

The calculations are as follows:

$$\text{variance}_{\text{portfolio}} = w_1^2 \sigma_1^2 + w_2^2 \sigma_2^2 + 2 w_1 w_2 \rho_{12} \sigma_1 \sigma_2$$

$$\sigma_{\text{portfolio}} = \sqrt{\text{variance}_{\text{portfolio}}}$$

$$\sigma_{\text{portfolio}} = \sqrt{w_1^2 \sigma_1^2 + w_2^2 \sigma_2^2 + 2 w_1 w_2 \rho_{12} \sigma_1 \sigma_2}$$

ρ = correlation = +1:

σ = portfolio standard deviation = 0.5(25%) + 0.5(18%) = **21.5%**

σ^2 = portfolio variance = 0.215^2 = 0.046225

ρ = correlation = 0.5:

$\sigma^2 = (0.5^2)0.0625 + (0.5^2)0.0324 + 2(0.5)(0.5)(\mathbf{0.5})(0.25)(0.18) = 0.034975$

σ = **18.70%**

ρ = correlation = 0:

$\sigma^2 = (0.5^2)0.0625 + (0.5^2)0.0324 = 0.023725$

σ = **15.40%**

ρ = correlation = −0.5:

$\sigma^2 = (0.5^2)0.0625 + (0.5^2)0.0324 + 2(0.5)(0.5)(\mathbf{-0.5})(0.25)(0.18) = 0.012475$

σ = **11.17%**

Note that portfolio risk falls as the correlation between the assets' returns decreases. This is an important result of the analysis of portfolio risk: The lower the correlation of asset returns, the greater the risk reduction (diversification) benefit of combining assets in a portfolio. If asset returns were perfectly negatively correlated, portfolio risk could be eliminated altogether for a specific set of asset weights.

We show these relations graphically in Figure 2 by plotting the portfolio risk and return for all portfolios of two risky assets, for assumed values of the assets' returns correlation.

Figure 2: Risk and Return for Different Values of ρ

[Figure 2 shows a graph with E(R_p) on the vertical axis and σ_p on the horizontal axis. Curves connect 100% Asset A (lower right) and 100% Asset B (upper right) for correlations ρ = −1, ρ = −0.5, ρ = 0, ρ = +0.5, and ρ = +1.]

From these analyses, the risk-reduction benefits of investing in assets with low return correlations should be clear. The desire to reduce risk is what drives investors to invest in not just domestic stocks, but also bonds, foreign stocks, real estate, and other assets.

LOS 42.g: Describe and interpret the minimum-variance and efficient frontiers of risky assets and the global minimum-variance portfolio.

For each level of expected portfolio return, we can vary the portfolio weights on the individual assets to determine the portfolio that has the least risk. These portfolios that have the lowest standard deviation of all portfolios with a given expected return are known as **minimum-variance portfolios**. Together they make up the **minimum-variance frontier**.

Assuming that investors are risk averse, investors prefer the portfolio that has the greatest expected return when choosing among portfolios that have the same standard deviation of returns. Those portfolios that have the greatest expected return for each level of risk (standard deviation) make up the **efficient frontier**. The efficient frontier coincides with the top portion of the minimum-variance frontier. A risk-averse investor would only choose portfolios that are on the efficient frontier because all available portfolios that are not on the efficient frontier have lower expected returns than an efficient portfolio with the same risk. The portfolio on the efficient frontier that has the least risk is the **global minimum-variance portfolio**.

These concepts are illustrated in Figure 3.

Figure 3: Minimum-Variance and Efficient Frontiers

[Figure showing E(R) on y-axis and σ on x-axis, with Global Minimum-Variance Portfolio labeled at the leftmost point of a curve, Efficient Frontier (All Efficient Portfolios) along the upper portion of the curve, Inefficient Portfolios shown as dots in the interior, and Individual Security labeled.]

LOS 42.h: Explain the selection of an optimal portfolio, given an investor's utility (or risk aversion) and the capital allocation line.

An investor's **utility function** represents the investor's preferences in terms of risk and return (i.e., his degree of risk aversion). An **indifference curve** is a tool from economics that, in this application, plots combinations of risk (standard deviation) and expected return among which an investor is indifferent. In constructing indifference curves for portfolios based on only their expected return and standard deviation of returns, we are assuming that these are the only portfolio characteristics that investors care about. In Figure 4, we show three indifference curves for an investor. The investor's expected utility is the same for all points along a single indifference curve. Indifference curve I_1 represents the most preferred portfolios in Figure 4; our investor will prefer any portfolio along I_1 to any portfolio on either I_2 or I_3.

Figure 4: Risk-Averse Investor's Indifference Curves

Indifference curves slope upward for risk-averse investors because they will only take on more risk (standard deviation of returns) if they are compensated with greater expected returns. An investor who is relatively more risk averse requires a relatively greater increase in expected return to compensate for a given increase in risk. In other words, a more risk-averse investor will have steeper indifference curves, reflecting a higher **risk aversion coefficient**.

In our previous illustration of efficient portfolios available in the market, we included only risky assets. Now we will introduce a risk-free asset into our universe of available assets, and we will consider the risk and return characteristics of a portfolio that combines a portfolio of risky assets and the risk-free asset. Recall from Quantitative Methods that we can calculate the expected return and standard deviation of a portfolio with weight W_A allocated to risky Asset A and weight W_B allocated to risky Asset B using the following formulas:

$$E(R_{portfolio}) = W_A E(R_A) + W_B E(R_B)$$

$$\sigma_{portfolio} = \sqrt{W_A^2 \sigma_A^2 + W_B^2 \sigma_B^2 + 2 W_A W_B \rho_{AB} \sigma_A \sigma_B}$$

Allow Asset B to be the risk-free asset and Asset A to be the risky asset portfolio. Because a risk-free asset has zero standard deviation and zero correlation of returns with those of a risky portfolio, this results in the reduced equation:

$$\sigma_{portfolio} = \sqrt{W_A^2 \sigma_A^2} = W_A \sigma_A$$

The intuition of this result is quite simple: If we put X% of our portfolio into the risky asset portfolio, the resulting portfolio will have standard deviation of returns equal to X% of the standard deviation of the risky asset portfolio. The relationship between portfolio risk and return for various portfolio allocations is linear, as illustrated in Figure 5.

Combining a risky portfolio with a risk-free asset is the process that supports the **two-fund separation theorem**, which states that all investors' optimum portfolios will be made up of some combination of an optimal portfolio of risky assets and the risk-free asset. The line representing these possible combinations of risk-free assets and the optimal risky asset portfolio is referred to as the **capital allocation line**.

Point X on the capital allocation line in Figure 5 represents a portfolio that is 40% invested in the risky asset portfolio and 60% invested in the risk-free asset. Its expected return will be $0.40[E(R_{risky\ asset\ portfolio})] + 0.60(R_f)$, and its standard deviation will be $0.40(\sigma_{risky\ asset\ portfolio})$.

Figure 5: Capital Allocation Line and Risky Asset Weights

Now that we have constructed a set of the possible efficient portfolios (the capital allocation line), we can combine this with indifference curves representing an individual's preferences for risk and return to illustrate the logic of selecting an optimal portfolio (i.e., one that maximizes the investor's expected utility). In Figure 6, we can see that Investor A, with preferences represented by indifference curves I_1, I_2, and I_3, can reach the level of expected utility on I_2 by selecting portfolio X. This is the optimal portfolio for this investor, as any portfolio that lies on I_2 is preferred to all portfolios that lie on I_3 (and in fact to any portfolios that lie between I_2 and I_3). Portfolios on I_1 are preferred to those on I_2, but none of the portfolios that lie on I_1 are available in the market.

Figure 6: Risk-Averse Investor's Indifference Curves

The final result of our analysis here is not surprising; investors who are less risk averse will select portfolios that are more risky. Recall that the less an investor's risk aversion, the flatter his indifference curves. As illustrated in Figure 7, the flatter indifference curve for Investor B (I_B) results in an optimal (tangency) portfolio that lies to the right of the one that results from a steeper indifference curve, such as that for Investor A (I_A). An investor who is less risk averse should optimally choose a portfolio with more invested in the risky asset portfolio and less invested in the risk-free asset.

Figure 7: Portfolio Choices Based on Investor's Indifference Curves

KEY CONCEPTS

LOS 42.a
Holding period return is used to measure an investment's return over a specific period. Arithmetic mean return is the simple average of a series of periodic returns. Geometric mean return is a compound annual rate.

Money-weighted rate of return is the IRR calculated using periodic cash flows into and out of an account and is the discount rate that makes the present value of cash inflows equal to the present value of cash outflows.

Gross return is total return after deducting commissions on trades and other costs necessary to generate the returns, but before deducting fees for the management and administration of the investment account. Net return is the return after management and administration fees have been deducted.

Pretax nominal return is the numerical percentage return of an investment, without considering the effects of taxes and inflation. After-tax nominal return is the numerical return after the tax liability is deducted, without adjusting for inflation. Real return is the increase in an investor's purchasing power, roughly equal to nominal return minus inflation. Leveraged return is the gain or loss on an investment as a percentage of an investor's cash investment.

LOS 42.b
As predicted by theory, asset classes with the greatest average returns have also had the highest risk.

Some of the major asset classes that investors consider when building a diversified portfolio include small-capitalization stocks, large-capitalization stocks, long-term corporate bonds, long-term Treasury bonds, and Treasury bills.

In addition to risk and return, when analyzing investments, investors also take into consideration an investment's liquidity, as well as non-normal characteristics such as skewness and kurtosis.

LOS 42.c

We can calculate the population variance, σ^2, when we know the return R_t for period t, the total number T of periods, and the mean μ of the population's distribution:

$$\text{population variance} = \sigma^2 = \frac{\sum_{t=1}^{T}(R_t - \mu)^2}{T}$$

In finance, we typically analyze only a sample of returns, so the sample variance applies instead:

$$\text{sample variance} = S^2 = \frac{\sum_{t=1}^{T}(R_t - \overline{R})^2}{T-1}$$

Covariance measures the extent to which two variables move together over time. Positive covariance means the variables (e.g., rates of return on two stocks) tend to move together. Negative covariance means that the two variables tend to move in opposite directions. Covariance of zero means there is no linear relationship between the two variables.

Correlation is a standardized measure of co-movement that is bounded by –1 and +1:

$$\rho_{1,2} = \frac{Cov_{1,2}}{\sigma_1 \sigma_2}$$

LOS 42.d

A risk-averse investor is one that dislikes risk. Given two investments that have equal expected returns, a risk-averse investor will choose the one with less risk. However, a risk-averse investor will hold risky assets if he feels that the extra return he expects to earn is adequate compensation for the additional risk. Assets in the financial markets are priced according to the preferences of risk-averse investors.

A risk-seeking (risk-loving) investor actually prefers more risk to less and, given investments with equal expected returns, will choose the more risky investment.

A risk-neutral investor has no preference regarding risk and would be indifferent between two investments with the same expected return but different standard deviation of returns.

LOS 42.e

The standard deviation of returns for a portfolio of two risky assets is calculated as follows:

$$\sigma_{portfolio} = \sqrt{w_1^2 \sigma_1^2 + w_2^2 \sigma_2^2 + 2w_1 w_2 \rho_{1,2} \sigma_1 \sigma_2}$$

LOS 42.f

The greatest portfolio risk will result when the asset returns are perfectly positively correlated. As the correlation decreases from +1 to –1, portfolio risk decreases. The lower the correlation of asset returns, the greater the risk reduction (diversification) benefit of combining assets in a portfolio.

LOS 42.g

For each level of expected portfolio return, the portfolio that has the least risk is known as a minimum-variance portfolio. Taken together, these portfolios form a line called the minimum-variance frontier.

On a risk versus return graph, the one risky portfolio that is farthest to the left (has the least risk) is known as the global minimum-variance portfolio.

Those portfolios that have the greatest expected return for each level of risk make up the efficient frontier. The efficient frontier coincides with the top portion of the minimum variance frontier. Risk-averse investors would only choose a portfolio that lies on the efficient frontier.

LOS 42.h

An indifference curve plots combinations of risk and expected return that an investor finds equally acceptable. Indifference curves generally slope upward because risk-averse investors will only take on more risk if they are compensated with greater expected returns. A more risk-averse investor will have steeper indifference curves.

Flatter indifference curves (less risk aversion) result in an optimal portfolio with higher risk and higher expected return. An investor who is less risk averse will optimally choose a portfolio with more invested in the risky asset portfolio and less invested in the risk-free asset.

Concept Checkers

1. An investor buys a share of stock for $40 at time t = 0, buys another share of the same stock for $50 at t = 1, and sells both shares for $60 each at t = 2. The stock paid a dividend of $1 per share at t = 1 and at t = 2. The periodic money-weighted rate of return on the investment is *closest* to:
   A. 22.2%.
   B. 23.0%.
   C. 23.8%.

2. Which of the following asset classes has historically had the highest returns and standard deviation?
   A. Small-cap stocks.
   B. Large-cap stocks.
   C. Long-term corporate bonds.

3. In a 5-year period, the annual returns on an investment are 5%, –3%, –4%, 2%, and 6%. The standard deviation of annual returns on this investment is *closest* to:
   A. 4.0%.
   B. 4.5%.
   C. 20.7%.

4. A measure of how the returns of two risky assets move in relation to each other is the:
   A. range.
   B. covariance.
   C. standard deviation.

5. Which of the following statements about correlation is *least accurate*?
   A. Diversification reduces risk when correlation is less than +1.
   B. If the correlation coefficient is 0, a zero variance portfolio can be constructed.
   C. The lower the correlation coefficient, the greater the potential benefits from diversification.

6. The variance of returns is 0.09 for Stock A and 0.04 for Stock B. The covariance between the returns of A and B is 0.006. The correlation of returns between A and B is:
   A. 0.10.
   B. 0.20.
   C. 0.30.

7. Which of the following statements about risk-averse investors is *most accurate*? A risk-averse investor:
   A. seeks out the investment with minimum risk, while return is not a major consideration.
   B. will take additional investment risk if sufficiently compensated for this risk.
   C. avoids participating in global equity markets.

Use the following data to answer Questions 8 and 9.

A portfolio was created by investing 25% of the funds in Asset A (standard deviation = 15%) and the balance of the funds in Asset B (standard deviation = 10%).

8. If the correlation coefficient is 0.75, what is the portfolio's standard deviation?
   A. 10.6%.
   B. 12.4%.
   C. 15.0%.

9. If the correlation coefficient is −0.75, what is the portfolio's standard deviation?
   A. 2.8%.
   B. 4.2%.
   C. 5.3%.

10. Which of the following statements about covariance and correlation is *least accurate*?
    A. A zero covariance implies there is no linear relationship between the returns on two assets.
    B. If two assets have perfect negative correlation, the variance of returns for a portfolio that consists of these two assets will equal zero.
    C. The covariance of a 2-stock portfolio is equal to the correlation coefficient times the standard deviation of one stock's returns times the standard deviation of the other stock's returns.

11. Which of the following available portfolios *most likely* falls below the efficient frontier?

	Portfolio	Expected return	Expected standard deviation
A.	A	7%	14%
B.	B	9%	26%
C.	C	12%	22%

12. The capital allocation line is a straight line from the risk-free asset through the:
    A. global maximum-return portfolio.
    B. optimal risky portfolio.
    C. global minimum-variance portfolio.

For more questions related to this topic review, log in to your Schweser online account and launch SchweserPro™ QBank; and for video instruction covering each LOS in this topic review, log in to your Schweser online account and launch the OnDemand video lectures, if you have purchased these products.

ANSWERS – CONCEPT CHECKERS

1. **C** Using the cash flow functions on your financial calculator, enter CF0 = –40; CF1 = –50 + 1 = –49; CF2 = 60 × 2 + 2 = 122; CPT IRR = 23.82%.

2. **A** Small-cap stocks have had the highest annual return and standard deviation of return over time. Large-cap stocks and bonds have historically had lower risk and return than small-cap stocks.

3. **B** Mean annual return = (5% – 3% – 4% + 2% + 6%) / 5 = 1.2%

   Squared deviations from the mean:

   5% – 1.2% = 3.8% 3.8^2 = 14.44
   –3% –1.2% = –4.2% -4.2^2 = 17.64
   –4% –1.2% = –5.2% -5.2^2 = 27.04
   2% –1.2% = 0.8% 0.8^2 = 0.64
   6% –1.2% = 4.8% 4.8^2 = 23.04

   Sum of squared deviations = 14.44 + 17.64 + 27.04 + 0.64 + 23.04 = 82.8

   Sample variance = 82.8 / (5 – 1) = 20.7

   Sample standard deviation = $20.7^{1/2}$ = 4.55%

4. **B** The covariance is defined as the co-movement of the returns of two assets or how well the returns of two risky assets move together. Range and standard deviation are measures of dispersion and measure risk, not how assets move together.

5. **B** A zero-variance portfolio can only be constructed if the correlation coefficient between assets is –1. Diversification benefits can be had when correlation is less than +1, and the lower the correlation, the greater the potential benefit.

6. **A** $\sqrt{A} = \sqrt{0.09} = 0.30$

   $\sqrt{B} = \sqrt{0.04} = 0.20$

   Correlation = 0.006 / [(0.30)(0.20)] = 0.10

7. **B** Risk-averse investors are generally willing to invest in risky investments, if the return of the investment is sufficient to reward the investor for taking on this risk. Participants in securities markets are generally assumed to be risk-averse investors.

8. **A** $\sqrt{(0.25)^2(0.15)^2 + (0.75)^2(0.10)^2 + 2(0.25)(0.75)(0.15)(0.10)(0.75)} =$

   $\sqrt{0.001406 + 0.005625 + 0.004219} = \sqrt{0.01125} = 0.106 = 10.6\%$

9. **C** $\sqrt{(0.25)^2(0.15)^2 + (0.75)^2(0.10)^2 + 2(0.25)(0.75)(0.15)(0.10)(-0.75)} =$

   $\sqrt{0.001406 + 0.005625 - 0.004219} = \sqrt{0.002812} = 0.053 = 5.3\%$

10. **B** If the correlation of returns between the two assets is –1, the set of possible portfolio risk/return combinations becomes two straight lines (see Figure 2). A portfolio of these two assets will have a positive returns variance unless the portfolio weights are those that minimize the portfolio variance. Covariance is equal to the correlation coefficient multiplied by the product of the standard deviations of the returns of the two stocks in a 2-stock portfolio. If covariance is zero, then correlation is also zero, which implies that there is no linear relationship between the two stocks' returns.

11. **B** Portfolio B must be the portfolio that falls below the Markowitz efficient frontier because there is a portfolio (Portfolio C) that offers a higher return and lower risk.

12. **B** An investor's optimal portfolio will lie somewhere on the capital allocation line, which begins at the risk-free asset and runs through the optimal risky portfolio.

The following is a review of the Portfolio Management principles designed to address the learning outcome statements set forth by CFA Institute. Cross-Reference to CFA Institute Assigned Reading #43.

PORTFOLIO RISK AND RETURN: PART II

Study Session 12

EXAM FOCUS

The concepts developed here are very important to finance theory and are also used extensively in practice. You must know this material completely—not only the formulas and definitions, but the ideas that underlie their use. A model assumption that diversification is costless leads to the conclusion that only systematic risk (which cannot be reduced by further diversification) is priced in equilibrium, so that bearing nonsystematic risk does not increase expected returns.

LOS 43.a: Describe the implications of combining a risk-free asset with a portfolio of risky assets.

In the previous topic review, we covered the mathematics of calculating the risk and return of a portfolio with a percentage weight of W_A invested in a risky portfolio (P) and a weight of $W_B = 1 - W_A$ invested in a risk-free asset.

$$E(R_P) = W_A E(R_A) + W_B E(R_B)$$

$$\sigma_P = \sqrt{W_A^2 \sigma_A^2 + W_B^2 \sigma_B^2 + 2 W_A W_B \rho_{AB} \sigma_A \sigma_B}$$

Because a risk-free asset has zero standard deviation and zero correlation of returns with a risky portfolio, allowing Asset B to be the risk-free asset and Asset A to be the risky asset portfolio results in the following reduced equation:

$$\sigma_P = \sqrt{W_A^2 \sigma_A^2} = W_A \sigma_A$$

Our result is that the risk (standard deviation of returns) and expected return of portfolios with varying weights in the risk-free asset and a risky portfolio can be plotted as a line that begins at the risk-free rate of return and extends through the risky portfolio. This result is illustrated in Figure 1.

Figure 1: Combining a Risk-Free Asset with a Risky Asset

[Figure: A graph with σ on the x-axis and $E(R_p)$ on the y-axis. A line starts at R_f on the y-axis and rises through a point labeled "Portfolio with W_A Invested in the Risky Asset" at coordinates ($\sigma_{portfolio} = W_A\sigma_A$, $E(R_{portfolio})$), continuing up to the "Risky Asset" point at (σ_A, $E(R_A)$).]

LOS 43.b: Explain the capital allocation line (CAL) and the capital market line (CML).

The line of possible portfolio risk and return combinations given the risk-free rate and the risk and return of a portfolio of risky assets is referred to as the **capital allocation line** (CAL). For an individual investor, the best CAL is the one that offers the most-preferred set of possible portfolios in terms of their risk and return. Figure 2 illustrates three possible investor CALs for three different risky portfolios A, B, and C. The optimal risky portfolio for this investor is Portfolio A because it results in the most preferred set of possible portfolios constructed by combining the risk-free asset with the risky portfolio. Of all the portfolios available to the investor, a combination of the risk-free asset with risky Portfolio A offers the investor the greatest expected utility.

Figure 2: Risky Portfolios and Their Associated Capital Allocation Lines

[Figure: E(R) vs σ graph showing an Indifference Curve tangent to three capital allocation lines labeled CAL$_A$, CAL$_B$, and CAL$_C$ with points A, B, and C marked on them respectively.]

If each investor has different expectations about the expected returns of, standard deviations of, or correlations between risky asset returns, each investor will have a different optimal risky asset portfolio and a different CAL.

A simplifying assumption underlying modern portfolio theory (and the capital asset pricing model, which is introduced later in this topic review) is that investors have homogeneous expectations (i.e., they all have the same estimates of risk, return, and correlations with other risky assets for all risky assets). Under this assumption, all investors face the same efficient frontier of risky portfolios and will all have the same optimal risky portfolio and CAL.

Figure 3 illustrates the determination of the optimal risky portfolio and optimal CAL for all investors under the assumption of homogeneous expectations. Note that, under this assumption, the optimal CAL for any investor is the one that is just tangent to the efficient frontier. Depending on their preferences for risk and return (their indifference curves), investors may choose different portfolio weights for the risk-free asset and the risky (tangency) portfolio. Every investor, however, will use the same risky portfolio. When this is the case, that portfolio must be the **market portfolio** of all risky assets because all investors that hold any risky assets hold the same portfolio of risky assets.

Study Session 12
Cross-Reference to CFA Institute Assigned Reading #43 – Portfolio Risk and Return: Part II

Figure 3: Determining the Optimal Risky Portfolio and Optimal CAL Assuming Homogeneous Expectations

[Figure: A graph with E(R) on the y-axis and σ on the x-axis. The Capital Market Line starts at R_f on the y-axis and is tangent to the Efficient Frontier curve at the Optimal Risky Portfolio (Market Portfolio).]

Under the assumption of homogeneous expectations, this optimal CAL for all investors is termed the **capital market line** (CML). Along this line, expected portfolio return, $E(R_P)$, is a linear function of portfolio risk, σ_P. The equation of this line is as follows:

$$E(R_P) = R_f + \left(\frac{E(R_M) - R_f}{\sigma_M}\right)\sigma_P$$

The *y*-intercept of this line is R_f and the slope (rise over run) of this line is as follows:

$$\left(\frac{E(R_M) - R_f}{\sigma_M}\right)$$

The intuition of this relation is straightforward. An investor who chooses to take on no risk ($\sigma_P = 0$) will earn the risk-free rate, R_f. The difference between the expected return on the market and the risk-free rate is termed the **market risk premium**. If we rewrite the CML equation as

$$E(R_P) = R_f + \left(E(R_M) - R_f\right)\left(\frac{\sigma_P}{\sigma_M}\right)$$

we can see that an investor can expect to get one unit of market risk premium in additional return (above the risk-free rate) for every unit of market risk, σ_M, that the investor is willing to accept.

If we assume that investors can both lend (invest in the risk-free asset) at the risk-free rate and borrow (as with a margin account) at the risk-free rate, they can select portfolios to the right of the market portfolio in Figure 3. An example will illustrate the calculations.

Example: Portfolio risk and return with borrowing and lending

Assume that the risk-free rate, R_f, is 5%; the expected rate of return on the market, $E(R_M)$, is 11%; and that the standard deviation of returns on the market portfolio, σ_M, is 20%. Calculate the expected return and standard deviation of returns for portfolios that are 25%, 75%, and 125% invested in the market portfolio. We will use R_M to represent these portfolio weights.

Expected portfolio returns are calculated as $E(R_p) = (1 - W_M) \times R_f + W_M \times E(R_M)$, so we have the following:

$W_M = 25\%$: $E(R_p) = 0.75 \times 5\% + 0.25 \times 11\% = 6.5\%$

$W_M = 75\%$: $E(R_p) = 0.25 \times 5\% + 0.75 \times 11\% = 9.5\%$

$W_M = 125\%$: $E(R_p) = -0.25 \times 5\% + 1.25 \times 11\% = 12.5\%$

Portfolio standard deviation is calculated as $\sigma_P = W_M \times \sigma_M$, so we have the following:

$\sigma_P = 0.25 \times 20\% = 5\%$

$\sigma_P = 0.75 \times 20\% = 15\%$

$\sigma_P = 1.25 \times 20\% = 25\%$

Figure 4: Borrowing and Lending Portfolios

> Note that with a weight (of investor assets) of 125% in the market portfolio, the investor borrows an amount equal to 25% of his portfolio assets at 5%. An investor with $10,000 would then borrow $2,500 and invest a total of $12,500 in the market portfolio. This leveraged portfolio will have an expected return of 12.5% and standard deviation of 25%.

Investors who believe market prices are informationally efficient often follow a **passive investment strategy** (i.e., invest in an index of risky assets that serves as a proxy for the market portfolio and allocate a portion of their investable assets to a risk-free asset, such as short-term government securities). In practice, many investors and portfolio managers believe their estimates of security values are correct and market prices are incorrect. Such investors will not use the weights of the market portfolio but will invest more than the market weights in securities that they believe are undervalued and less than the market weights in securities which they believe are overvalued. This is referred to as **active portfolio management** to differentiate it from a passive investment strategy that utilizes a market index for the optimal risky asset portfolio.

LOS 43.c: Explain systematic and nonsystematic risk, including why an investor should not expect to receive additional return for bearing nonsystematic risk.

When an investor diversifies across assets that are not perfectly correlated, the portfolio's risk is less than the weighted average of the risks of the individual securities in the portfolio. The risk that is eliminated by diversification is called **unsystematic risk** (also called *unique, diversifiable,* or *firm-specific risk*). Because the market portfolio contains *all* risky assets, it must be a well-diversified portfolio. All the risk that can be diversified away has been. The risk that remains cannot be diversified away and is called the **systematic risk** (also called *nondiversifiable risk* or *market risk*).

The concept of systematic risk applies to individual securities as well as to portfolios. Some securities' returns are highly correlated with overall market returns. Examples of firms that are highly correlated with market returns are luxury goods manufacturers such as Ferrari automobiles and Harley Davidson motorcycles. These firms have high systematic risk (i.e., they are very responsive to market, or systematic, changes). Other firms, such as utility companies, respond very little to changes in the systematic risk factors. These firms have very little systematic risk. Hence, total risk (as measured by standard deviation) can be broken down into its component parts: unsystematic risk and systematic risk. Mathematically:

total risk = systematic risk + unsystematic risk

> *Professor's Note: Know this concept!*

Do you actually have to buy all the securities in the market to diversify away unsystematic risk? No. Academic studies have shown that as you increase the number of stocks in a portfolio, the portfolio's risk falls toward the level of market risk. One study showed that it only took about 12 to 18 stocks in a portfolio to achieve 90% of the maximum diversification possible. Another study indicated it took 30 securities. Whatever the number, it is significantly less than *all* the securities. Figure 5 provides a general representation of this concept. Note, in the figure, that once you get to 30 or so securities in a portfolio, the standard deviation remains constant. The remaining risk is systematic, or nondiversifiable, risk. We will develop this concept later when we discuss beta, a measure of systematic risk.

Figure 5: Risk vs. Number of Portfolio Assets

Systematic Risk is Relevant in Portfolios

One important conclusion of capital market theory is that equilibrium security returns depend on a stock's or a portfolio's systematic risk, not its total risk as measured by standard deviation. One of the assumptions of the model is that diversification is free. The reasoning is that investors will not be compensated for bearing risk that can be eliminated at no cost. If you think about the costs of a no-load index fund compared to buying individual stocks, diversification is actually very low cost if not actually free.

The implications of this conclusion are very important to asset pricing (expected returns). The riskiest stock, with risk measured as standard deviation of returns, does not necessarily have the greatest expected return. Consider a biotech stock with one new drug product that is in clinical trials to determine its effectiveness. If it turns out that the drug is effective and safe, stock returns will be quite high. If, on the other hand, the subjects in the clinical trials are killed or otherwise harmed by the drug, the stock will fall to approximately zero and returns will be quite poor. This describes a stock with high standard deviation of returns (i.e., high total risk).

The high risk of our biotech stock, however, is primarily from firm-specific factors, so its unsystematic risk is high. Because market factors such as economic growth rates have little to do with the eventual outcome for this stock, systematic risk is a small proportion of the total risk of the stock. Capital market theory says that the equilibrium return on this stock may be less than that of a stock with much less firm-specific risk but more sensitivity to the factors that drive the return of the overall market. An established manufacturer of machine tools may not be a very risky investment in terms of total risk, but may have a greater sensitivity to market (systematic) risk factors (e.g., GDP growth rates) than our biotech stock. Given this scenario, the stock with more total risk (the biotech stock) has less systematic risk and will therefore have a lower equilibrium rate of return according to capital market theory.

Note that holding many biotech firms in a portfolio will diversify away the firm-specific risk. Some will have blockbuster products and some will fail, but you can imagine that when 50 or 100 such stocks are combined into a portfolio, the uncertainty about the portfolio return is much less than the uncertainty about the return of a single biotech firm stock.

To sum up, unsystematic risk is not compensated in equilibrium because it can be eliminated for free through diversification. Systematic risk is measured by the contribution of a security to the risk of a well-diversified portfolio, and the expected equilibrium return (required return) on an individual security will depend only on its systematic risk.

LOS 43.d: Explain return generating models (including the market model) and their uses.

Return generating models are used to estimate the expected returns on risky securities based on specific factors. For each security, we must estimate the sensitivity of its returns to each specific factor. Factors that explain security returns can be classified as macroeconomic, fundamental, and statistical factors. **Multifactor models** most commonly use macroeconomic factors such as GDP growth, inflation, or consumer confidence, along with fundamental factors such as earnings, earnings growth, firm size, and research expenditures. Statistical factors often have no basis in finance theory and are suspect in that they may represent only relations for a specific time period which have been identified by data mining (repeated tests on a single data set).

The general form of a multifactor model with *k* factors is as follows:

$$E(R_i) - R_f = \beta_{i1} \times E(\text{Factor 1}) + \beta_{i2} \times E(\text{Factor 2}) + \ldots + \beta_{ik} \times E(\text{Factor k})$$

This model states that the expected excess return (above the risk-free rate) for Asset *i* is the sum of each **factor sensitivity** or **factor loading** (the βs) for Asset *i* multiplied by the expected value of that factor for the period. The first factor is often the expected excess return on the market, $E(R_m - R_f)$.

One multifactor model that is often used is that of Fama and French. They estimated the sensitivity of security returns to three factors: firm size, firm book value to market value ratio, and the return on the market portfolio minus the risk-free rate (excess return on the market portfolio). Carhart suggests a fourth factor that measures price momentum using prior period returns. Together, these four factors do a relatively good job of explaining returns differences for U.S. equity securities over the period for which the model has been estimated.

The simplest factor model is a single-factor model. A single-factor model with the return on the market, R_m, as its only risk factor can be written (in excess returns form) as:

$$E(R_i) - R_f = \beta_i \times [E(R_m) - R_f]$$

Here, the expected excess return (return above the risk-free rate) is the product of the factor weight or factor sensitivity, Beta i, and the risk factor, which in this model is the excess return on the market portfolio or market index, so that this is also sometimes called a **single-index model**.

A simplified form of a single-index model is the **market model**, which is used to estimate a security's (or portfolio's) beta and to estimate a security's abnormal return (return above its expected return) based on the actual market return.

The form of the market model is as follows:

$$R_i = \alpha_i + \beta_i R_m + e_i$$

where:
R_i = Return on Asset i
R_m = Market return
β_i = Slope coefficient
α_i = Intercept
e_i = Abnormal return on Asset i

The intercept α_i and slope coefficient β_i are estimated from historical return data. We can require that α_i is the risk-free rate times $(1 - \beta_i)$ to be consistent with the general form of a single-index model in excess returns form.

The expected return on Asset i is $\alpha_i + \beta_i E(R_m)$. A deviation from the expected return in a given period is the abnormal return on Asset i, e_i, or $R_i - (\alpha_i + \beta_i R_m)$.

In the market model, the factor sensitivity or beta for Asset i is a measure of how sensitive the return on Asset i is to the return on the overall market portfolio (market index).

LOS 43.e: Calculate and interpret beta.

The sensitivity of an asset's return to the return on the market index in the context of the market model is referred to as its **beta**. Beta is a standardized measure of the covariance of the asset's return with the market return. Beta can be calculated as follows:

$$\beta_i = \frac{\text{covariance of Asset } i\text{'s return with the market return}}{\text{variance of the market return}} = \frac{\text{Cov}_{im}}{\sigma_m^2}$$

We can use the definition of the correlation between the returns on Asset i with the returns on the market index:

$$\rho_{im} = \frac{Cov_{im}}{\sigma_i \sigma_m}$$

to get $Cov_{im} = \rho_{im} \sigma_i \sigma_m$.

Substituting for Cov_{im} in the equation for B_i, we can also calculate beta as:

$$\beta_i = \frac{\rho_{im} \sigma_i \sigma_m}{\sigma_m^2} = \rho_{im} \frac{\sigma_i}{\sigma_m}$$

> **Example: Calculating an asset's beta**
>
> The standard deviation of the return on the market index is estimated as 20%.
>
> 1. If Asset A's standard deviation is 30% and its correlation of returns with the market index is 0.8, what is Asset A's beta?
>
>   Using the formula $\beta_i = \rho_{im} \frac{\sigma_i}{\sigma_m}$, we have: $\beta_i = 0.80 \left(\frac{0.30}{0.20} \right) = 1.2$.
>
> 2. If the covariance of Asset A's returns with the returns on the market index is 0.048, what is the beta of Asset A?
>
>   Using the formula $\beta_i = \frac{Cov_{im}}{\sigma_m^2}$, we have $\beta_i = \frac{0.048}{0.2^2} = 1.2$.
>
> *Professor's Note: Candidates should be prepared to calculate beta in either of the two ways in the example.*

In practice, we estimate asset betas by regressing returns on the asset on those of the market index. While regression is a Level II concept, for our purposes, you can think of it as a mathematical estimation procedure that fits a line to a data plot. In Figure 5, we represent the excess returns on Asset i as the dependent variable and the excess returns on the market index as the independent variable. The *least squares regression line* is the line that minimizes the sum of the squared distances of the points plotted from the line (this is what is meant by the line of *best fit*). The slope of this line is our estimate of beta. In Figure 6, the line is steeper than 45 degrees, the slope is greater than one, and the asset's estimated beta is greater than one. Our interpretation is that the returns on Asset i are more variable in response to systematic risk factors than is the overall market, which has a beta of one.

Figure 6: Regression of Asset Excess Returns against Market Asset Returns

This regression line is referred to as the asset's **security characteristic line**. Mathematically, the slope of the security characteristic line is $\frac{Cov_{im}}{\sigma_m^2}$, which is the same formula we used earlier to calculate beta.

LOS 43.f: Explain the capital asset pricing model (CAPM), including its assumptions, and the security market line (SML).

Given that the only relevant (priced) risk for an individual Asset i is measured by the covariance between the asset's returns and the returns on the market, $Cov_{i,mkt}$, we can plot the relationship between risk and return for individual assets using $Cov_{i,mkt}$ as our measure of systematic risk. The resulting line, plotted in Figure 7, is one version of what is referred to as the **security market line** (SML).

Figure 7: Security Market Line

[Figure: Security Market Line plot with E(R_i) on vertical axis and Systematic Risk (Cov_{i,mkt}) on horizontal axis. The SML line starts at R_f on the vertical axis and rises through the Market Portfolio point at coordinates (cov_{mkt,mkt} = σ²_{mkt}, E(R_{mkt})).]

The equation of the SML is:

$$E(R_i) = R_f + \frac{E(R_{mkt}) - R_f}{\sigma^2_{mkt}}(Cov_{i,mkt})$$

which can be rearranged and stated as:

$$E(R_i) = R_f + \frac{Cov_{i,mkt}}{\sigma^2_{mkt}}[E(R_{mkt}) - R_f]$$

The line described by this last equation is presented in Figure 8, where we let the standardized covariance term, $\frac{Cov_{i,mkt}}{\sigma^2_{mkt}}$, be defined as beta, β_i.

This is the most common means of describing the SML, and this relation between beta (systematic risk) and expected return is known as the **capital asset pricing model** (CAPM).

Figure 8: The Capital Asset Pricing Model

So, we can define beta, $\beta = \dfrac{Cov_{i,mkt}}{\sigma^2_{mkt}}$, as a standardized measure of systematic risk.

Beta measures the relation between a security's excess returns and the excess returns to the market portfolio.

Formally, the CAPM is stated as:

$$E(R_i) = R_f + \beta_i[E(R_{mkt}) - R_f]$$

The CAPM holds that, in equilibrium, the expected return on risky asset $E(R_i)$ is the risk-free rate (R_f) plus a beta-adjusted market risk premium, $\beta_i[E(R_{mkt}) - R_f]$. Beta measures systematic (market or covariance) risk.

The **assumptions of the CAPM** are:

- *Risk aversion.* To accept a greater degree of risk, investors require a higher expected return.
- *Utility maximizing investors.* Investors choose the portfolio, based on their individual preferences, with the risk and return combination that maximizes their (expected) utility.
- *Frictionless markets.* There are no taxes, transaction costs, or other impediments to trading.
- *One-period horizon.* All investors have the same one-period time horizon.
- *Homogeneous expectations.* All investors have the same expectations for assets' expected returns, standard deviation of returns, and returns correlations between assets.
- *Divisible assets.* All investments are infinitely divisible.
- *Competitive markets.* Investors take the market price as given and no investor can influence prices with their trades.

Comparing the CML and the SML

It is important to recognize that the CML and SML are very different. Recall the equation of the CML:

$$E(R_P) = R_f + \sigma_P \left\{ \frac{[E(R_M) - R_f]}{\sigma_M} \right\}$$

The CML uses total risk = σ_p on the x-axis. Hence, only efficient portfolios will plot on the CML. On the other hand, the SML uses beta (systematic risk) on the x-axis. So in a CAPM world, *all properly priced securities and portfolios of securities will plot on the SML*, as shown in Figure 9.

Figure 9: Comparing the CML and the SML

(a) Capital Market Line

(b) Security Market Line

Portfolios that are not well diversified (efficient) plot inside the efficient frontier and are represented by risk-return combinations such as points A, B, and C in panel (a) of Figure 9. Individual securities are one example of such inefficient portfolios. According to the CAPM, the expected returns on all portfolios, well diversified or not, are determined by their systematic risk. Thus, according to the CAPM, Point A represents a high-beta stock or portfolio, Point B a stock or portfolio with a beta of one, and Point C a low-beta stock or portfolio. We know this because the expected return at Point B is equal to the expected return on the market, and the expected returns at Point A and C are greater and less than the expected return on the market (tangency) portfolio, respectively.

Note that a low-beta stock, such as represented by Point C, is not necessarily low-risk when total risk is considered. While its contribution to the risk of a well-diversified portfolio may be low, its risk when held by itself can be considered quite high. A firm whose only activity is developing a new, but as yet unproven, drug may be quite speculative with highly uncertain returns. It may also have quite low systematic risk if the uncertainty about its future returns depends primarily on firm-specific factors.

All stocks and portfolios that plot along the line labeled $\beta = 1$ in Figure 9 have the same expected return as the market portfolio and, thus, according to the CAPM, have the same systematic risk as the market portfolio (i.e., they all have betas of one).

All points on the CML (except the tangency point) represent the risk-return characteristics of portfolios formed by either combining the market portfolio with the risk-free asset or borrowing at the risk-free rate in order to invest more than 100% of the portfolio's net value in the risky market portfolio (investing on margin). Point D in Figure 9 represents a portfolio that combines the market portfolio with the risk-free asset, while points above the point of tangency, such as Point E, represent portfolios created by borrowing at the risk-free rate to invest in the market portfolio. Portfolios that do not lie on the CML are not efficient and therefore have risk that will not be rewarded with higher expected returns in equilibrium.

According to the CAPM, all securities and portfolios, diversified or not, will plot on the SML in equilibrium. In fact, all stocks and portfolios along the line labeled $\beta = 1$ in Figure 9, including the market portfolio, will plot at the same point on the SML. They will plot at the point on the SML with beta equal to one and expected return equal to the expected return on the market, regardless of their total risk.

LOS 43.g: Calculate and interpret the expected return of an asset using the CAPM.

The CAPM is one of the most fundamental concepts in investment theory. The CAPM is an equilibrium model that predicts the expected return on a stock, given the expected return on the market, the stock's beta coefficient, and the risk-free rate.

Study Session 12
Cross-Reference to CFA Institute Assigned Reading #43 – Portfolio Risk and Return: Part II

Example: Capital asset pricing model

The expected return on the market is 15%, the risk-free rate is 8%, and the beta for Stock A is 1.2. Compute the rate of return that would be expected (required) on this stock.

Answer:

$E(R_A) = 0.08 + 1.2 (0.15 - 0.08) = 0.164$

Note: $\beta_A > 1$, so $E(R_A) > E(R_{mkt})$

Professor's Note: Know this calculation!

Example: Capital asset pricing model

The expected return on the market is 15%, the risk-free rate is 8%, and the beta for Stock B is 0.8. Compute the rate of return that would be expected (required) on this stock.

Answer:

$E(R_B) = 0.08 + 0.8 (0.15 - 0.08) = 0.136$

Note: Beta < 1 so $E(R_B) < E(R_{mkt})$

LOS 43.h: Describe and demonstrate applications of the CAPM and the SML.

We have used beta to estimate a security's expected return based on our estimate of the risk-free rate and the expected return on the market. In equilibrium, a security's expected return and its required return (by investors) are equal. Therefore, we can use the CAPM to estimate a security's required return, as in the following example.

Example: Using beta to estimate a required return

Acme, Inc., has a capital structure that is 40% debt and 60% equity. The expected return on the market is 12%, and the risk-free rate is 4%. What discount rate should an analyst use to calculate the NPV of a project with an equity beta of 0.9 if the firm's after-tax cost of debt is 5%?

Answer:

The required return on equity for this project is $0.04 + 0.9(0.12 - 0.04) = 11.2\%$.

The appropriate discount rate is a weighted average of the costs of debt and equity for this project, $0.4(5\%) + 0.6(11.2\%) = 8.72\%$.

Because the SML shows the equilibrium (required) return for any security or portfolio based on its beta (systematic risk), analysts often compare their forecast of a security's return to its required return based on its beta risk. The following example illustrates this technique.

> **Example: Identifying mispriced securities**
>
> The following figure contains information based on analyst's forecasts for three stocks. Assume a risk-free rate of 7% and a market return of 15%. Compute the expected and required return on each stock, determine whether each stock is undervalued, overvalued, or properly valued, and outline an appropriate trading strategy.
>
> **Forecast Data**
>
> | Stock | Price Today | E(Price) in 1 Year | E(Dividend) in 1 Year | Beta |
> |-------|-------------|--------------------|-----------------------|------|
> | A | $25 | $27 | $1.00 | 1.0 |
> | B | 40 | 45 | 2.00 | 0.8 |
> | C | 15 | 17 | 0.50 | 1.2 |
>
> **Answer:**
>
> Expected and required returns computations are shown in the following figure.
>
> **Forecasts vs. Required Returns**
>
> | Stock | Forecast Return | Required Return |
> |-------|-----------------|-----------------|
> | A | ($27 − $25 + $1) / $25 = 12.0% | 0.07 + (1.0)(0.15 − 0.07) = 15.0% |
> | B | ($45 − $40 + $2) / $40 = 17.5% | 0.07 + (0.8)(0.15 − 0.07) = 13.4% |
> | C | ($17 − $15 + $0.5) / $15 = 16.6% | 0.07 + (1.2)(0.15 − 0.07) = 16.6% |
>
> - Stock A is *overvalued*. It is expected to earn 12%, but based on its systematic risk, it should earn 15%. It plots *below* the SML.
> - Stock B is *undervalued*. It is expected to earn 17.5%, but based on its systematic risk, it should earn 13.4%. It plots *above* the SML.
> - Stock C is *properly valued*. It is expected to earn 16.6%, and based on its systematic risk, it should earn 16.6%. It plots *on* the SML.
>
> The appropriate trading strategy is:
>
> - Short sell Stock A.
> - Buy Stock B.
> - Buy, sell, or ignore Stock C.
>
> We can do this same analysis graphically. The expected return/beta combinations of all three stocks are graphed in the following figure relative to the SML.

Identifying Mispriced Securities

E(R) axis with points B (beta 0.8, above SML), A (beta 1, below SML), C (beta 1.2, on SML). SML line starting from 7 on the E(R) axis. Horizontal axis: beta risk.

> *Professor's Note: If the estimated return plots "over" the SML, the security is "under" valued. If the estimated return plots "under" the SML, the security is "over" valued.*

Remember, all stocks should plot on the SML; any stock not plotting on the SML is mispriced. Notice that Stock A falls below the SML, Stock B lies above the SML, and Stock C is on the SML. If you plot a stock's expected return and it falls below the SML, the stock is overpriced. That is, the stock's expected return is too low given its systematic risk. If a stock plots above the SML, it is underpriced and is offering an expected return greater than required for its systematic risk. If it plots on the SML, the stock is properly priced.

Because the equation of the SML is the capital asset pricing model, you can determine if a stock is over- or underpriced graphically or mathematically. Your answers will always be the same.

When we evaluate the performance of a portfolio with risk that differs from that of a benchmark, we need to adjust the portfolio returns for the risk of the portfolio. There are several measures of risk-adjusted returns that are used to evaluate relative portfolio performance.

One such measure is the **Sharpe ratio** $\left(\dfrac{R_P - R_f}{\sigma_P}\right)$.

The Sharpe ratio of a portfolio is its *excess returns per unit of total portfolio risk*, and higher Sharpe ratios indicate better risk-adjusted portfolio performance. Note that this is a slope measure and, as illustrated in Figure 9, the Sharpe ratios of all portfolios along the CML are the same. Because the Sharpe ratio uses total risk, rather than systematic risk, it accounts for any unsystematic risk that the portfolio manager has taken. Note that the value of the Sharpe ratio is only useful for comparison with the Sharpe ratio of another portfolio.

Study Session 12
Cross-Reference to CFA Institute Assigned Reading #43 – Portfolio Risk and Return: Part II

Professor's Note: We introduced the Sharpe ratio in Quantitative Methods.

In Figure 10, we illustrate that the Sharpe ratio is the slope of the CAL for the portfolio and can be compared to the slope of the CML, which is the Sharpe ratio for any portfolio along the CML.

Figure 10: Sharpe Ratios as Slopes

CAL slope = $\dfrac{R_{P2} - R_f}{\sigma_{P2}}$ CML slope = $\dfrac{R_M - R_f}{\sigma_M} = \dfrac{R_{P1} - R_f}{\sigma_{P1}}$

The **M-squared** (M^2) measure produces the same portfolio rankings as the Sharpe ratio but is stated in percentage terms. It is calculated as $(R_P - R_f)\dfrac{\sigma_M}{\sigma_P} - (R_M - R_f)$.

The intuition of this measure is that the first term is the excess return on a Portfolio P*, constructed by taking a leveraged position in Portfolio P so that P* has the same total risk, σ_M, as the market portfolio. As shown in Figure 11, the excess return on such a leveraged portfolio is greater than the return on the market portfolio by the vertical distance M^2.

Figure 11: M-squared for a Portfolio

Two measures of risk-adjusted returns based on systematic risk (beta) rather than total risk are the **Treynor measure** and **Jensen's alpha**. They are similar to the Sharpe ratio and M^2 in that the Treynor measure is based on slope and Jensen's alpha is a measure of percentage returns in excess of those from a portfolio that has the same beta but lies on the SML.

The Treynor measure is calculated as $\dfrac{R_P - R_f}{\beta_P}$, interpreted as excess returns per unit of systematic risk, and represented by the slope of a line as illustrated in Figure 12. Jensen's alpha for Portfolio P is calculated as $\alpha_P = R_P - [R_f + \beta_P(R_M - R_f)]$ and is the percentage portfolio return above that of a portfolio (or security) with the same beta as the portfolio that lies on the SML, as illustrated in Figure 12.

Figure 12: Treynor Measure and Jensen's Alpha

Whether risk adjustment should be based on total risk or systematic risk depends on whether a fund bears the nonsystematic risk of a manager's portfolio. If a single manager is used, then the total risk (including any nonsystematic risk) is the relevant measure and risk adjustment using total risk, as with the Sharpe and M^2 measures, is appropriate. If a fund uses multiple managers so that the overall fund portfolio is well diversified (has no nonsystematic risk), then performance measures based on systematic (beta) risk, such as the Treynor measure and Jensen's alpha, are appropriate.

These measures of risk-adjusted returns are often used to compare the performance of actively managed funds to passively managed funds. Note in Figures 10 and 11 that portfolios that lie above the CML have Sharpe ratios greater than those of any portfolios along the CML and have positive M^2 measures. Similarly, in Figure 12, we can see that portfolios that lie above the SML have Treynor measures greater than those of any security or portfolio that lies along the SML and also have positive values for Jensen's alpha.

One final note of caution is that estimating the values needed to apply these theoretical models and performance measures is often difficult and is done with error. The expected return on the market, and thus the market risk premium, may not be equal to its average historical value. Estimating security and portfolio betas is done with error as well.

Study Session 12
Cross-Reference to CFA Institute Assigned Reading #43 – Portfolio Risk and Return: Part II

KEY CONCEPTS

LOS 43.a
The availability of a risk-free asset allows investors to build portfolios with superior risk-return properties. By combining a risk-free asset with a portfolio of risky assets, the overall risk and return can be adjusted to appeal to investors with various degrees of risk aversion.

LOS 43.b
On a graph of return versus risk, the various combinations of a risky asset and the risk-free asset form the capital allocation line (CAL). In the specific case where the risky asset is the market portfolio, the combinations of the risky asset and the risk-free asset form the capital market line (CML).

LOS 43.c
Systematic (market) risk is due to factors, such as GDP growth and interest rate changes, that affect the values of all risky securities. Systematic risk cannot be reduced by diversification. Unsystematic (firm-specific) risk can be reduced by portfolio diversification.

Because one of the assumptions underlying the CAPM is that portfolio diversification to eliminate unsystematic risk is costless, investors cannot increase expected equilibrium portfolio returns by taking on unsystematic risk.

LOS 43.d
A return generating model is an equation that estimates the expected return of an investment, based on a security's exposure to one or more macroeconomic, fundamental, or statistical factors.

The simplest return generating model is the market model, which assumes the return on an asset is related to the return on the market portfolio in the following manner:

$$R_i = \alpha_i + \beta_i R_m + e_i$$

LOS 43.e
Beta can be calculated using the following equation:

$$\beta_i = \frac{[Cov(R_i, R_m)]}{\sigma_m^2} = \frac{\rho_{i,m}\sigma_i}{\sigma_m}$$

where $[Cov(R_i, R_m)]$ and $\rho_{i,m}$ are the covariance and correlation between the asset and the market, and σ_i and σ_m are the standard deviations of asset returns and market returns.

The theoretical average beta of stocks in the market is 1. A beta of zero indicates that a security's return is uncorrelated with the returns of the market.

©2016 Kaplan, Inc.

LOS 43.f
The capital asset pricing model (CAPM) requires several assumptions:
- Investors are risk averse, utility maximizing, and rational.
- Markets are free of frictions like costs and taxes.
- All investors plan using the same time period.
- All investors have the same expectations of security returns.
- Investments are infinitely divisible.
- Prices are unaffected by an investor's trades.

The security market line (SML) is a graphical representation of the CAPM that plots expected return versus beta for any security.

LOS 43.g
The CAPM relates expected return to the market factor (beta) using the following formula:

$$E(R_i) - R_f = \beta_i [E(R_m) - R_f]$$

LOS 43.h
The CAPM and the SML indicate what a security's equilibrium required rate of return should be based on the security's exposure to market risk. An analyst can compare his expected rate of return on a security to the required rate of return indicated by the SML to determine whether the security is overvalued, undervalued, or properly valued.

The Sharpe ratio measures excess return per unit of total risk and is useful for comparing portfolios on a risk-adjusted basis. The M-squared measure provides the same portfolio rankings as the Sharpe ratio but is stated in percentage terms:

$$\text{Sharpe ratio} = \left(\frac{R_P - R_f}{\sigma_P} \right)$$

$$\text{M-squared} = (R_P - R_f)\frac{\sigma_M}{\sigma_P} - (R_M - R_f)$$

The Treynor measure measures a portfolio's excess return per unit of systematic risk. Jensen's alpha is the difference between a portfolio's return and the return of a portfolio on the SML that has the same beta:

$$\text{Treynor measure} = \frac{R_P - R_f}{\beta_P}$$

$$\text{Jensen's alpha} = \alpha_P = R_P - [R_f + \beta_P (R_M - R_f)]$$

CONCEPT CHECKERS

1. An investor put 60% of his portfolio into a risky asset offering a 10% return with a standard deviation of returns of 8% and put the balance of his portfolio in a risk-free asset offering 5%. What is the expected return and standard deviation of his portfolio?

	Expected return	Standard deviation
A.	6.0%	6.8%
B.	8.0%	4.8%
C.	10.0%	6.6%

2. What is the risk measure associated with the capital market line (CML)?
    A. Beta risk.
    B. Unsystematic risk.
    C. Total risk.

3. A portfolio to the right of the market portfolio on the CML is:
    A. a lending portfolio.
    B. a borrowing portfolio.
    C. an inefficient portfolio.

4. As the number of stocks in a portfolio increases, the portfolio's systematic risk:
    A. can increase or decrease.
    B. decreases at a decreasing rate.
    C. decreases at an increasing rate.

5. Total risk equals:
    A. unique plus diversifiable risk.
    B. market plus nondiversifiable risk.
    C. systematic plus unsystematic risk.

6. A return generating model is *least likely* to be based on a security's exposure to:
    A. statistical factors.
    B. macroeconomic factors.
    C. fundamental factors.

7. The covariance of the market's returns with a stock's returns is 0.005 and the standard deviation of the market's returns is 0.05. What is the stock's beta?
    A. 1.0.
    B. 1.5.
    C. 2.0.

8. The covariance of the market's returns with the stock's returns is 0.008. The standard deviation of the market's returns is 0.08, and the standard deviation of the stock's returns is 0.11. What is the correlation coefficient of the returns of the stock and the returns of the market?
    A. 0.91.
    B. 1.00.
    C. 1.25.

9. According to the CAPM, what is the expected rate of return for a stock with a beta of 1.2, when the risk-free rate is 6% and the market rate of return is 12%?
   A. 7.2%.
   B. 12.0%.
   C. 13.2%.

10. According to the CAPM, what is the required rate of return for a stock with a beta of 0.7, when the risk-free rate is 7% and the expected market rate of return is 14%?
    A. 11.9%.
    B. 14.0%.
    C. 16.8%.

11. The risk-free rate is 6%, and the expected market return is 15%. A stock with a beta of 1.2 is selling for $25 and will pay a $1 dividend at the end of the year. If the stock is priced at $30 at year-end, it is:
    A. overpriced, so short it.
    B. underpriced, so buy it.
    C. underpriced, so short it.

12. A stock with a beta of 0.7 currently priced at $50 is expected to increase in price to $55 by year-end and pay a $1 dividend. The expected market return is 15%, and the risk-free rate is 8%. The stock is:
    A. overpriced, so do not buy it.
    B. underpriced, so buy it.
    C. properly priced, so buy it.

13. Which of the following statements about the SML and the CML is *least accurate*?
    A. Securities that plot above the SML are undervalued.
    B. Investors expect to be compensated for systematic risk.
    C. Securities that plot on the SML have no value to investors.

For more questions related to this topic review, log in to your Schweser online account and launch SchweserPro™ QBank; and for video instruction covering each LOS in this topic review, log in to your Schweser online account and launch the OnDemand video lectures, if you have purchased these products.

Answers – Concept Checkers

1. **B** Expected return: (0.60 × 0.10) + (0.40 × 0.05) = 0.08, or 8.0%.

   Standard deviation: 0.60 × 0.08 = 0.048, or 4.8%.

2. **C** The capital market line (CML) plots return against *total risk* which is measured by standard deviation of returns.

3. **B** A portfolio to the right of a portfolio on the CML has more risk than the market portfolio. Investors seeking to take on more risk will *borrow* at the risk-free rate to purchase more of the market portfolio.

4. **A** When you increase the number of stocks in a portfolio, *unsystematic risk* will decrease at a decreasing rate. However, the portfolio's *systematic risk* can be increased by adding higher-beta stocks or decreased by adding lower-beta stocks.

5. **C** Total risk equals systematic plus unsystematic risk. Unique risk is diversifiable and is unsystematic. Market (systematic) risk is nondiversifiable risk.

6. **A** Macroeconomic, fundamental, and statistical factor exposures can be included in a return generating model to estimate the expected return of an investment. However, statistical factors may not have any theoretical basis, so analysts prefer macroeconomic and fundamental factor models.

7. **C** Beta = covariance / market variance

   Market variance = 0.05^2 = 0.0025

   Beta = 0.005 / 0.0025 = 2.0

8. **A** $\rho_{1,2} = \dfrac{Cov_{1,2}}{\sigma_1 \sigma_2} = \dfrac{0.008}{(0.08)(0.11)} = 0.909$

9. **C** 6 + 1.2(12 − 6) = 13.2%

10. **A** 7 + 0.7(14 − 7) = 11.9%

11. **B** Required rate = 6 + 1.2(15 − 6) = 16.8%

    Return on stock = (30 − 25 + 1) / 25 = 24%

    Based on risk, the stock plots above the SML and is underpriced, so buy it.

12. **A** Required rate = 8 + 0.7(15 − 8) = 12.9%

    Return on stock = (55 − 50 + 1) / 50 = 12%

    The stock falls below the SML so it is *overpriced*.

13. **C** Securities that plot on the SML are expected to earn their equilibrium rate of return and, therefore, do have value to an investor and may have diversification benefits as well. The other statements are true.

The following is a review of the Portfolio Management principles designed to address the learning outcome statements set forth by CFA Institute. Cross-Reference to CFA Institute Assigned Reading #44.

BASICS OF PORTFOLIO PLANNING AND CONSTRUCTION

Study Session 12

EXAM FOCUS

There is nothing difficult here, but the material is important because it is the foundation for the portfolio construction material at Level II and especially Level III. You should be ready to explain why investment policy statements are created and what their major components are. You should be familiar with the objectives (risk and return) and the constraints: liquidity, legal, time horizon, tax treatment, and unique circumstances. Know the difference between ability and willingness to take risk, the factors that define an asset class, and how asset allocation is used in constructing portfolios.

LOS 44.a: Describe the reasons for a written investment policy statement (IPS).

An investment manager is very unlikely to produce a good result for a client without understanding that client's needs, circumstances, and constraints.

A written **investment policy statement** will typically begin with the investor's goals in terms of risk and return. These should be determined jointly, as the goals of high returns and low risk (while quite popular) are likely to be mutually exclusive in practice. Investor expectations in terms of returns must be compatible with investor's tolerance for risk (uncertainty about portfolio performance).

LOS 44.b: Describe the major components of an IPS.

The major components of an IPS typically address the following:

- *Description of Client* circumstances, situation, and investment objectives.
- *Statement of the Purpose* of the IPS.
- *Statement of Duties and Responsibilities* of investment manager, custodian of assets, and the client.
- *Procedures* to update IPS and to respond to various possible situations.
- *Investment Objectives* derived from communications with the client.
- *Investment Constraints* that must be considered in the plan.
- *Investment Guidelines* such as how the policy will be executed, asset types permitted, and leverage to be used.

- *Evaluation of Performance*, the benchmark portfolio for evaluating investment performance, and other information on evaluation of investment results.
- *Appendices* containing information on strategic (baseline) asset allocation and permitted deviations from policy portfolio allocations, as well as how and when the portfolio allocations should be rebalanced.

In any case, the IPS will, at a minimum, contain a clear statement of client circumstances and constraints, an investment strategy based on these, and some benchmark against which to evaluate the account performance.

LOS 44.c: Describe risk and return objectives and how they may be developed for a client.

The **risk objectives** in an IPS may take several forms. An **absolute risk objective** might be to "have no decrease in portfolio value during any 12-month period" or to "not decrease in value by more than 2% at any point over any 12-month period." Low absolute percentage risk objectives such as these may result in portfolios made up of securities that offer guaranteed returns (e.g., U.S. Treasury bills).

Absolute risk objectives can also be stated in terms of the probability of specific portfolio results, either percentage losses or dollar losses, rather than strict limits on portfolio results. Examples are as follows:

- "No greater than a 5% probability of returns below –5% in any 12-month period."
- "No greater than a 4% probability of a loss of more than $20,000 over any 12-month period."

An absolute return objective may be stated in nominal terms, such as "an overall return of at least 6% per annum," or in real returns, such as "a return of 3% more than the annual inflation rate each year."

Relative risk objectives relate to a specific benchmark and can also be strict, such as, "Returns will not be less than 12-month euro LIBOR over any 12-month period," or stated in terms of probability, such as, "No greater than a 5% probability of returns more than 4% below the return on the MSCI World Index over any 12-month period."

Return objectives can be relative to a benchmark portfolio return, such as, "Exceed the return on the S&P 500 Index by 2% per annum." For a bank, the return objective may be relative to the bank's cost of funds (deposit rate). While it is possible for an institution to use returns on peer portfolios, such as an endowment with a stated objective to be in the top quartile of endowment fund returns, peer performance benchmarks suffer from not being *investable* portfolios. There is no way to match this investment return by portfolio construction before the fact.

In any event, the account manager must make sure that the stated risk and return objectives are compatible, given the reality of expected investment results and uncertainty over time.

LOS 44.d: Distinguish between the willingness and the ability (capacity) to take risk in analyzing an investor's financial risk tolerance.

An investor's **ability to bear risk** depends on financial circumstances. Longer investment horizons (20 years rather than 2 years), greater assets versus liabilities (more wealth), more insurance against unexpected occurrences, and a secure job all suggest a greater ability to bear investment risk in terms of uncertainty about periodic investment performance.

An investor's **willingness to bear risk** is based primarily on the investor's attitudes and beliefs about investments (various asset types). The assessment of an investor's attitude about risk is quite subjective and is sometimes done with a short questionnaire that attempts to categorize the investor's risk aversion or risk tolerance.

When the adviser's assessments of an investor's ability and willingness to take investment risk are compatible, there is no real problem selecting an appropriate level of investment risk. If the investor's willingness to take on investment risk is high but the investor's ability to take on risk is low, the low ability to take on investment risk will prevail in the adviser's assessment.

In situations where ability is high but willingness is low, the adviser may attempt to educate the investor about investment risk and correct any misconceptions that may be contributing to the investor's low stated willingness to take on investment risk. However, the adviser's job is not to change the investor's personality characteristics that contribute to a low willingness to take on investment risk. The approach will most likely be to conform to the lower of the investor's ability or willingness to bear risk, as constructing a portfolio with a level of risk that the client is clearly uncomfortable with will not likely lead to a good outcome in the investor's view.

LOS 44.e: Describe the investment constraints of liquidity, time horizon, tax concerns, legal and regulatory factors, and unique circumstances and their implications for the choice of portfolio assets.

Professor's Note: When I was studying for the CFA exams over 20 years ago, we memorized R-R-T-T-L-L-U as a checklist for addressing the important points of portfolio construction, and it still works today. Then, as now, the important points to cover in an IPS were Risk, Return, Time horizon, Tax situation, Liquidity, Legal restrictions, and the Unique constraints of a specific investor.

Investment constraints include the investor's liquidity needs, time horizon, tax considerations, legal and regulatory constraints, and unique needs and preferences.

Liquidity: Liquidity refers to the ability to turn investment assets into spendable cash in a short period of time without having to make significant price concessions to do so. Investor needs for money to pay tuition, to pay for a parent's assisted living expenses, or to fund other possible spending needs may all require that some liquid assets be held. As we noted in an earlier topic review discussing property and casualty insurance companies, claims arrive unpredictably to some extent and therefore their portfolios must hold a significant proportion of liquid (or maturing) securities in order to be prepared to honor these claims. Illiquid investments in hedge funds and private equity funds, which typically are not traded and have restrictions on redemptions, are not suitable for an investor who may unexpectedly need access to the funds.

Time horizon: In general, the longer an investor's time horizon, the more risk and less liquidity the investor can accept in the portfolio. While the expected returns on a broad equities portfolio may not be too risky for an investor with a 20-year investment horizon, they likely are too risky for an investor who must fund a large purchase at the end of this year. For such an investor, government securities or a bank certificate of deposit may be the most appropriate investments because of their low risk and high liquidity at the time when the funds will be needed.

Tax situation: Besides an individual's overall tax rate, the tax treatment of various types of investment accounts is also a consideration in portfolio construction. For a fully taxable account, investors subject to higher tax rates may prefer tax-free bonds (U.S.) to taxable bonds or prefer equities that are expected to produce capital gains, which are often taxed at a lower rate than other types of income. A focus on expected after-tax returns over time in relation to risk should correctly account for differences in tax treatments as well as investors' overall tax rates.

Some types of investment accounts, such as retirement accounts, may be tax exempt or tax deferred. Investors with such accounts may choose to put securities that generate fully taxed income, such as corporate bond interest, in accounts that are tax deferred, while seeking long-term capital gains, tax-exempt interest income, and dividend income (in jurisdictions where dividends receive preferential tax treatment) in their personal accounts, which have no tax deferral benefit.

Legal and regulatory: In addition to financial market regulations that apply to all investors, more specific legal and regulatory constraints may apply to particular investors. Trust, corporate, and qualified investment accounts may all be restricted by law from investing in particular types of securities and assets. There may also be restrictions on percentage allocations to specific types of investments in such accounts. Corporate officers and directors face legal restrictions on trading in the securities of their firms that the account manager should be aware of.

Unique circumstances: Each investor, whether individual or institutional, may have specific preferences or restrictions on which securities and assets may be purchased for the account. Ethical preferences, such as prohibiting investment in securities issued by tobacco or firearms producers, are not uncommon. Restrictions on investments in companies or countries where human rights abuses are suspected or documented would also fall into this category. Religious preferences may preclude investment in securities that make explicit interest payments. Unique investor preferences may also be based on diversification needs when the investor's income depends heavily on the prospects for one company or industry. An investor who has founded or runs a company may not want any investment in securities issued by a competitor to that company.

LOS 44.f: Explain the specification of asset classes in relation to asset allocation.

After having determined the investor objectives and constraints through the exercise of creating an IPS, a **strategic asset allocation** is developed which specifies the percentage allocations to the included asset classes. In choosing which asset classes to consider when developing the strategic asset allocation for the account, the correlations of returns *within* an asset class should be relatively high, indicating that the assets within the class are similar in their investment performance. On the other hand, it is low correlations of returns *between* asset classes that leads to risk reduction through portfolio diversification.

Historically, only the broad categories of equities, bonds, cash, and real estate were considered. More recently, a group of several investable asset classes, referred to collectively as alternative investments, has gained more prominence. Alternative investment asset classes include hedge funds of various types, private equity funds, managed or passively constructed commodity funds, artwork, and intellectual property rights.

We can further divide equities by whether the issuing companies are domestic or foreign, large or small, or whether they are traded in emerging or developed markets. An example of specifying asset classes is world equities. A U.S. investor may want to divide world equities into different regions. Figure 1 shows the correlation matrix, annualized returns, and volatilities among four different regions and the United States.

Figure 1: World Equities Asset Class Correlation Matrix
Monthly Index Returns from MSCI Price Returns
10 Year Period from June 28, 2001, to June 29, 2012

	1	2	3	4	5
1. MSCI USA	1.00				
2. MSCI Emerging Markets Europe	0.74	1.00			
3. MSCI Emerging Markets Asia	0.79	0.80	1.00		
4. MSCI Emerging Markets Latin America	0.79	0.85	0.82	1.00	
5. MSCI Frontier Markets Africa	0.35	0.41	0.33	0.34	1.00
Annualized Volatility	15.86%	32.52%	24.54%	28.65%	27.47%
Annualized Return	3.44%	11.20%	9.31%	17.01%	9.33%

Source: www.msci.com/products/indices/

With bonds, we can divide the overall universe of bonds into asset classes based on maturities or on criteria such as whether they are foreign or domestic, government or corporate, or investment grade or speculative (high yield). Overall, the asset classes considered should approximate the universe of permissible investments specified in the IPS.

Once the universe of asset classes has been specified, the investment manager will collect data on the returns, standard deviation of returns, and correlations of returns with those of other asset classes for each asset class.

Figure 2 illustrates the strategic asset allocation for a pension fund.

Figure 2: Strategic Asset Allocation

The Vermont Pension Investment Committee manages about $3 billion in retirement assets for various teachers and state and municipal employees in that state. VPIC's investment policy specifies the following strategic asset allocation:

Asset Class	Target
Cash	0.0%
U.S. large-cap equity	11.0%
U.S. small-/mid-cap equity	6.5%
Established international equity	10.0%
Emerging market equity	6.0%
U.S. bonds	18.0%
Global bonds	3.0%
High-yield bonds	6.0%
Emerging market debt	5.0%
Inflation-protected bonds	3.0%
Real estate	4.5%
Hedge funds	5.0%
Private equity	0.0%
Commodities	2.0%
Global asset allocation and other	20.0%
	100%

Source: State of Vermont, Office of the State Treasurer. Target allocation as of March 31, 2012. www.vermonttreasurer.gov/pension-funds.

LOS 44.g: Describe the principles of portfolio construction and the role of asset allocation in relation to the IPS.

Once the portfolio manager has identified the investable asset classes for the portfolio and the risk, return, and correlation characteristics of each asset class, an *efficient frontier*, analogous to one constructed from individual securities, can be constructed using a computer program. By combining the return and risk objectives from the IPS with the actual risk and return properties of the many portfolios along the efficient frontier, the manager can identify that portfolio which best meets the risk and return requirements of the investor. The asset allocation for the efficient portfolio selected is then the strategic asset allocation for the portfolio.

So far, we have not concerned ourselves with deviations from strategic asset allocations or with selection of individual securities within individual asset classes. These activities are referred to as active (versus passive) portfolio management strategies. A manager who varies from strategic asset allocation weights in order to take advantage of perceived short-term opportunities is adding **tactical asset allocation** to the portfolio strategy. **Security selection** refers to deviations from index weights on individual securities within an asset class. For example, a portfolio manager might overweight energy stocks and underweight financial stocks, relative to the index weights for U.S. large-cap equities as an asset class. For some asset classes, such as hedge funds, individual real estate properties, and artwork, investable indexes are not available. For these asset classes, selection of individual assets is required by the nature of the asset class.

While each of these active strategies may produce higher returns, they each also increase the risk of the portfolio compared to a passive portfolio of asset class indexes. A practice known as **risk budgeting** sets an overall risk limit for the portfolio and budgets (allocates) a portion of the permitted risk to the systematic risk of the strategic asset allocation, the risk from tactical asset allocation, and the risk from security selection.

Active portfolio management has two specific issues to consider.

1. An investor may have multiple managers actively managing to the same benchmark for the same asset class (or may have significant benchmark overlap). In this case, one manager may overweight an index stock while another may underweight the same stock. Taken together, there is no net active management risk, although each manager has reported active management risk. Overall, the risk budget is underutilized as there is less net active management than gross active management.

2. When all managers are actively managing portfolios relative to an index, trading may be excessive overall. This extra trading could have negative tax consequences, specifically potentially higher capital gains taxes, compared to an overall efficient tax strategy.

One way to address these issues is to use a **core-satellite approach**. The core-satellite approach invests the majority, or core, portion of the portfolio in passively managed indexes and invests a smaller, or satellite, portion in active strategies. This approach reduces the likelihood of excessive trading and offsetting active positions.

Clearly, the success of security selection will depend on the manager's skill and the opportunities (mispricings or inefficiencies) within a particular asset class. Similarly, the success of tactical asset allocation will depend both on the existence of short-term opportunities in specific asset classes and on the manager's ability to identify them.

Key Concepts

LOS 44.a
A written investment policy statement, the first step in the portfolio management process, is a plan for achieving investment success. An IPS forces investment discipline and ensures that goals are realistic by requiring investors to articulate their circumstances, objectives, and constraints.

LOS 44.b
Many IPS include the following sections:
- Introduction—Describes the client.
- Statement of Purpose—The intentions of the IPS.
- Statement of Duties and Responsibilities—Of the client, the asset custodian, and the investment managers.
- Procedures—Related to keeping the IPS updated and responding to unforeseen events.
- Investment Objectives—The client's investment needs, specified in terms of required return and risk tolerance.
- Investment Constraints—Factors that may hinder the ability to meet investment objectives; typically categorized as time horizon, taxes, liquidity, legal and regulatory, and unique needs.
- Investment Guidelines—For example, whether leverage, derivatives, or specific kinds of assets are allowed.
- Evaluation and Review—Related to feedback on investment results.
- Appendices—May specify the portfolio's strategic asset allocation (policy portfolio) or the portfolio's rebalancing policy.

LOS 44.c
Risk objectives are specifications for portfolio risk that are developed to embody a client's risk tolerance. Risk objectives can be either absolute (e.g., no losses greater than 10% in any year) or relative (e.g., annual return will be within 2% of FTSE return).

Return objectives are typically based on an investor's desire to meet a future financial goal, such as a particular level of income in retirement. Return objectives can be absolute (e.g., 9% annual return) or relative (e.g., outperform the S&P 500 by 2% per year).

The achievability of an investor's return expectations may be hindered by the investor's risk objectives.

LOS 44.d
Willingness to take financial risk is related to an investor's psychological factors, such as personality type and level of financial knowledge.

Ability or capacity to take risk depends on financial factors, such as wealth relative to liabilities, income stability, and time horizon.

A client's overall risk tolerance depends on both his ability to take risk and his willingness to take risk. A willingness greater than ability, or vice versa, is typically resolved by choosing the more conservative of the two and counseling the client.

LOS 44.e
Investment constraints include:
- Liquidity—The need to draw cash from the portfolio for anticipated or unexpected future spending needs. High liquidity needs often translate to a high portfolio allocation to bonds or cash.
- Time horizon—Often the period over which assets are accumulated and before withdrawals begin. Risky or illiquid investments may be inappropriate for an investor with a short time horizon.
- Tax considerations—Concerns the tax treatments of the investor's various accounts, the relative tax treatment of capital gains and income, and the investor's marginal tax bracket.
- Legal and regulatory—Constraints such as government restrictions on portfolio contents or laws against insider trading.
- Unique circumstances—Restrictions due to investor preferences (religious, ethical, etc.) or other factors not already considered.

LOS 44.f
An asset class is a group of securities with similar risk and performance characteristics. Examples of major asset classes include equity, fixed income, cash, and real estate. Portfolio managers also use more narrowly defined asset classes, such as large-cap U.S. equities or speculative international bonds, and alternative asset classes, such as commodities or investments in hedge funds.

LOS 44.g
Strategic asset allocation is a set of percentage allocations to various asset classes that is designed to meet the investor's objectives. The strategic asset allocation is developed by combining the objectives and constraints in the IPS with the performance expectations of the various asset classes. The strategic asset allocation provides the basic structure of a portfolio.

Tactical asset allocation refers to an allocation that deviates from the baseline (strategic) allocation in order to profit from a forecast of shorter-term opportunities in specific asset classes.

CONCEPT CHECKERS

1. The investment policy statement is *most accurately* considered the:
   A. starting point of the portfolio management process.
   B. key intermediate step in the portfolio management process.
   C. end product of the portfolio management process.

2. The component of an investment policy statement that defines the investment objectives is *most likely* to include information about:
   A. the investor's risk tolerance.
   B. unique needs and preferences of the investor.
   C. permitted asset types and use of leverage in the investment account.

3. A client exhibits an above-average willingness to take risk but a below-average ability to take risk. When assigning an overall risk tolerance, the investment adviser is *most likely* to assess the client's overall risk tolerance as:
   A. above average.
   B. average.
   C. below average.

4. Which of the following is *least likely* an example of a portfolio constraint?
   A. Higher tax rate on dividend income than on capital gains.
   B. Significant spending requirements in the near future.
   C. Minimum total return requirement of 8%.

5. In determining the appropriate asset allocation for a client's investment account, the manager should:
   A. consider only the investor's risk tolerance.
   B. incorporate forecasts of future economic conditions.
   C. consider the investor's risk tolerance and future needs, but not forecasts of market conditions.

For more questions related to this topic review, log in to your Schweser online account and launch SchweserPro™ QBank; and for video instruction covering each LOS in this topic review, log in to your Schweser online account and launch the OnDemand video lectures, if you have purchased these products.

ANSWERS – CONCEPT CHECKERS

1. **A** An investment policy statement is considered to be the starting point of the portfolio management process. The IPS is a plan for achieving investment success.

2. **A** Investment objectives are defined based on both the investor's return requirements and risk tolerance. Investment constraints include the investor's time horizon, liquidity needs, tax considerations, legal and regulatory requirements, and unique needs and preferences. Policies regarding permitted asset types and the amount of leverage to use are best characterized as investment guidelines.

3. **C** When assigning an overall risk tolerance, the prudent approach is to use the lower of ability to take risk and willingness to take risk.

4. **C** Return objectives are part of a policy statement's objectives, not constraints.

5. **B** An adviser's forecasts of the expected returns and expected volatilities (risk) of different asset classes are an important part of determining an appropriate asset allocation.

Self-Test: Portfolio Management

You have now finished the Portfolio Management topic section. To get immediate feedback on how effective your study has been for this material, log in to your Schweser online account and take the self-test for this topic area. The number of questions on this test is equal to the number of questions for the topic on one-half of the actual Level I CFA exam. Questions are more exam-like than typical Concept Checkers or QBank questions; a score of less than 70% indicates that your study likely needs improvement. These tests are timed and allow 1.5 minutes per question.

The following is a review of the Equity: Market Organization, Market Indices, and Market Efficiency principles designed to address the learning outcome statements set forth by CFA Institute. Cross-Reference to CFA Institute Assigned Reading #45.

MARKET ORGANIZATION AND STRUCTURE

Study Session 13

EXAM FOCUS

There is a great deal of introductory material in this review. Almost all of the types of securities discussed are covered in detail elsewhere in the curriculum. We introduce the terminology you will need but leave many of the details to the topic reviews specific to each security type. You should understand the concept of purchasing stock on margin and be able to calculate the return on an investment using margin. Be able to differentiate between market and limit orders as well as between quote-driven, order-driven, and brokered markets. Know that market regulation should increase informational, allocational, and operational market efficiency.

LOS 45.a: Explain the main functions of the financial system.

The three main functions of the financial system are to:

1. Allow entities to save and borrow money, raise equity capital, manage risks, trade assets currently or in the future, and trade based on their estimates of asset values.

2. Determine the returns (i.e., interest rates) that equate the total supply of savings with the total demand for borrowing.

3. Allocate capital to its most efficient uses.

The financial system allows the transfer of assets and risks from one entity to another as well as across time. Entities who utilize the financial system include individuals, firms, governments, charities, and others.

Achievement of Purposes in the Financial System

The financial system allows entities to save, borrow, issue equity capital, manage risks, exchange assets, and to utilize information. The financial system is best at fulfilling these roles when the markets are liquid, transactions costs are low, information is readily available, and when regulation ensures the execution of contracts.

Savings. Individuals will save (e.g., for retirement) and expect a return that compensates them for risk and the use of their money. Firms save a portion of their sales to fund future expenditures. Vehicles used for saving include stocks, bonds, certificates of deposit, real assets, and other assets.

Borrowing. Individuals may borrow in order to buy a house, fund a college education, or for other purposes. A firm may borrow in order to finance capital expenditures and for other activities. Governments may issue debt to fund their expenditures. Lenders can require collateral to protect them in the event of borrower defaults, take an equity position, or investigate the credit risk of the borrower.

Issuing equity. Another method of raising capital is to issue equity, where the capital providers will share in any future profits. Investment banks help with issuance, analysts value the equity, and regulators and accountants encourage the dissemination of information.

Risk management. Entities face risks from changing interest rates, currency values, commodities values, and defaults on debt, among other things. For example, a firm that owes a foreign currency in 90 days can lock in the price of this foreign currency in domestic currency units by entering into a forward contract. Future delivery of the foreign currency is guaranteed at a domestic-currency price set at inception of the contract. In this transaction, the firm would be referred to as a *hedger*. This hedging allows the firm to enter a market that it would otherwise be reluctant to enter by reducing the risk of the transaction. Hedging instruments are available from exchanges, investment banks, insurance firms, and other institutions.

Exchanging assets. The financial system also allows entities to exchange assets. For example, Proctor and Gamble may sell soap in Europe but have costs denominated in U.S. dollars. Proctor and Gamble can exchange their euros from soap sales for dollars in the currency markets.

Utilizing information. Investors with information expect to earn a return on that information in addition to their usual return. Investors who can identify assets that are currently undervalued or overvalued in the market can earn extra returns from investing based on their information (when their analysis is correct).

Return Determination

The financial system also provides a mechanism to determine the rate of return that equates the amount of borrowing with the amount of lending (saving) in an economy. Low rates of return increase borrowing but reduce saving (increase current consumption). High rates of return increase saving but reduce borrowing. The **equilibrium interest rate** is the rate at which the amount individuals, businesses, and governments desire to borrow is equal to the amount that individuals, businesses, and governments desire to lend. Equilibrium rates for different types of borrowing and lending will differ due to differences in risk, liquidity, and maturity.

Allocation of Capital

With limited availability of capital, one of the most important functions of a financial system is to allocate capital to its most efficient uses. Investors weigh the expected risks and returns of different investments to determine their most preferred investments. As long as investors are well informed regarding risk and return and markets function well, this results in an allocation to capital to its most valuable uses.

LOS 45.b: Describe classifications of assets and markets.

Financial assets include securities (stocks and bonds), derivative contracts, and currencies. **Real assets** include real estate, equipment, commodities, and other physical assets.

Financial securities can be classified as debt or equity. **Debt securities** are promises to repay borrowed funds. **Equity securities** represent ownership positions.

Public (publicly traded) securities are traded on exchanges or through securities dealers and are subject to regulatory oversight. Securities that are not traded in public markets are referred to as **private securities**. Private securities are often illiquid and not subject to regulation.

Derivative contracts have values that depend on (are derived from) the values of other assets. **Financial derivative contracts** are based on equities, equity indexes, debt, debt indexes, or other financial contracts. **Physical derivative contracts** derive their values from the values of physical assets such as gold, oil, and wheat.

Markets for immediate delivery are referred to as **spot markets**. Contracts for the future delivery of physical and financial assets include forwards, futures, and options. Options provide the buyer the right, but not the obligation, to purchase (or sell) assets over some period or at some future date at predetermined prices.

The **primary market** is the market for newly issued securities. Subsequent sales of securities are said to occur in the **secondary market**.

Money markets refer to markets for debt securities with maturities of one year or less. **Capital markets** refer to markets for longer-term debt securities and equity securities that have no specific maturity date.

Traditional investment markets refer to those for debt and equity. **Alternative markets** refer to those for hedge funds, commodities, real estate, collectibles, gemstones, leases, and equipment. Alternative assets are often more difficult to value, illiquid, require investor due diligence, and therefore often sell at a discount.

Study Session 13
Cross-Reference to CFA Institute Assigned Reading #45 – Market Organization and Structure

LOS 45.c: Describe the major types of securities, currencies, contracts, commodities, and real assets that trade in organized markets, including their distinguishing characteristics and major subtypes.

Assets can be classified as securities, currencies, contracts, commodities, and real assets. Their characteristics and subtypes are as follows.

Securities

Securities can be classified as fixed income or equity securities, and individual securities can be combined in pooled investment vehicles. Corporations and governments are the most common issuers of individual securities. The initial sale of a security is called an **issue** when the security is sold to the public.

Fixed income securities typically refer to debt securities that are promises to repay borrowed money in the future. Short-term fixed income securities generally have a maturity of less than one or two years; long-term term maturities are longer than five to ten years, and intermediate term maturities fall in the middle of the maturity range.

Although the terms are used loosely, *bonds* are generally long term, whereas *notes* are intermediate term. *Commercial paper* refers to short-term debt issued by firms. Governments issue *bills* and banks issue *certificates of deposit*. In *repurchase agreements*, the borrower sells a high-quality asset and has both the right and obligation to repurchase it (at a higher price) in the future. Repurchase agreements can be for terms as short as one day.

Convertible debt is debt that an investor can exchange for a specified number of equity shares of the issuing firm.

Equity securities represent ownership in a firm and include common stock, preferred stock, and warrants.

- **Common stock** is a residual claim on a firm's assets. Common stock dividends are paid only after interest is paid to debtholders and dividends are paid to preferred stockholders. Furthermore, in the event of firm liquidation, debtholders and preferred stockholders have priority over common stockholders and are usually paid in full before common stockholders receive any payment.
- **Preferred stock** is an equity security with scheduled dividends that typically do not change over the security's life and must be paid before any dividends on common stock may be paid.
- **Warrants** are similar to options in that they give the holder the right to buy a firm's equity shares (usually common stock) at a fixed exercise price prior to the warrant's expiration.

Pooled investment vehicles include mutual funds, depositories, and hedge funds. The term refers to structures that combine the funds of many investors in a portfolio of investments. The investor's ownership interests are referred to as *shares, units, depository receipts*, or *limited partnership interests*.

- **Mutual funds** are pooled investment vehicles in which investors can purchase shares, either from the fund itself (open-end funds) or in the secondary market (closed-end funds).
- **Exchange-traded funds** (ETFs) and **exchange-traded notes** (ETNs) trade like closed-end funds but have special provisions allowing conversion into individual portfolio securities, or exchange of portfolio shares for ETF shares, that keep their market prices close to the value of their proportional interest in the overall portfolio. These funds are sometimes referred to as *depositories*, with their shares referred to as *depository receipts*.
- **Asset-backed securities** represent a claim to a portion of a pool of financial assets such as mortgages, car loans, or credit card debt. The return from the assets is passed through to investors, with different classes of claims (referred to as *tranches*) having different levels of risk.
- **Hedge funds** are organized as limited partnerships, with the investors as the limited partners and the fund manager as the general partner. Hedge funds utilize various strategies and purchase is usually restricted to investors of substantial wealth and investment knowledge. Hedge funds often use leverage. Hedge fund managers are compensated based on the amount of assets under management as well as on their investment results.

Professor's Note: Asset-backed securities are described in more detail in the Study Session on fixed income. Mutual funds and ETFs are discussed in the Study Session on portfolio management. Hedge funds are discussed in the Study Session on alternative investments.

Currencies

Currencies are issued by a government's central bank. Some are referred to as **reserve currencies**, which are those held by governments and central banks worldwide. These include the dollar and euro and, secondarily, the British pound, Japanese yen, and Swiss franc. In spot currency markets, currencies are traded for immediate delivery.

Contracts

Contracts are agreements between two parties that require some action in the future, such as exchanging an asset for cash. Financial contracts are often based on securities, currencies, commodities, or security indexes (portfolios). They include futures, forwards, options, swaps, and insurance contracts.

A **forward contract** is an agreement to buy or sell an asset in the future at a price specified in the contract at its inception. An agreement to purchase 100 ounces of gold 90 days from now for $1,000 per ounce is a forward contract. Forward contracts are not traded on exchanges or in dealer markets.

Futures contracts are similar to forward contracts except that they are standardized as to amount, asset characteristics, and delivery time and are traded on an exchange (in a secondary market) so that they are liquid investments.

In a **swap contract**, two parties make payments that are equivalent to one asset being traded (swapped) for another. In a simple *interest rate swap*, floating rate interest payments are exchanged for fixed-rate payments over multiple settlement dates. A *currency swap* involves a loan in one currency for the loan of another currency for a period of time. An *equity swap* involves the exchange of the return on an equity index or portfolio for the interest payment on a debt instrument.

An **option contract** gives its owner the right to buy or sell an asset at a specific exercise price at some specified time in the future. A **call option** gives the option buyer the right (but not the obligation) to buy an asset. A **put option** gives the option buyer the right (but not the obligation) to sell an asset.

Sellers, or writers, of call (put) options receive a payment, referred to as the *option premium*, when they sell the options but incur the obligation to sell (buy) the asset at the specified price if the option owner chooses to exercise it.

Options on currencies, stocks, stock indexes, futures, swaps, and precious metals are traded on exchanges. Customized options contracts are also sold by dealers in the over-the-counter market.

An **insurance contract** pays a cash amount if a future event occurs. They are used to hedge against unfavorable, unexpected events. Examples include life, liability, and automobile insurance contracts. Insurance contracts can sometimes be traded to other parties and often have tax-advantaged payouts.

Credit default swaps are a form of insurance that makes a payment if an issuer defaults on its bonds. They can be used by bond investors to hedge default risk. They can also be used by parties that will experience losses if an issuer experiences financial distress and by others who are speculating that the issuer will experience more or less financial trouble than is currently expected.

Commodities

Commodities trade in spot, forward, and futures markets. They include precious metals, industrial metals, agricultural products, energy products, and credits for carbon reduction.

Futures and forwards allow both hedgers and speculators to participate in commodity markets without having to deliver or store the physical commodities.

Real Assets

Examples of **real assets** are real estate, equipment, and machinery. Although they have been traditionally held by firms for their use in production, real assets are increasingly held by institutional investors both directly and indirectly.

Buying real assets directly often provides income, tax advantages, and diversification benefits. However, they often entail substantial management costs. Furthermore, because of their heterogeneity, they usually require the investor to do substantial due diligence before investing. They are illiquid because their specialization may result in a limited pool of investors for a particular real asset.

Rather than buying real assets directly, an investor may choose to buy them indirectly through an investment such as a *real estate investment trust* (REIT) or *master limited partnership* (MLP). The investor owns an interest in these vehicles, which hold the assets directly. Indirect ownership interests are typically more liquid than ownership of the assets themselves. Another indirect ownership method is to buy the stock of firms that have large ownership of real assets.

LOS 45.d: Describe types of financial intermediaries and services that they provide.

Financial intermediaries stand between buyers and sellers, facilitating the exchange of assets, capital, and risk. Their services allow for greater efficiency and are vital to a well-functioning economy. Financial intermediaries include brokers and exchanges, dealers, securitizers, depository institutions, insurance companies, arbitrageurs, and clearinghouses.

Brokers, Dealers, and Exchanges

Brokers help their clients buy and sell securities by finding counterparties to trades in a cost efficient manner. They may work for large brokerage firms, for banks, or at exchanges.

Block brokers help with the placement of large trades. Typically, large trades are difficult to place without moving the market. For example, a large sell order might cause a security's price to decrease before the order can be fully executed. Block brokers help conceal their clients' intentions so that the market does not move against them.

Investment banks help corporations sell common stock, preferred stock, and debt securities to investors. They also provide advice to firms, notably about mergers, acquisitions, and raising capital.

Exchanges provide a venue where traders can meet. Exchanges sometimes act as brokers by providing electronic order matching. Exchanges regulate their members and require firms that list on the exchange to provide timely financial disclosures and to promote shareholder democratization. Exchanges acquire their regulatory power through member agreement or from their governments.

Alternative trading systems (ATS), which serve the same trading function as exchanges but have no regulatory function, are also known as **electronic communication networks** (ECNs) or **multilateral trading facilities** (MTFs). ATS that do not reveal current client orders are known as *dark pools*.

Dealers facilitate trading by buying for or selling from their own inventory. Dealers provide liquidity in the market and profit primarily from the spread (difference) between the price at which they will buy (bid price) and the price at which they will sell (ask price) the security or other asset.

Some dealers also act as brokers. **Broker-dealers** have an inherent conflict of interest. As brokers, they should seek the best prices for their clients, but as dealers, their goal is to profit through prices or spreads. As a result, traders typically place limits on how their orders are filled when they transact with broker-dealers.

Dealers that trade with central banks when the banks buy or sell government securities in order to affect the money supply are referred to as **primary dealers**.

Securitizers

Securitizers pool large amounts of securities or other assets and then sell interests in the pool to other investors. The returns from the pool, net of the securitizer's fees, are passed through to the investors. By securitizing the assets, the securitizer creates a diversified pool of assets with more predictable cash flows than the individual assets in the pool. This creates liquidity in the assets because the ownership interests are more easily valued and traded. There are also economies of scale in the management costs of large pools of assets and potential benefits from the manager's selection of assets.

Assets that are often securitized include mortgages, car loans, credit card receivables, bank loans, and equipment leases. The primary benefit of securitization is to decrease the funding costs for the assets in the pool. A firm may set up a *special purpose vehicle* (SPV) or *special purpose entity* (SPE) to buy firm assets, which removes them from the firm's balance sheet and may increase their value by removing the risk that financial trouble at the firm will give other investors a claim to the assets' cash flows.

The cash flows from securitized assets can be segregated by risk. The different risk categories are called *tranches*. The senior tranches provide the most certain cash flows, while the junior tranches have greater risk.

Depository Institutions

Examples of **depository institutions** include banks, credit unions, and savings and loans. They pay interest on customer deposits and provide transaction services such as checking accounts. These financial intermediaries then make loans with the funds, which offer diversification benefits. The intermediaries have expertise in evaluating credit quality and managing the risk of a portfolio of loans of various types.

Other intermediaries, such as payday lenders and factoring companies, lend money to firms and individuals on the basis of their wages, accounts receivable, and other future cash flows. These intermediaries often finance the loans by issuing commercial paper or other debt securities.

Securities brokers provide loans to investors who purchase securities on margin. When this margin lending is to hedge funds and other institutions, the brokers are referred to as *prime brokers*.

The equity owners (stockholders) of banks, brokers, and other intermediaries absorb any loan losses before depositors and other lenders. The more equity capital an intermediary has, the less risk for depositors. Poorly capitalized intermediaries (those with less equity) have less incentive to reduce the risk of their loan portfolios because they have less capital at risk.

Insurance Companies

Insurance companies are intermediaries, in that they collect insurance premiums in return for providing risk reduction to the insured. The insurance firm can do this efficiently because it provides protection to a diversified pool of policyholders, whose risks of loss are typically uncorrelated. This provides more predictable losses and cash flows compared to a single insurance contract, in the same way that a bank's diversified portfolio of loans diversifies the risk of loan defaults.

Insurance firms also provide a benefit to investors by managing the risks inherent in insurance: moral hazard, adverse selection, and fraud. **Moral hazard** occurs because the insured may take more risks once he is protected against losses. **Adverse selection** occurs when those most likely to experience losses are the predominant buyers of insurance. In **fraud**, the insured purposely causes damage or claims fictitious losses so he can collect on his insurance policy.

Arbitrageurs

In its pure (riskless) form, **arbitrage** refers to buying an asset in one market and reselling it in another at a higher price. By doing so, arbitrageurs act as intermediaries, providing liquidity to participants in the market where the asset is purchased and transferring the asset to the market where it is sold.

In markets with good information, pure arbitrage is rare because traders will favor the markets with the best prices. More commonly, arbitrageurs try to exploit pricing differences for similar instruments. For example, a dealer who sells a call option will often also buy the stock because the call and stock price are highly correlated. Likewise, arbitrageurs will attempt to exploit discrepancies in the pricing of the call and stock. Many (risk) arbitrageurs use complex models for valuation of related securities and for risk control. Creating similar positions using different assets is referred to as *replication*. This is also a form of intermediation because similar risks are traded in different forms and in different markets.

Clearinghouses and Custodians

Clearinghouses act as intermediaries between buyers and sellers in financial markets and provide:

- Escrow services (transferring cash and assets to the respective parties).
- Guarantees of contract completion.
- Assurance that margin traders have adequate capital.
- Limits on the aggregate net order quantity (buy orders minus sell orders) of members.

Through these activities, clearinghouses limit **counterparty risk**, the risk that the other party to a transaction will not fulfill its obligation. In some markets, the clearinghouse ensures only the trades of its member brokers and dealers, who, in turn, ensure the trades of their retail customers.

Custodians also improve market integrity by holding client securities and preventing their loss due to fraud or other events that affect the broker or investment manager.

LOS 45.e: Compare positions an investor can take in an asset.

An investor who owns an asset, or has the right or obligation under a contract to purchase an asset, is said to have a **long position**. A **short position** can result from borrowing an asset and selling it, with the obligation to replace the asset in the future (a short sale). The party to a contract who must sell or deliver an asset in the future is also said to have a short position. In general, investors who are long benefit from an increase in the price of an asset and those who are short benefit when the asset price declines.

Hedgers use short positions in one asset to hedge an existing risk from a long position in another asset that has returns that are strongly correlated with the returns of the asset shorted. For example, wheat farmers may take a short position in (i.e., sell) wheat futures contracts. If wheat prices fall, the resulting increase in the value of the short futures position offsets, partially or fully, the loss in the value of the farmer's crop.

> *Professor's Note: As a rule of thumb, hedgers must "do in the futures market what they must do in the future." Thus, the farmer who must sell wheat in the future can reduce the risk from wheat price fluctuations by selling wheat futures.*

The buyer of an option contract is said to be long the option. The seller is short the option and is said to have written the option. Note that an investor who is long (buys) a call option on an asset profits when the value of the underlying asset increases in value, while the party short the option has losses. A long position in a put option on an asset has the right to sell the asset at a specified price and profits when the price of the underlying asset falls, while the party short the option has losses.

In swaps, each party is long one asset and short the other, so the designation of the long and short side is often arbitrary. Usually, however, the side that benefits from an increase in the quoted price or rate is referred to as the long side.

In a currency contract, each party is long one currency and short the other. For example, the buyer of a euro futures contract priced in dollars is long the euro and short the dollar.

Short Sales and Positions

In a **short sale**, the short seller (1) simultaneously borrows and sells securities through a broker, (2) must return the securities at the request of the lender or when the short sale is closed out, and (3) must keep a portion of the proceeds of the short sale on deposit with the broker. Short sellers hope to profit from a fall in the price of the security or asset sold short, buying at a lower price in the future in order to repay the loan of the asset originally sold at a higher price. The repayment of the borrowed security or other asset is referred to as "covering the short position."

In a short sale, the short seller must pay all dividends or interest that the lender would have received from the security that has been loaned to the short seller. These payments are called **payments-in-lieu** of dividends or interest. The short seller must also deposit the proceeds of the short sale as collateral to guarantee the eventual repurchase of the security. The broker then earns interest on these funds and may return a portion of this interest to the short seller at a rate referred to as the **short rebate rate**. The short rebate rate is usually only provided to institutional investors and is typically 0.1% less than overnight interest rates. If the security is difficult to borrow, the short rebate rate may be lower or negative. The difference between the interest earned on the proceeds from the short sale and the short rebate paid is the return to the lender of the securities. A short sale may also require the short seller to deposit additional margin in the form of cash or short-term riskless securities.

Leveraged Positions

The use of borrowed funds to purchase an asset results in a **leveraged position** and the investor is said to be using leverage. Investors who use leverage to buy securities by borrowing from their brokers are said to buy on **margin** and the borrowed funds are referred to as a **margin loan**. The interest rate paid on the funds is the **call money rate**, which is generally higher than the government bill rate. The call money rate is lower for larger investors with better collateral.

At the time of a new margin purchase, investors are required to provide a minimum amount of equity, referred to as the **initial margin requirement**. This requirement may be set by the government, exchange, clearinghouse, or broker. Lower risk in an investor's portfolio will often result in the broker lending more funds.

The use of leverage magnifies both the gains and losses from changes in the value of the underlying asset. The additional risk from the use of borrowed funds is referred to as risk from **financial leverage**.

Study Session 13
Cross-Reference to CFA Institute Assigned Reading #45 – Market Organization and Structure

LOS 45.f: Calculate and interpret the leverage ratio, the rate of return on a margin transaction, and the security price at which the investor would receive a margin call.

The **leverage ratio** of a margin investment is the value of the asset divided by the value of the equity position. For example, an investor who satisfies an initial margin requirement of 50% equity has a 2-to-1 leverage ratio so that a 10% increase (decrease) in the price of the asset results in a 20% increase (decrease) in the investor's equity amount.

Example: Margin transaction

Given the following information:

Shares purchased	1,000
Purchase price per share	$100
Annual dividend per share	$2.00
Initial margin requirement	40%
Call money rate	4%
Commission per share	$0.05
Stock price after one year	$110

Calculate (1) the leverage ratio and (2) the investor's return on the margin transaction (return on equity) if the stock is sold at the end of one year.

Answer:

1. The leverage ratio = 1 / 0.40 = 2.5.

2. The total purchase price is 1,000 × $100 = $100,000. The investor must post initial margin of 40% × $100,000 = $40,000. The remaining $60,000 is borrowed. The commission on the purchase is 1,000 × $0.05 = $50. Thus, the total initial equity investment is $40,050.

At the end of one year, the stock value is 1,000 × $110 = $110,000, for a gain of $9,950. Dividends received are 1,000 × $2.00 = $2,000. Interest paid is $60,000 × 4% = $2,400. The commission on the sale is 1,000 × $0.05 = $50.

The gain on the transaction in one year is $9,950 + $2,000 – $2,400 – $50 = $9,500. The return on the equity investment is $9,500 / $40,050 = 23.72%. The investor's net return is less than the asset total return (10% price appreciation + 2% dividend = 12%) multiplied by the leverage ratio (12% × 2.5 = 30%) because of the loan interest and commissions.

We can also solve for the return on the margin transaction with the cash flow functions on a financial calculator. The initial cash outflow is the $40,000 initial margin + $50 purchase commission = $40,050. The inflow after one year is the $110,000 stock value + $2,000 dividends – $60,000 margin repayment – $2,400 margin interest – $50 sale commission = $49,550. Using the cash flow functions: CF_0 = –40,050; CF_1 = 49,550; CPT IRR = 23.72%.

To ensure that the loan is covered by the value of the asset, an investor must maintain a minimum equity percentage, called the **maintenance margin requirement**, in the account. This minimum is typically 25% of the current position value, but brokers may require a greater minimum equity percentage for volatile stocks.

If the percentage of equity in a margin account falls below the maintenance margin requirement, the investor will receive a **margin call**, a request to bring the equity percentage in the account back up to the maintenance margin percentage. An investor can satisfy this request by depositing additional funds or depositing other unmargined securities that will bring the equity percentage up to the minimum requirement. If the investor does not meet the margin call, the broker must sell the position.

The stock price which results in a margin call can be calculated by using the following formula:

$$\text{margin call price} = P_0 \left(\frac{1 - \text{initial margin}}{1 - \text{maintenance margin}} \right)$$

where:
P_0 = initial purchase price

> **Example: Margin call price**
>
> If an investor purchases a stock for $40 per share with an initial margin requirement of 50% and the maintenance margin requirement is 25%, at what price will the investor get a margin call?
>
> **Answer:**
>
> $$\frac{\$40(1 - 0.5)}{1 - 0.25} = \$26.67$$
>
> A margin call is triggered at a price below $26.67.

In a short sale, the investor must deposit initial margin equal to a percentage of the value of the shares sold short to protect the broker in case the share price increases. An increase in the share price can decrease the margin percentage below the maintenance margin percentage and generate a margin call.

LOS 45.g: Compare execution, validity, and clearing instructions.

LOS 45.h: Compare market orders with limit orders.

Securities dealers provide prices at which they will buy and sell shares. The **bid price** is the price at which a dealer will buy a security. The **ask** or **offer price** is the price at which a dealer will sell a security. The difference between the bid and ask prices is referred to as the **bid-ask spread** and is the source of a dealer's compensation. The bid and ask are quoted for specific trade sizes (**bid size** and **ask size**).

> *Professor's Note: Calculations with bid and ask prices are unlikely to appear on the Level I exam but they do appear at Level II. If you need to work with bid and ask prices, just remember that the price you get will be the one that is **worse** for you.*
>
> - *Securities: If you are buying, you must pay the higher price. If you are selling, you only receive the lower price.*
> - *Currencies: The bid or ask price you get is the one that gives you **less** of the currency you are acquiring. This works regardless of which way the exchange rate is quoted.*

The quotation in the market is the highest dealer bid and lowest dealer ask from among all dealers in a particular security. More liquid securities have market quotations with bid-ask spreads that are lower (as a percentage of share price) and therefore have lower transactions costs for investors. Traders who post bids and offers are said to *make a market*, while those who trade with them at posted prices are said to *take the market*.

When investors want to buy or sell, they must enter orders that specify the size of the trade and whether to buy or sell. The order can also include *execution instructions* that specify how to trade, *validity instructions* that specify when the order can be filled, and *clearing instructions* that specify how to settle the trade.

Execution Instructions

The most common orders, in terms of execution instructions, are market or limit orders. A **market order** instructs the broker to execute the trade immediately at the best possible price. A **limit order** places a minimum execution price on sell orders and a maximum execution price on buy orders. For example, a buy order with a limit of $6 will be executed immediately as long as the shares can be purchased for $6 or less.

A market order is often appropriate when the trader wants to execute quickly, as when the trader has information she believes is not yet reflected in market prices. The disadvantage of market orders is that they may execute at unfavorable prices, especially if the security has low trading volume relative to the order size. A market buy order may execute at a high price or a market sell order may execute at a low price. Executing at an unfavorable price represents a concession by the trader for immediate liquidity. Unfortunately, these price concessions are unpredictable.

To avoid price execution uncertainty, a trader can place a limit order instead of the market order. The disadvantage of the limit order is that it might not be filled. For example, if a trader places a limit buy order of $50 and no one is willing to sell at $50, the order will not be filled. Furthermore, if the stock price rises over time, the trader misses out on the gains.

A limit buy order above the best ask or a limit sell order below the best bid are said to be *marketable* or *aggressively priced* because at least part of the order is likely to execute immediately. If the limit price is between the best bid and the best ask, a limit order is said to be *making a new market* or *inside the market*. Limit orders waiting to execute are called **standing limit orders**.

A limit buy order at the best bid or a limit sell order at the best ask are said to *make the market*. Again, the order might not be filled. A buy order with a limit price below the best bid, or a sell order with a limit price above the best ask, is said to be *behind the market*. It will likely not execute until security prices move toward the limit price. A limit buy order with a price considerably lower than the best bid, or a limit sell order with a price significantly higher than the best ask, is said to be *far from the market*.

Other execution instructions concern the volume of the trade. **All-or-nothing orders** execute only if the whole order can be filled. Orders can specify the minimum size of a trade, which is beneficial when trading costs depend on the number of executed trades rather than the size of the order.

Trade visibility can also be specified. **Hidden orders** are those for which only the broker or exchange knows the trade size. These are useful for investors that have a large amount to trade and do not want to reveal their intentions. Traders can also specify **display size**, where some of the trade is visible to the market, but the rest is not. These are also referred to as **iceberg orders** because part of most of the order is hidden from view. They allow the investor to advertise some of the trade, with the rest of the trade potentially executed once the visible part has executed. Sometimes entering trades for part of the position the trader wishes to establish is a way to estimate the liquidity of, or the buying interest in, the security in question.

Validity Instructions

Validity instructions specify when an order should be executed. Most orders are **day orders**, meaning they expire if unfilled by the end of the trading day. **Good-till-cancelled** orders last until they are filled. **Immediate-or-cancel** orders are cancelled unless they can be filled immediately. They are also known as **fill-or-kill** orders. **Good-on-close** orders are only filled at the end of the trading day. If they are market orders, they are referred to as **market-on-close** orders. These are often used by mutual funds because their portfolios are valued using closing prices. There are also **good-on-open** orders.

Stop Orders

Stop orders are those that are not executed unless the stop price has been met. They are often referred to as **stop loss orders** because they can be used to prevent losses or to protect profits. Suppose an investor purchases a stock for $50. If the investor wants to sell out of the position if the price falls 10% to $45, he can enter a **stop-sell order** at $45. If the stock trades down to $45 or lower, this *triggers* a market order to sell. There is no guarantee that the order will execute at $45, and a rapidly falling stock could be sold at a price significantly lower than $45.

A **stop-buy** is entered with at stop (trigger) above the current market price. There are two primary reasons a trader would enter a stop-buy order. (1) A trader with a short position could attempt to limit losses from an increasing stock price with a stop-buy order. (2) It is often said, "You don't get paid for being right until the market agrees with you." With this in mind, an investor who believes a stock is undervalued, but does not wish to own it until there are signs that market participants are being convinced of this undervaluation, may place a stop-buy order at a price some specific percentage above the current price.

Note that stop orders reinforce market momentum. Stop-sell orders execute when market prices are falling, and stop-buy orders execute when the market is rising. Execution prices for stop orders are therefore often unfavorable.

Example: Using stop orders

Raymond Flowers believes that the shares of Acme Corp. that he owns are overvalued currently but knows that stocks often continue to increase above their intrinsic values for some time before correcting. What type of order should Flowers place if he wants to sell his shares when the price begins to fall a significant amount?

Answer:

Flowers should enter a good-till-cancelled stop-sell order at a price some percentage below the current level. If, for example, the shares are trading at 40, he could enter a stop-sell order at 36, 10% below the current level. Investors sometimes move these stops up as a stock continues to increase in price. In response to a price increase to 42, Flowers might move his stop-sell order up to 37.80, 10% below the new price. Note that a limit order to sell with a limit price below the current market price would likely execute immediately.

Clearing Instructions

Clearing instructions tell the trader how to clear and settle a trade. They are usually standing instructions and not attached to an order. Retail trades are typically cleared and settled by the broker, whereas institutional trades may be settled by a custodian or another broker, which might be the trader's prime broker. Using two brokers allows the investor to keep one broker as her prime broker for margin and custodial services while using a variety of other brokers for specialized execution.

One important clearing instruction is whether a sell order is a short sale or long sale. In the former, the broker must confirm that the security can be borrowed and in the latter, that the security can be delivered.

LOS 45.i: Define primary and secondary markets and explain how secondary markets support primary markets.

Primary capital markets refer to the sale of newly issued securities. New equity issues involve either:

- New shares issued by firms whose shares are already trading in the marketplace. These issues are called **seasoned offerings** or **secondary issues**.
- First-time issues by firms whose shares are not currently publicly traded. These are called **initial public offerings** (IPOs).

Secondary financial markets are where securities trade after their initial issuance. Placing a buy order on the London Stock Exchange is an order in the secondary market and will result in purchase of existing shares from their current owner.

Primary Market: Public Offerings

Corporate stock or bond issues are almost always sold with the assistance of an investment banking firm. The investment bank finds investors who agree to buy part of the issue. These are not actual orders but are referred to as **indications of interest**. When the number of shares covered by indications of interest are greater (less) than the number of shares to be offered, the offering price may be adjusted upward (downward). This process of gathering indications of interest is referred to as **book building**. In London, the book builder is referred to as the **book runner**. In Europe, an **accelerated book build** occurs when securities must be issued quickly. To build a book, the investment bank disseminates information about the firm's financials and prospects. The issuer must also make disclosures including how the funds will be used.

The most common way an investment bank assists with a security issuance is through an **underwritten offering**. Here, the investment bank agrees to purchase the entire issue at a price that is negotiated between the issuer and bank. If the issue is undersubscribed, the investment bank must buy the unsold portion. In the case of an IPO, the investment bank also agrees to make a market in the stock for a period after the issuance to provide price support for the issue.

An investment bank can also agree to distribute shares of an IPO on a **best efforts** basis, rather than agreeing to purchase the whole issue. If the issue is undersubscribed, the bank is not obligated to buy the unsold portion.

Note that investment banks have a conflict of interest in an underwritten offer. As the issuer's agents, they should set the price high to raise the most funds for the issuer. But, as underwriters, they would prefer that the price be set low enough that the whole issue sells. This also allows them to allocate portions of an undervalued IPO to their clients. This results in IPOs typically being underpriced. Issuers also could have an interest in underpricing the IPO because of the negative publicity when an undersubscribed IPO initially trades at a price below the IPO price investors pay. An IPO that is oversubscribed and has the expectation of trading significantly above its IPO price is referred to as a hot issue.

Study Session 13
Cross-Reference to CFA Institute Assigned Reading #45 – Market Organization and Structure

Primary Market: Private Placements and Other Transactions

In a **private placement**, securities are sold directly to qualified investors, typically with the assistance of an investment bank. Qualified investors are those with substantial wealth and investment knowledge. Private placements do not require the issuer to disclose as much information as they must when the securities are being sold to the public. The issuance costs are less with a private placement and the offer price is also lower because the securities cannot be resold in public markets, making them less valuable than shares registered for public trading.

In a **shelf registration**, a firm makes its public disclosures as in a regular offering but then issues the registered securities over time when it needs capital and when the markets are favorable.

A **dividend reinvestment plan** (DRP or DRIP) allows existing shareholders to use their dividends to buy new shares from the firm at a slight discount.

In a **rights offering**, existing shareholders are given the right to buy new shares at a discount to the current market price. Shareholders tend to dislike rights offerings because their ownership is diluted unless they exercise their rights and buy the additional shares. However, rights can be traded separately from the shares themselves in some circumstances.

In addition to firms issuing securities, governments issue short-term and long-term debt, either by auction or through investment banks.

Importance of the Secondary Market

Secondary markets are important because they provide liquidity and price/value information. Liquid markets are those in which a security can be sold quickly without incurring a discount from the current price. The better the secondary market, the easier it is for firms to raise external capital in the primary market, which results in a lower cost of capital for firms with shares that have adequate liquidity.

LOS 45.j: Describe how securities, contracts, and currencies are traded in quote-driven, order-driven, and brokered markets.

The trading of securities in the secondary market has encouraged the development of market structures to facilitate trading. Trading can be examined according to when securities are traded and how they are traded.

Securities markets may be structured as call markets or continuous markets. In **call markets**, the stock is only traded at specific times. Call markets are potentially very liquid when in session because all traders are present, but they are obviously illiquid between sessions. In a call market, all trades, bids, and asks are declared, and then one negotiated price is set that clears the market for the stock. This method is used in smaller markets but is also used to set opening prices and prices after trading halts on major exchanges.

In **continuous markets**, trades occur at any time the market is open. The price is set by either the auction process or by dealer bid-ask quotes.

Market Structures

There are three main categories of securities markets: *quote-driven markets* where investors trade with dealers, *order-driven markets* where rules are used to match buyers and sellers, and *brokered markets* where investors use brokers to locate a counterparty to a trade.

Quote-Driven Markets

In **quote-driven markets**, traders transact with dealers (market makers) who post bid and ask prices. Dealers maintain an inventory of securities. Quote-driven markets are thus sometimes called **dealer markets**, **price-driven markets**, or **over-the-counter markets**. Most securities other than stocks trade in quote-driven markets. Trading often takes place electronically.

Order-Driven Markets

In **order-driven markets**, orders are executed using trading rules, which are necessary because traders are usually anonymous. Exchanges and automated trading systems are examples of order-driven markets. Two sets of rules are used in these markets: order matching rules and trade pricing rules.

Order matching rules establish an *order precedence hierarchy.* **Price priority** is one criteria, where the trades given highest priority are those at the highest bid (buy) and lowest ask (sell). If orders are at the same prices, a **secondary precedence rule** gives priority to non-hidden orders and earliest arriving orders. These rules encourage traders to price their trades aggressively, display their entire orders, and trade earlier, thereby improving liquidity.

After orders are created using order matching rules, **trade pricing rules** are used to determine the price. Under the *uniform pricing rule*, all orders trade at the same price, which is the price that results in the highest volume of trading. The *discriminatory pricing rule* uses the limit price of the order that arrived first as the trade price.

In an electronic crossing network, the typical trader is an institution. Orders are batched together and crossed (matched) at fixed points in time during the day at the average of the bid and ask quotes from the exchange where the stock primarily trades. This pricing rule is referred to as the *derivative pricing rule* because it is derived from the security's main market. The price is not determined by orders in the crossing network.

Brokered Markets

In **brokered markets**, brokers find the counterparty in order to execute a trade. This service is especially valuable when the trader has a security that is unique or illiquid. Examples are large blocks of stock, real estate, and artwork. Dealers typically do not carry an inventory of these assets and there are too few trades for these assets to trade in order-driven markets.

Market Information

A market is said to be **pre-trade transparent** if investors can obtain pre-trade information regarding quotes and orders. A market is **post-trade transparent** if investors can obtain post-trade information regarding completed trade prices and sizes.

Buy-side traders value transparency because it allows them to better understand security values and trading costs. Dealers, on the other hand, prefer opaque markets because this provides them with an informational advantage over traders who trade less frequently in the security. Transactions costs and bid-ask spreads are larger in opaque markets.

LOS 45.k: Describe characteristics of a well-functioning financial system.

A well-functioning financial system allows entities to achieve their purposes. More specifically, **complete markets** fulfill the following:

- Investors can save for the future at fair rates of return.
- Creditworthy borrowers can obtain funds.
- Hedgers can manage their risks.
- Traders can obtain the currencies, commodities, and other assets they need.

If a market can perform these functions at low trading costs (including commissions, bid-ask spreads, and price impacts), it is said to be **operationally efficient**. If security prices reflect all the information associated with fundamental value in a timely fashion, then the financial system is **informationally efficient**. A well-functioning financial system has complete markets that are operationally and informationally efficient, with prices that reflect fundamental values.

A well-functioning financial system has financial intermediaries that:

- Organize trading venues, including exchanges, brokerages, and alternative trading systems.
- Supply liquidity.
- Securitize assets so that borrowers can obtain funds inexpensively.
- Manage banks that use depositor capital to fund borrowers.
- Manage insurance firms that pool unrelated risks.
- Manage investment advisory services that assist investors with asset management inexpensively.
- Provide clearinghouses that settle trades.
- Manage depositories that provide for asset safety.

The benefits of a well-functioning financial system are tremendous. Savers can fund entrepreneurs who need capital to fund new companies. Company risks can be shared so that risky companies can be funded. These benefits are enhanced because the transactions can occur among strangers, widening the opportunities for capital formation and risk sharing in the economy.

Furthermore, in informationally efficiently markets, capital is allocated to its most productive use. That is, they are **allocationally efficient**. Informational efficiency is brought about by traders who bid prices up and down in response to new information that changes estimates of securities' fundamental values. If markets are operationally efficient, security prices will be more informationally efficient because low trading costs encourage trading based on new information. The existence of accounting standards and financial reporting requirements also reduces the costs of obtaining information and increases security values.

LOS 45.l: Describe objectives of market regulation.

Without market regulation, many problems could persist in financial markets:

- *Fraud and theft*: In complex financial markets, the potential for theft and fraud increases because investment managers and others can take advantage of unsophisticated investors. Furthermore, if returns are often random, it is difficult for investors to determine if their agents (e.g., investment managers and brokers) are performing well.
- *Insider trading*: If investors believe traders with inside information will exploit them, they will exit the market and liquidity will be reduced.
- *Costly information*: If obtaining information is relatively expensive, markets will not be as informationally efficient and investors will not invest as much.
- *Defaults:* Parties might not honor their obligations in markets.

To solve these problems, market regulation should:

- Protect unsophisticated investors so that trust in the markets is preserved.
- Require minimum standards of competency and make it easier for investors to evaluate performance. The CFA Program and the Global Investment Performance Standards are part of this effort.
- Prevent insiders from exploiting other investors.
- Require common financial reporting requirements (e.g., those of the International Accounting Standards Board) so that information gathering is less expensive.
- Require minimum levels of capital so that market participants will be able to honor their long-term commitments. This is especially important for insurance companies and pension funds that individuals depend on for their financial future. With capital at stake, market participants have more incentive to be careful about the risks they take.

Regulation can be provided by governments as well as industry groups. For example, most exchanges, clearinghouses, and dealer trade organizations are self-regulating organizations (SROs), meaning that they regulate their members. Governments sometimes delegate regulatory authority to SROs.

When they fail to address the problems mentioned above, financial markets do not function well. Liquidity declines, firms shun risky projects, new ideas go unfunded, and economic growth slows.

Key Concepts

LOS 45.a
The three main functions of the financial system are to:
1. Allow entities to save, borrow, issue equity capital, manage risks, exchange assets, and utilize information.

2. Determine the return that equates aggregate savings and borrowing.

3. Allocate capital efficiently.

LOS 45.b
Assets and markets can be classified as:
- Financial assets (e.g., securities, currencies, derivatives) versus real assets (e.g., real estate, equipment).
- Debt securities versus equity securities.
- Public securities that trade on exchanges or through dealers versus private securities.
- Physical derivative contracts (e.g., on grains or metals) versus financial derivative contracts (e.g., on bonds or equity indexes).
- Spot versus future delivery markets.
- Primary markets (issuance of new securities) versus secondary markets (trading of previously issued securities).
- Money markets (short-term debt instruments) versus capital markets (longer-term debt instruments and equities).
- Traditional investment markets (bonds, stocks) versus alternative investment markets (e.g., real estate, hedge funds, fine art).

LOS 45.c
The major types of assets are securities, currencies, contracts, commodities, and real assets.

Securities include fixed income (e.g., bonds, notes, commercial paper), equity (common stock, preferred stock, warrants), and pooled investment vehicles (mutual funds, exchange-traded funds, hedge funds, asset-backed securities).

Contracts include futures, forwards, options, swaps, and insurance contracts.

Commodities include agricultural products, industrial and precious metals, and energy products and are traded in spot, forward, and futures markets.

Most national currencies are traded in spot markets and some are also traded in forward and futures markets.

LOS 45.d
Financial intermediaries perform the following roles:
- Brokers, exchanges, and alternative trading systems connect buyers and sellers of the same security at the same location and time. They provide a centralized location for trading.
- Dealers match buyers and sellers of the same security at different points in time.
- Arbitrageurs connect buyers and sellers of the same security at the same time but in different venues. They also connect buyers and sellers of non-identical securities of similar risk.
- Securitizers and depository institutions package assets into a diversified pool and sell interests in it. Investors obtain greater liquidity and choose their desired risk level.
- Insurance companies create a diversified pool of risks and manage the risk inherent in providing insurance.
- Clearinghouses reduce counterparty risk and promote market integrity.

LOS 45.e
A long position in an asset represents current or future ownership. A long position benefits when the asset increases in value.

A short position represents an agreement to sell or deliver an asset or results from borrowing an asset and selling it (i.e., a short sale). A short position benefits when the asset decreases in value.

When an investor buys a security by borrowing from a broker, the investor is said to buy on margin and has a leveraged position. The risk of investing borrowed funds is referred to as financial leverage. More leverage results in greater risk.

LOS 45.f
The leverage ratio is the value of the asset divided by the value of the equity position. Higher leverage ratios indicate greater risk.

The return on a margin transaction is the increase in the value of the position after deducting selling commissions and interest charges, divided by the amount of funds initially invested, including purchase commissions.

The maintenance margin is the minimum percentage of equity that a margin investor is required to maintain in his account. If the investor's equity falls below the maintenance margin, the investor will receive a margin call. The stock price that will result in a margin call is:

$$\text{margin call price} = P_0 \left(\frac{1 - \text{initial margin}}{1 - \text{maintenance margin}} \right)$$

where:
P_0 = initial purchase price

LOS 45.g

Execution instructions specify how to trade. Market orders and limit orders are examples of execution instructions.

Validity instructions specify when an order can be filled. Day orders, good-til-cancelled orders, and stop orders are examples of validity instructions.

Clearing instructions specify how to settle a trade.

LOS 45.h

A market order is an order to execute the trade immediately at the best possible price. A market order is appropriate when the trader wants to execute a transaction quickly. The disadvantage of a market order is that it may execute at an unfavorable price.

A limit order is an order to trade at the best possible price, subject to the price satisfying the limit condition. A limit order avoids price execution uncertainty. The disadvantage of a limit order is that it may not be filled. A buy (sell) order with a limit of $18 will only be executed if the security can be bought (sold) at a price of $18 or less (more).

LOS 45.i

New issues of securities are sold in primary capital markets. Secondary financial markets are where securities trade after their initial issuance.

In an underwritten offering, the investment bank guarantees that the issue will be sold at a price that is negotiated between the issuer and bank. In a best efforts offering, the bank acts only as a broker.

In a private placement, a firm sells securities directly to qualified investors, without the disclosures of a public offering.

A liquid secondary market makes it easier for firms to raise external capital in the primary market, which results in a lower cost of capital for firms.

LOS 45.j

There are three main categories of securities markets:
1. Quote-driven markets: Investors trade with dealers that maintain inventories of securities, currencies, or contracts.

2. Order-driven markets: Order-matching and trade-pricing rules are used to match the orders of buyers and sellers.

3. Brokered markets: Brokers locate a counterparty to take the other side of a buy or sell order.

In call markets, securities are only traded at specific times. In continuous markets, trades occur at any time the market is open.

Study Session 13
Cross-Reference to CFA Institute Assigned Reading #45 – Market Organization and Structure

LOS 45.k
A well-functioning financial system has the following characteristics:
- Complete markets: Savers receive a return, borrowers can obtain capital, hedgers can manage risks, and traders can acquire needed assets.
- Operational efficiency: Trading costs are low.
- Informational efficiency: Prices reflect fundamental information quickly.
- Allocational efficiency: Capital is directed to its highest valued use.

LOS 45.l
The objectives of market regulation are to:
- Protect unsophisticated investors.
- Establish minimum standards of competency.
- Help investors to evaluate performance.
- Prevent insiders from exploiting other investors.
- Promote common financial reporting requirements so that information gathering is less expensive.
- Require minimum levels of capital so that market participants will be able to honor their commitments and be more careful about their risks.

CONCEPT CHECKERS

1. Daniel Ferramosco is concerned that a long-term bond he holds might default. He therefore buys a contract that will compensate him in the case of default. What type of contract does he hold?
    A. Physical derivative contract.
    B. Primary derivative contract.
    C. Financial derivative contract.

2. A financial intermediary buys a stock and then resells it a few days later at a higher price. Which intermediary would this *most likely* describe?
    A. Broker.
    B. Dealer.
    C. Arbitrageur.

3. Which of the following is *most* similar to a short position in the underlying asset?
    A. Buying a put.
    B. Writing a put.
    C. Buying a call.

4. An investor buys 1,000 shares of a stock on margin at a price of $50 per share. The initial margin requirement is 40% and the margin lending rate is 3%. The investor's broker charges a commission of $0.01 per share on purchases and sales. The stock pays an annual dividend of $0.30 per share. One year later, the investor sells the 1,000 shares at a price of $56 per share. The investor's rate of return is *closest* to:
    A. 12%.
    B. 27%.
    C. 36%.

5. A stock is selling at $50. An investor's valuation model estimates its intrinsic value to be $40. Based on her estimate, she would *most likely* place a:
    A. short-sale order.
    B. stop order to buy.
    C. market order to buy.

6. Which of the following limit buy orders would be the *most likely* to go unexecuted?
    A. A marketable order.
    B. An order behind the market.
    C. An order making a new market.

7. New issues of securities are transactions in the:
    A. primary market.
    B. secondary market.
    C. seasoned market.

8. In which of the following types of markets do stocks trade any time the market is open?
   A. Exchange markets.
   B. Call markets.
   C. Continuous markets.

9. A market is said to be informationally efficient if it features:
   A. market prices that reflect all available information about the value of the securities traded.
   B. timely and accurate information about current supply and demand conditions.
   C. many buyers and sellers that are willing to trade at prices above and below the prevailing market price.

10. Which of the following would *least likely* be an objective of market regulation?
    A. Reduce burdensome accounting standards.
    B. Make it easier for investors to evaluate performance.
    C. Prevent investors from using inside information in securities trading.

For more questions related to this topic review, log in to your Schweser online account and launch SchweserPro™ QBank; and for video instruction covering each LOS in this topic review, log in to your Schweser online account and launch the OnDemand video lectures, if you have purchased these products.

Study Session 13
Cross-Reference to CFA Institute Assigned Reading #45 – Market Organization and Structure

ANSWERS – CONCEPT CHECKERS

1. **C** Daniel holds a derivative contract that has a value determined by another financial contract; in this case, the long-term bond.

2. **B** This situation best describes a dealer. A dealer buys an asset for its inventory in the hopes of reselling it later at a higher price. Brokers stand between buyers and sellers of the same security at the same location and time. Arbitrageurs trade in the same security simultaneously in different markets.

3. **A** Buying a put is most similar to a short position in the underlying asset because the put increases in value if the underlying asset value decreases. The writer of a put and the holder of a call have a long exposure to the underlying asset because their positions increase in value if the underlying asset value increases.

4. **B** The total purchase price is 1,000 × $50 = $50,000. The investor must post initial margin of 40% × $50,000 = $20,000. The remaining $30,000 is borrowed. The commission on the purchase is 1,000 × $0.01 = $10. Thus, the initial equity investment is $20,010.

   In one year, the sales price is 1,000 × $56 = $56,000. Dividends received are 1,000 × $0.30 = $300. Interest paid is $30,000 × 3% = $900. The commission on the sale is 1,000 × $0.01 = $10. Thus the ending value is $56,000 − $30,000 + $300 − $900 − $10 = $25,390.

   The return on the equity investment is $25,390 / $20,010 − 1 = 26.89%.

5. **A** If the investor believes the stock is overvalued in the market, the investor should place a short-sale order, which would be profitable if the stock moves toward her value estimate.

6. **B** A behind-the-market limit order would be least likely executed. In the case of a buy, the limit buy order price is below the best bid. It will likely not execute until security prices decline. A marketable buy order is the most likely to trade because it is close to the best ask price. In an order that is making a new market or inside the market, the limit buy order price is between the best bid and ask.

7. **A** The primary market refers to the market for newly issued securities.

8. **C** Continuous markets are defined as markets where stocks can trade any time the market is open. Some exchange markets are call markets where orders are accumulated and executed at specific times.

9. **A** Informational efficiency means the prevailing price reflects all available information about the value of the asset, and the price reacts quickly to new information.

10. **A** Market regulation should require financial reporting standards so that information gathering is less expensive and the informational efficiency of the markets is enhanced.

The following is a review of the Equity: Market Organization, Market Indices, and Market Efficiency principles designed to address the learning outcome statements set forth by CFA Institute. Cross-Reference to CFA Institute Assigned Reading #46.

SECURITY MARKET INDICES

Study Session 13

EXAM FOCUS

Security market indexes are used to measure the performance of markets and investment managers. Understand the construction, calculation, and weaknesses of price-weighted, market capitalization-weighted, and equal-weighted indexes. Be familiar with the various security indexes and their potential weaknesses.

LOS 46.a: Describe a security market index.

A **security market index** is used to represent the performance of an asset class, security market, or segment of a market. They are usually created as portfolios of individual securities, which are referred to as the **constituent securities** of the index. An index has a numerical value that is calculated from the market prices (actual when available, or estimated) of its constituent securities at a point in time. An index return is the percentage change in the index's value over a period of time.

LOS 46.b: Calculate and interpret the value, price return, and total return of an index.

An index return may be calculated using a **price index** or a **return index**. A price index uses only the prices of the constituent securities in the return calculation. A rate of return that is calculated based on a price index is referred to as a **price return**.

A return index includes both prices and income from the constituent securities. A rate of return that is calculated based on a return index is called a **total return**. If the assets in an index produce interim cash flows such as dividends or interest payments, the total return will be greater than the price return.

Once returns are calculated for each period, they then can be compounded together to arrive at the return for the measurement period:

$$R_P = (1 + R_{S1})(1 + R_{S2})(1 + R_{S3})(1 + R_{S4})...(1 + R_{Sk}) - 1$$

where:
R_P = portfolio return during the measurement period
k = total number of subperiods
R_{Sk} = portfolio return during the subperiod k

For example, if the returns for the first two periods were 0.50% and 1.04%, they would be geometrically linked to produce 1.55%:

$$R_P = (1 + R_{S1})(1 + R_{S2}) - 1 = (1.005)(1.0104) - 1 = 0.0155 \text{ or } 1.55\%$$

If the starting index value is 100, its value after two periods would be 100 × 1.0155 = 101.55.

LOS 46.c: Describe the choices and issues in index construction and management.

Index providers must make several decisions:

- What is the *target market* the index is intended to measure?
- Which securities from the target market should be included?
- How should the securities be weighted in the index?
- How often should the index be rebalanced?
- When should the selection and weighting of securities be re-examined?

The target market may be defined very broadly (e.g., stocks in the United States) or narrowly (e.g., small-cap value stocks in the United States). It may also be defined by geographic region or by economic sector (e.g., cyclical stocks). The constituent stocks in the index could be all the stocks in that market or just a representative sample. The selection process may be determined by an objective rule or subjectively by a committee.

LOS 46.d: Compare the different weighting methods used in index construction.

Weighting schemes for stock indexes include price weighting, equal weighting, market capitalization weighting, float-adjusted market capitalization weighting, and fundamental weighting.

A **price-weighted index** is simply an arithmetic average of the prices of the securities included in the index. The divisor of a price-weighted index is adjusted for stock splits and changes in the composition of the index when securities are added or deleted, such that the index value is unaffected by such changes.

The advantage of a price-weighted index is that its computation is simple. One disadvantage is that a given percentage change in the price of a higher priced stock has a greater impact on the index's value than does an equal percentage change in the price of a lower priced stock. Put another way, higher priced stocks have more weight in the calculation of a price-weighted index. Additionally, a stock's weight in the index going forward changes if the firm splits its stock, repurchases stock, or issues stock dividends, as all of these actions will affect the price of the stock and therefore its weight in the index. A portfolio that has an equal number of shares in each of the constituent stocks will have price returns (ignoring dividends) that will match the returns of a price-weighted index.

Two major price-weighted indexes are the Dow Jones Industrial Average (DJIA) and the Nikkei Dow Jones Stock Average. The DJIA is a price-weighted index based on 30 U.S. stocks. The Nikkei Dow is constructed from the prices of 225 stocks that trade in the first section of the Tokyo Stock Exchange.

An **equal-weighted index** is calculated as the arithmetic average return of the index stocks and, for a given time period, would be matched by the returns on a portfolio that had equal dollar amounts invested in each index stock. As with a price-weighted index, an advantage of an equal-weighted index is its simplicity.

One complication with an equal-weighted index return is that a matching portfolio would have to be adjusted periodically (rebalanced) as prices change so that the values of all security positions are made equal each period. The portfolio rebalancing required to match the performance of an equal-weighted index creates high transactions costs that would decrease portfolio returns.

Another concern with an equal-weighted index is that the weights placed on the returns of the securities of smaller capitalization firms are greater than their proportions of the overall market value of the index stocks. Conversely, the weights on the returns of large capitalization firms in the index are smaller than their proportions of the overall market value of the index stocks.

The Value Line Composite Average and the Financial Times Ordinary Share Index are well-known examples of equal-weighted indexes.

A **market capitalization-weighted index** (or **value-weighted index**) has weights based on the market capitalization of each index stock (current stock price multiplied by the number of shares outstanding) as a proportion of the total market capitalization of all the stocks in the index. A market capitalization-weighted index return can be matched with a portfolio in which the value of each security position in the portfolio is the same proportion of the total portfolio value as the proportion of that security's market capitalization to the total market capitalization of all of the securities included in the index. This weighting method more closely represents changes in aggregate investor wealth than price weighting. Because the weight of an index stock is based on its market capitalization, a market capitalization-weighted index does not need to be adjusted when a stock splits or pays a stock dividend.

An alternative to using a firm's market capitalization to calculate its weight in an index is to use its **market float**. A firm's market float is the total value of the shares that are actually available to the investing public and excludes the value of shares held by controlling stockholders because they are unlikely to sell their shares. For example, the float for Microsoft would exclude shares owned by Bill Gates and Paul Allen (the founders) and those of certain other large shareholders as well. The market float is often calculated excluding those shares held by corporations or governments as well. Sometimes the market float calculation excludes shares that are not available to foreign buyers and is then referred to as the **free float**. The reason for this is to better match the index weights of stocks to their proportions of the total value of all the shares of index stocks that are actually available to investors.

A **float-adjusted market capitalization-weighted index** is constructed like a market capitalization-weighted index. The weights, however, are based on the proportionate value of each firm's shares that are available to investors to the total market value of the shares of index stocks that are available to investors. Firms with relatively large percentages of their shares held by controlling stockholders will have less weight than they have in an unadjusted market-capitalization index.

The advantage of market capitalization-weighted indexes of either type is that index security weights represent proportions of total market value. The primary disadvantage of value-weighted indexes is that the relative impact of a stock's return on the index increases as its price rises and decreases as its price falls. This means that stocks that are possibly overvalued are given disproportionately high weights in the index and stocks that are possibly undervalued are given disproportionately low weights. Holding a portfolio that tracks a value-weighted index is, therefore, similar to following a momentum strategy, under which the most successful stocks are given the greatest weights and poor performing stocks are underweighted.

The Standard and Poor's 500 (S&P 500) Index Composite is an example of a market capitalization-weighted index.

An index that uses **fundamental weighting** uses weights based on firm fundamentals, such as earnings, dividends, or cash flow. In contrast to market capitalization index weights, these weights are unaffected by the share prices of the index stocks (although related to them over the long term). Fundamental weights can be based on a single measure or some combination of fundamental measures.

An advantage of a fundamental-weighted index is that it avoids the bias of market capitalization-weighted indexes toward the performance of the shares of overvalued firms and away from the performance of the shares of undervalued firms. A fundamental-weighted index will actually have a value tilt, overweighting firms with high value-based metrics such as book-to-market ratios or earnings yields. Note that a firm with a high earnings yield (total earnings to total market value) relative to other index firms will by construction have a higher weight in an earnings-weighted index because, among index stocks, its earnings are high relative to its market value.

LOS 46.e: Calculate and analyze the value and return of an index given its weighting method.

Price Weighting

A price-weighted index adds the market prices of each stock in the index and divides this total by the number of stocks in the index. The divisor, however, must be adjusted for stock splits and other changes in the index portfolio to maintain the continuity of the series over time.

$$\text{price-weighted index} = \frac{\text{sum of stock prices}}{\text{number of stocks in index adjusted for splits}}$$

Example: Price-weighted index

Given the information for the three stocks presented in the following figure, calculate a price-weighted index return over a 1-month period.

Index Firm Data

	Share Price December 31, 20X6	Share Price January 31, 20X7
Stock X	$10	$20
Stock Y	$20	$15
Stock Z	$60	$40

Answer:

The price-weighted index is (10 + 20 + 60) / 3 = 30 as of December 31 and (20 + 15 + 40) / 3 = 25 as of January 31. Hence, the price-weighted 1-month percentage return is:

$$\frac{25}{30} - 1 = -16.7\%$$

Example: Adjusting a price-weighted index for stock splits

At the market close on day 1, Stock A has a price of $10, Stock B has a price of $20, and Stock C has a price of $90. The value of a price-weighted index of these three stocks is (10 + 20 + 90) / 3 = 40 at the close of trading. If Stock C splits 2-for-1, effective on day 2, what is the new denominator for the index?

Answer:

The effect of the split on the price of Stock C, in the absence of any change from the price at the end of day 1, would be to reduce it to $90 / 2 = $45. The index denominator will be adjusted so that the index value would remain at 40 if there were no changes in the stock prices other than to adjust for the split. The new denominator, d, must satisfy (10 + 20 + 45) / d = 40 and equals 1.875.

The returns on a price-weighted index could be matched by purchasing an equal number of shares of each stock represented in the index. Because the index is price weighted, a percentage change in a high-priced stock will have a relatively greater effect on the index than the same percentage change in a low-priced stock.

Market Capitalization Weighting

A market capitalization-weighted index is calculated by summing the total value (current stock price multiplied by the number of shares outstanding) of all the stocks in the index. This sum is then divided by a similar sum calculated during the selected base period. The ratio is then multiplied by the index's base value (typically 100).

For example, if the total market values of the index portfolio on December 31 and January 31 are $80 million and $95 million, respectively, the index value at the end of January is:

$$\text{current index value} = \frac{\text{current total market value of index stocks}}{\text{base year total market value of index stocks}} \times \text{base year index value}$$

$$\text{current index value} = \frac{\$95 \text{ million}}{\$80 \text{ million}} \times 100 = 118.75$$

Thus, the market capitalization-weighted index percentage return is:

(118.75 / 100) − 1 = 18.75%

The following example of price-weighting versus market value-weighting shows how these two indexes are calculated and how they differ.

> **Example: Price-weighted vs. market capitalization-weighted indexes**
>
> Consider the three firms described below. Compare the effects on a price-weighted index and a market capitalization-weighted index if Stock A doubles in price or if Stock C doubles in price. Assume the period shown in the table is the base period for the market capitalization-weighted index and that its base value is 100.
>
> **Index Firm Data**
>
> | Company | Number of Shares Outstanding (000s) | Stock Price | Capitalization (000s) |
> |---|---|---|---|
> | A | 100 | $100 | $10,000 |
> | B | 1,000 | $10 | $10,000 |
> | C | 20,000 | $1 | $20,000 |

Answer:

The price-weighted index equals:

$$\frac{100+10+1}{3} = 37$$

If Stock A doubles in price to $200, the price-weighted index value is:

$$\frac{200+10+1}{3} = 70.33$$

If Stock C doubles in price to $2, the price-weighted index value is:

$$\frac{100+10+2}{3} = 37.33$$

If Stock A doubles in value, the index goes up 33.33 points, while if Stock C doubles in value, the index only goes up 0.33 points. Changes in the value of the firm with the highest stock price have a disproportionately large influence on a price-weighted index.

For a market capitalization-weighted index, the base period market capitalization is (100,000 × $100) + (1,000,000 × $10) + (20,000,000 × $1) = $40,000,000.

If Stock A doubles in price to $200, the index goes to:

$$\frac{100,000 \times \$200 + 1,000,000 \times \$10 + 20,000,000 \times \$1}{\$40,000,000} \times 100 = 125$$

If Stock C doubles in price to $2, the index goes to:

$$\frac{100,000 \times \$100 + 1,000,000 \times \$10 + 20,000,000 \times \$2}{\$40,000,000} \times 100 = 150$$

In the market capitalization-weighted index, the returns on Stock C have the greatest influence on the index return because Stock C's market capitalization is larger than that of Stock A or Stock B.

Equal Weighting

An equal-weighted index places an equal weight on the returns of all index stocks, regardless of their prices or market values. A $2 change in the price of a $20 stock has the same effect on the index as a $30 change in the price of a $300 stock regardless of the size of the company. The return of an equal-weighted index over a given period is often calculated as a simple average of the returns of the index stocks.

> **Example: Equally weighted index**
>
> Calculate the equal-weighted index value for the three stocks described below, assuming an initial index value of 131.
>
> **Equal-Weighted Index Data**
>
> | Stock | Initial Price | Current Price | Price Change |
> |-------|---------------|---------------|--------------|
> | A | $12 | $15 | +25.0% |
> | B | $52 | $48 | −7.7% |
> | C | $38 | $45 | +18.4% |
>
> **Answer:**
>
> $$\text{change in index} = \frac{25\% - 7.7\% + 18.4\%}{3} = 11.9\%$$
>
> new index value = 131(1 + 0.119) = 146.59

Note that for a total return index, period returns would include any dividends paid over the period.

LOS 46.f: Describe rebalancing and reconstitution of an index.

Rebalancing refers to adjusting the weights of securities in a portfolio to their target weights after price changes have affected the weights. For index calculations, rebalancing to target weights on the index securities is done on a periodic basis, usually quarterly. Because the weights in price- and value-weighted indexes (portfolios) are adjusted to their correct values by changes in prices, rebalancing is an issue primarily for equal-weighted indexes. As noted previously, the weights on security returns in an (initially) equal-weighted portfolio are not equal as securities prices change over time. Therefore, rebalancing the portfolio at the end of each period used to calculate index returns is necessary for the portfolio return to match the index return.

Index **reconstitution** refers to periodically adding and deleting securities that make up an index. Securities are deleted if they no longer meet the index criteria and are replaced by other securities that do. Indexes are reconstituted to reflect corporate events such as bankruptcy or delisting of index firms and are at the subjective judgment of a committee.

When a security is added to an index, its price tends to rise as portfolio managers seeking to track that index in a portfolio buy the security. The prices of deleted securities tend to fall as portfolio managers sell them. Note that additions and deletions also require that the weights on the returns of other index stocks be adjusted to conform to the desired weighting scheme.

LOS 46.g: Describe uses of security market indices.

Security market indexes have several uses:

- *Reflection of market sentiment.* Indexes provide a representative market return and thus reflect investor confidence. Although the Dow Jones Industrial Average is a popular index, it reflects the performance of only 30 stocks and thus may not be a good measure of sentiment with regard to the broader market.
- *Benchmark of manager performance.* An index can be used to evaluate the performance of an active manager. Because portfolio performance depends to a large degree on its chosen style, the benchmark should be consistent with the manager's investment approach and style to assess the manager's skill accurately. The index stocks should be those that the manager will actually choose from. For example, a value manager should be compared against a value index, not a broad market index, because portfolio securities will be selected from among value stocks.
- *Measure of market return and risk.* In asset allocation, estimates of the expected return and standard deviation of returns for various asset classes are based on historical returns for an index of securities representing that asset class.
- *Measure of beta and risk-adjusted return.* The use of the capital asset pricing model (CAPM) to determine a stock's expected return requires an estimate of its beta and the return on the market. Index portfolio returns are used as a proxy for the returns on the market portfolio, both in estimating a stock's beta, and then again in calculating its expected return based on its systematic (beta) risk. Expected returns can then be compared to actual stock returns to determine systematic risk-adjusted returns.
- *Model portfolio for index funds.* Investors who wish to invest passively can invest in an index fund, which seeks to replicate the performance of a market index. There are index mutual funds and index exchange-traded funds, as well as private portfolios that are structured to match the return of an index.

LOS 46.h: Describe types of equity indices.

Investors can use a variety of equity market indexes. These equity indexes can be classified as follows:

- *Broad market index.* Provides a measure of a market's overall performance and usually contains more than 90% of the market's total value. For example, the Wilshire 5000 Index contains more than 6,000 equity securities and is, therefore, a good representation of the overall performance of the U.S. equity market.
- *Multi-market index.* Typically constructed from the indexes of markets in several countries and is used to measure the equity returns of a geographic region (e.g., Latin America indexes), markets based on their stage of economic development (e.g., emerging markets indexes), or the entire world (e.g., MSCI World Index).
- *Multi-market index with fundamental weighting.* Uses market capitalization-weighting for the country indexes but then weights the country index returns in the global index by a fundamental factor (e.g., GDP). This prevents a country with previously high stock returns from being overweighted in a multi-market index.

- *Sector index.* Measures the returns for an industry sector such as health care, financial, or consumer goods firms. Investors can use these indexes in cyclical analysis because some sectors do better than others in various phases of the business cycle. Sector indexes can be for a particular country or global. These indexes are used to evaluate portfolio managers and to construct index portfolios.
- *Style index.* Measures the returns to market capitalization and value or growth strategies. Some indexes reflect a combination of the two (e.g., small-cap value fund). Because there is no widely accepted definition of large-cap, mid-cap, or small-cap stocks, different indexes use different definitions. These definitions may be specified values of market capitalization or relative definitions, such as defining large-cap stocks as the largest 500 firms in a given market. In constructing value stock and growth stock indexes, price-to-earnings ratios or dividend yields are often used to identify value and growth stocks. Over time, stocks can migrate from one classification to another. For example, a successful small-cap company might grow to become a mid-cap or large-cap company. This causes style indexes to typically have higher turnover of constituent firms than broad market indexes.

LOS 46.i: Describe types of fixed-income indices.

Fixed income securities vary widely with respect to their coupon rates, ratings, maturities, and embedded options such as convertibility to common stock. Consequently, a wide variety of fixed income indexes is available. Like equity indexes, fixed income indexes are created for various sectors, geographic regions, and levels of country economic development. They can also be constructed based on type of issuer or collateral, coupon, maturity, default risk, or inflation protection. Broad market indexes, sector indexes, style indexes, and other specialized indexes are available.

Investors should be aware of several issues with the construction of fixed income indexes:

- *Large universe of securities.* The fixed income security universe is much broader than the universe of stocks. Fixed income securities are issued not just by firms, but also by governments and government agencies. Each of these entities may also issue various types of fixed income securities. Also, unlike stocks, bonds mature and must be replaced in fixed income indexes. As a result, turnover is high in fixed income indexes.
- *Dealer markets and infrequent trading.* Fixed income securities are primarily traded by dealers, so index providers must depend on dealers for recent prices. Because fixed income securities are typically illiquid, a lack of recent trades may require index providers to estimate the value of index securities from recent prices of securities with similar characteristics.

The large number of fixed income securities results in large differences in the number of index securities among fixed income indexes. Illiquidity, transactions costs, and high turnover of constituent securities make it both difficult and expensive for fixed income portfolio managers to replicate a fixed income index.

LOS 46.j: Describe indices representing alternative investments.

Alternative assets are of interest to investors because of their potential diversification benefits. Three of the most widely held alternative assets are commodities, real estate, and hedge funds.

Commodity indexes represent futures contracts on commodities such as grains, livestock, metals, and energy. Examples include the Commodity Research Bureau Index and the S&P GSCI (previously the Goldman Sachs Commodity Index).

The issues in commodity indexes relevant for investors are as follows:

- *Weighting method.* Commodity index providers use a variety of weighting schemes. Some use equal weighting, others weight commodities by their global production values, and others use fixed weights that the index provider determines. As a result, different indexes have significantly different commodity exposures and risk and return characteristics. For example, one index may have a large exposure to the prices of energy commodities while another has a large exposure to the prices of agricultural products.
- *Futures vs. actual.* Commodity indexes are based on the prices of commodity futures contracts, not the spot prices of commodities. Commodity futures contracts reflect the risk-free rate of return, changes in futures prices, and the roll yield. Furthermore, the contracts mature and must be replaced over time by other contracts. For these reasons, the return on commodity futures differs from the returns on a long position in the commodity itself.

Real estate indexes can be constructed using returns based on appraisals of properties, repeat property sales, or the performance of Real Estate Investment Trusts (REITs). REITs are similar to closed-end mutual funds in that they invest in properties or mortgages and then issue ownership interests in the pool of assets to investors. While real properties are quite illiquid, REIT shares trade like any common shares and many offer very good liquidity to investors. FTSE International produces a family of REIT indexes.

Hedge funds pool investor money and invest in nontraditional assets, using leverage (borrowed money or derivative contracts) and both long and short positions. Most **hedge fund indexes** equally weight the returns of the hedge funds included in the index.

Hedge funds are largely unregulated and are not required to report their performance to index providers. Consequently, some funds will report to one index but not another. The performance of different indexes can thus vary substantially.

Furthermore, it is often the case that those funds that report are the funds that have been successful, as the poorly performing funds do not want to publicize their performance. Funds that have reported in the past but have recently had poor returns may stop reporting their performance. The result is an upward bias in index returns, with hedge funds appearing to be better investments than they actually are.

> *Professor's Note: Commodities (including the components of return on a commodity investment), real estate, and hedge funds (including hedge fund performance biases) are discussed further in the Study Session on alternative investments.*

LOS 46.k: Compare types of security market indices.

The following table summarizes some of the noteworthy characteristics of various global indexes. Notice from the table that most security market indexes are market capitalization-weighted and often adjusted for the float (securities actually available for purchase). The number of securities in many of these indexes can vary.

Index	Reflects	Number of Constituent Securities	Weighting Method	Notes
Dow Jones Industrial Average	Large U.S. stocks	30	Price	Stocks are chosen by Wall Street Journal editors
Nikkei Stock Average	Large Japanese stocks	225	Modified price	Contains some illiquid stocks, price weighting and adjusted for high-priced shares
TOPIX	All stocks on the Tokyo Stock Exchange First Section	Variable	Market capitalization, adjusted for float	Has a large number of small illiquid stocks making it hard to replicate. Contains 93% of the market cap of Japanese equities
MSCI All Country World Index	Stocks in 23 developed and 22 emerging markets	Variable	Market capitalization, adjusted for float	Available in both U.S. dollars and local currency
S&P Developed Ex-U.S. BMI Energy Sector Index	Global energy stocks outside the United States	Variable	Market capitalization, adjusted for float	Is the model portfolio for an ETF
Barclays Capital Global Aggregate Bond Index	Global investment-grade bonds	Variable	Market capitalization	Formerly compiled by Lehman Brothers
Markit iBoxx Euro High-Yield Bond Indexes	Below investment-grade bonds	Variable	Market capitalization	Represents liquid portion of market and rebalanced monthly
FTSE EPRA/ NAREIT Global Real Estate Index	Global real estate	335	Market capitalization, adjusted for float	Represents publicly traded REITs

Index	Reflects	Number of Constituent Securities	Weighting Method	Notes
HFRX Global Hedge Fund Index	Global hedge funds	Variable	Asset weighted	Contains a variety of hedge fund strategies and is weighted based on the amount invested in each hedge fund
HFRX Equal Weighted Strategies EUR Index	Global hedge funds	Variable	Equal weighted	Contains same strategy funds as HFRX Global Hedge Fund Index and is equal weighted
Morningstar Style Indexes	U.S. stocks grouped by value/growth and market cap	Variable	Market capitalization, adjusted for float	Nine categories classified by combinations of three cap categories and three value/growth categories

Key Concepts

LOS 46.a
A security market index represents the performance of an asset class, security market, or segment of a market. The performance of the market or segment over a period of time is represented by the percentage change in (i.e., the return on) the value of the index.

LOS 46.b
A price index uses only the prices of the constituent securities in the return calculation. The rate of return is called a price return.

A total return index uses both the price of and the income from the index securities in the return calculation.

LOS 46.c
Decisions that index providers must make when constructing and managing indexes include:
- The target market the index will measure.
- Which securities from the target market to include.
- The appropriate weighting method.
- How frequently to rebalance the index to its target weights.
- How frequently to re-examine the selection and weighting of securities.

LOS 46.d
A price-weighted index is the arithmetic mean of the prices of the index securities. The divisor, which is initially equal to the number of securities in the index, must be adjusted for stock splits and changes in the composition of the index over time.

An equal-weighted index assigns the same weight to each of its constituent securities.

A market capitalization-weighted index gives each constituent security a weight equal to its proportion of the total market value of all securities in the index. Market capitalization can be adjusted for a security's market float or free float to reflect the fact that not all outstanding shares are available for purchase.

A fundamental-weighted index uses weights that are independent of security prices, such as company earnings, revenue, assets, or cash flow.

LOS 46.e

$$\text{Price-weighted index} = \frac{\text{sum of stock prices}}{\text{number of stocks in index adjusted for splits}}.$$

Market capitalization-weighted index =

$$\frac{\text{current total market value of index stocks}}{\text{base year total market value of index stocks}} \times \text{base year index value}.$$

Equal-weighted index = $(1 + \text{average percentage change in index stocks}) \times \text{initial index value}.$

LOS 46.f
Index providers periodically rebalance the weights of the constituent securities. This is most important for equal-weighted indexes.

Reconstitution refers to changing the securities that are included in an index. This is necessary when securities mature or when they no longer have the required characteristics to be included.

LOS 46.g
Indexes are used for the following purposes:
- Reflection of market sentiment.
- Benchmark of manager performance.
- Measure of market return.
- Measure of beta and excess return.
- Model portfolio for index funds.

LOS 46.h
Broad market equity indexes represent the majority of stocks in a market.

Multi-market equity indexes contain the indexes of several countries. Multi-market equity indexes with fundamental weighting use market capitalization weighting for the securities within a country's market but then weight the countries within the global index by a fundamental factor.

Sector indexes measure the returns for a sector (e.g., health care) and are useful because some sectors do better than others in certain business cycle phases. These indexes are used to evaluate portfolio managers and as models for sector investment funds.

Style indexes measure the returns to market capitalization and value or growth strategies. Stocks tend to migrate among classifications, which causes style indexes to have higher constituent turnover than broad market indexes.

LOS 46.i
Fixed income indexes can be classified by issuer, collateral, coupon, maturity, credit risk (e.g., investment grade versus high-yield), and inflation protection. They can be delineated as broad market, sector, style, or other specialized indexes. Indexes exist for various sectors, regions, and levels of development.

The fixed income security universe is much broader than the equity universe, and fixed income indexes have higher turnover. Index providers must depend on dealers for fixed income security prices, and the securities are often illiquid. Fixed income security indexes vary widely in their numbers of constituent securities and can be difficult and expensive to replicate.

LOS 46.j

Indexes have been developed to represent markets for alternative assets such as commodities, real estate, and hedge funds.

Issues in creating commodity indexes include the weighting method (different indexes can have vastly different commodity weights and resulting risk and return) and the fact that commodity indexes are based on the performance of commodity futures contracts, not the actual commodities, which can result in different performance for a commodity index versus the actual commodity.

Real estate indexes include appraisal indexes, repeat property sales indexes, and indexes of real estate investment trusts.

Because hedge funds report their performance to index providers voluntarily, the performance of different hedge fund indexes can vary substantially and index returns have an upward bias.

LOS 46.k

Security market indexes available from commercial providers represent a variety of asset classes and reflect target markets that can be classified by:
- Geographic location, such as country, regional, or global indexes.
- Sector or industry, such as indexes of energy producers.
- Level of economic development, such as emerging market indexes.
- Fundamental factors, such as indexes of value stocks or growth stocks.

Study Session 13
Cross-Reference to CFA Institute Assigned Reading #46 – Security Market Indices

CONCEPT CHECKERS

Use the information in the following table to answer Questions 1 through 3.

	As of January 1		As of December 31	
	Share Price	Number of Shares Outstanding (thousands)	Share Price	Number of Shares Outstanding (thousands)
Stock A	$22	1,500	$28	1,500
Stock B	$40	10,000	$50	10,000
Stock C	$34	3,000	$30	3,000

1. The 1-year return on a price-weighted index of these three stocks is *closest* to:
   A. 12.5%.
   B. 13.5%.
   C. 18.0%.

2. The 1-year return on an equal-weighted index of these three stocks is *closest* to:
   A. 12.0%.
   B. 12.5%.
   C. 13.5%.

3. The 1-year return on a market capitalization-weighted index of these stocks is *closest* to:
   A. 12.5%.
   B. 13.5%.
   C. 18.0%.

4. Market float of a stock is *best* described as its:
   A. total outstanding shares.
   B. shares that are available to domestic investors.
   C. outstanding shares excluding those held by controlling shareholders.

5. For which of the following indexes will rebalancing occur *most* frequently?
   A. A price-weighted index.
   B. An equal-weighted index.
   C. A market capitalization-weighted index.

6. Which of the following would *most likely* represent an inappropriate use of an index?
   A. As a reflection of market sentiment.
   B. Comparing a small-cap manager against a broad market.
   C. Using the CAPM to determine the expected return and beta.

7. Which of the following is *least accurate* regarding fixed income indexes?
   A. Replicating the return on a fixed income security index is difficult for investors.
   B. There is a great deal of heterogeneity in the composition of fixed income security indexes.
   C. Due to the large universe of fixed income security issues, data for fixed income securities are relatively easy to obtain.

8. Most of the widely used global security indexes are:
   A. price-weighted.
   B. equal-weighted.
   C. market capitalization-weighted.

For more questions related to this topic review, log in to your Schweser online account and launch SchweserPro™ QBank; and for video instruction covering each LOS in this topic review, log in to your Schweser online account and launch the OnDemand video lectures, if you have purchased these products.

ANSWERS – CONCEPT CHECKERS

1. A $\frac{22+40+34}{3}=32$, $\frac{28+50+30}{3}=36$, $\frac{36}{32}-1=0.125=12.5\%$

2. C $\left[\left(\frac{28}{22}-1\right)+\left(\frac{50}{40}-1\right)+\left(\frac{30}{34}-1\right)\right]\left(\frac{1}{3}\right)=0.135=13.5\%$

3. C Total portfolio value January 1:

    $22(1,500)+40(10,000)+34(3,000)=\$535,000$

    Total portfolio value December 31:

    $28(1,500)+50(10,000)+30(3,000)=\$632,000$

    $\frac{632}{535}-1=0.1813\approx 18\%$

    From a base value of 100, the December 31 index value would be $\frac{632}{535}\times 100=118.13$.

4. C Market float represents shares available to the investing public and excludes shares held by controlling shareholders. Free float is a narrower measure that also excludes shares that are not available to foreign investors.

5. B An equal-weighted index will be rebalanced most frequently because as stock prices change, their representation in the index needs to be adjusted. Price-weighted and market capitalization-weighted indexes do not usually need rebalancing.

6. B Comparing a small-cap manager against a broad market would be an inappropriate use of an index. A benchmark should be consistent with the manager's investment approach and style. A manager's performance will depend to a large degree on its chosen style.

7. C Fixed income securities are largely traded by dealers and trade infrequently. Data are therefore difficult to obtain.

8. C Most global security indexes are market capitalization-weighted with a float adjustment to reflect the amount of shares available to investors.

The following is a review of the Equity: Market Organization, Market Indices, and Market Efficiency principles designed to address the learning outcome statements set forth by CFA Institute. Cross-Reference to CFA Institute Assigned Reading #47.

MARKET EFFICIENCY

Study Session 13

EXAM FOCUS

The informational efficiency of market prices is a very important concept to a portfolio manager. When markets are truly efficient, careful analysis and security selection using publicly available information will not lead to positive risk-adjusted returns on average. For the exam, you must understand the three forms of market efficiency and know the evidence from tests of each form of market efficiency. Focus your attention on the implications of this evidence about the value of technical and fundamental analysis and about the role of portfolio managers in the investment process. Finally, be familiar with market anomalies listed and the perspective provided by behavioral finance.

LOS 47.a: Describe market efficiency and related concepts, including their importance to investment practitioners.

An **informationally efficient capital market** is one in which the current price of a security fully, quickly, and rationally reflects all available information about that security. This is really a statistical concept. An academic might say, "Given all available information, current securities prices are unbiased estimates of their values, so that the expected return on any security is just the equilibrium return necessary to compensate investors for the risk (uncertainty) regarding its future cash flows." This concept is often put more intuitively as, "You can't beat the market."

In a perfectly efficient market, investors should use a **passive investment** strategy (i.e., buying a broad market index of stocks and holding it) because **active investment** strategies will underperform due to transactions costs and management fees. However, to the extent that market prices are inefficient, active investment strategies can generate positive risk-adjusted returns.

One method of measuring a market's efficiency is to determine the time it takes for trading activity to cause information to be reflected in security prices (i.e., the lag from the time information is disseminated to the time prices reflect the value implications of that information). In some very efficient markets, such as foreign currency markets, this lag can be as short as a minute. If there is a significant lag, informed traders can use the information to potentially generate positive risk-adjusted returns.

Note that market prices should not be affected by the release of information that is well anticipated. Only new information (information that is unexpected and changes expectations) should move prices. The announcement that a firm's earnings were up 45% over the last quarter may be good news if the expected increase was 20%. On the other hand, this may be bad news if a 70% increase was anticipated or no news at all if market participants correctly anticipated quarterly earnings.

LOS 47.b: Distinguish between market value and intrinsic value.

The **market value** of an asset is its current price. The **intrinsic value** or **fundamental value** of an asset is the value that a rational investor with full knowledge about the asset's characteristics would willingly pay. For example, a bond investor would fully know and understand a bond's coupon, maturity, default risk, liquidity, and other characteristics and would use these to estimate its intrinsic value.

In markets that are highly efficient, investors can typically expect market values to reflect intrinsic values. If markets are not completely efficient, active managers will buy assets for which they think intrinsic values are greater than market values and sell assets for which they think intrinsic values are less than market values.

Intrinsic values cannot be known with certainty and are estimated by investors who will have differing estimates of an asset's intrinsic value. The more complex an asset, the more difficult it is to estimate its intrinsic value. Furthermore, intrinsic value is constantly changing as new (unexpected) information becomes available.

LOS 47.c: Explain factors that affect a market's efficiency.

Markets are generally neither perfectly efficient nor completely inefficient. The degree of informational efficiency varies across countries, time, and market types. The following factors affect the degree of market efficiency.

Number of market participants. The larger the number of investors, analysts, and traders who follow an asset market, the more efficient the market. The number of participants can vary through time and across countries. For example, some countries prevent foreigners from trading in their markets, reducing market efficiency.

Availability of information. The more information is available to investors, the more efficient the market. In large, developed markets such as the New York Stock Exchange, information is plentiful and markets are quite efficient. In emerging markets, the availability of information is lower, and consequently, market prices are relatively less efficient. Some assets, such as bonds, currencies, swaps, forwards, mortgages, and money market securities that trade in over-the-counter (OTC) markets, may have less available information.

Access to information should not favor one party over another. Therefore, regulations such as the U.S. Securities and Exchange Commission's Regulation FD (fair disclosure) require that firms disclose the same information to the public that they disclose to stock analysts. Traders with material inside information about a firm are prohibited from trading on that information.

Impediments to trading. Arbitrage refers to buying an asset in one market and simultaneously selling it at a higher price in another market. This buying and selling of assets will continue until the prices in the two markets are equal. Impediments to arbitrage, such as high transactions costs or lack of information, will limit arbitrage activity and allow some price inefficiencies (i.e., mispricing of assets) to persist.

Short selling improves market efficiency. The sales pressure from short selling prevents assets from becoming overvalued. Restrictions on short selling, such as an inability to borrow stock cheaply, can reduce market efficiency.

Transaction and information costs. To the extent that the costs of information, analysis, and trading are greater than the potential profit from trading misvalued securities, market prices will be inefficient. It is generally accepted that markets are efficient if, after deducting costs, there are no risk-adjusted returns to be made from trading based on publicly available information.

LOS 47.d: Contrast weak-form, semi-strong-form, and strong-form market efficiency.

Professor Eugene Fama originally developed the concept of market efficiency and identified three forms of market efficiency. The difference among them is that each is based on a different set of information.

1. **Weak-form market efficiency.** The weak form of the efficient markets hypothesis (EMH) states that current security prices *fully reflect all currently available security market data.* Thus, past price and volume (market) information will have no predictive power about the future direction of security prices because price changes will be independent from one period to the next. In a weak-form efficient market, an investor cannot achieve positive risk-adjusted returns on average by using technical analysis.

2. **Semi-strong form market efficiency.** The semi-strong form of the EMH holds that security prices rapidly adjust without bias to the arrival of all new public information. As such, current security prices *fully reflect all publicly available information*. The semi-strong form says security prices include all past security market information and nonmarket information available to the public. The implication is that an investor cannot achieve positive risk-adjusted returns on average by using fundamental analysis.

3. **Strong-form market efficiency.** The strong form of the EMH states that security prices *fully reflect all information from both public and private sources*. The strong form includes all types of information: past security market information, public, and private (inside) information. This means that no group of investors has monopolistic access to information relevant to the formation of prices, and none should be able to consistently achieve positive abnormal returns.

Given the prohibition on insider trading in most markets, it would be unrealistic to expect markets to reflect all private information. The evidence supports the view that markets are not strong-form efficient.

> *Professor's Note: As a base level knowledge of the EMH, you should know that the weak form is based on past security market information; the semi-strong form is based on all public information (including market information); and the strong form is based on both public information and inside or private information.*

LOS 47.e: Explain the implications of each form of market efficiency for fundamental analysis, technical analysis, and the choice between active and passive portfolio management.

Abnormal profit (or **risk-adjusted returns**) calculations are often used to test market efficiency. To calculate abnormal profits, the expected return for a trading strategy is calculated given its risk, using a model of expected returns such as the CAPM or a multifactor model. If returns are, on average, greater than equilibrium expected returns, we can reject the hypothesis of efficient prices with respect to the information on which the strategy is based.

The results of tests of the various forms of market efficiency have implications about the value of technical analysis, fundamental analysis, and portfolio management in general.

Technical analysis seeks to earn positive risk-adjusted returns by using historical price and volume (trading) data. Tests of weak-form market efficiency have examined whether technical analysis produces abnormal profits. Generally, the evidence indicates that technical analysis does not produce abnormal profits, so we cannot reject the hypothesis that markets are weak-form efficient. However, technical analysis has been shown to have success in emerging markets, and there are so many possible technical analysis trading strategies that they cannot all be tested. As noted previously, the success of any technical analysis strategy should be evaluated considering the costs of information, analysis, and trading.

Fundamental analysis is based on public information such as earnings, dividends, and various accounting ratios and estimates. The semi-strong form of market efficiency suggests that all public information is already reflected in stock prices. As a result, investors should not be able to earn abnormal profits by trading on this information.

One method of testing the semi-strong form is an **event study**. Event studies examine abnormal returns before and after the release of new information that affects a firm's intrinsic value, such as earnings announcements or dividend changes. The null hypothesis is that investors should not be able to earn positive abnormal returns on average by trading based on firm events because prices will rapidly reflect news about a firm's prospects. The evidence in developed markets indicates that markets are generally semi-strong form efficient. However, there is evidence of semi-strong form inefficiency in some emerging markets.

The evidence that developed markets are generally semi-strong form efficient raises questions about the usefulness of fundamental analysis. It must be fundamental analysis, however, that results in informationally efficient market prices. Fundamental analysis can also be of use to those exceptionally skilled investors who can generate abnormal profits through its use and to those who act rapidly before new information is reflected in prices.

Professor's Note: Markets can be weak-form efficient without being semi-strong or strong-form efficient. If markets are semi-strong form efficient, they must be weak-form efficient because public information includes market information, but semi-strong form efficient markets need not be strong-form efficient.

Active vs. Passive Portfolio Management

If markets are semi-strong form efficient, investors should invest passively (i.e., invest in an index portfolio that replicates the returns on a market index). Indeed, the evidence shows that most mutual fund managers cannot outperform a passive index strategy over time.

If so, what is the role of a portfolio manager? Even if markets are efficient, portfolio managers can add value by establishing and implementing portfolio risk and return objectives and by assisting clients with portfolio diversification, asset allocation, and tax management.

LOS 47.f: Describe market anomalies.

An anomaly is something that deviates from the common rule. Tests of the EMH are frequently called *anomaly studies*, so in the efficient markets literature, a **market anomaly** is something that would lead us to reject the hypothesis of market efficiency.

Just by chance, some variables will be related to abnormal returns over a given period, although in fact these relationships are unlikely to persist over time. Thus, analysts using historical data can find patterns in security returns that appear to violate market efficiency but are unlikely to recur in the future. If the analyst uses a 5% significance level and examines the relationship between stock returns and 40 variables, two of the variables are expected to show a statistically significant relationship with stock returns by random chance. Recall that the significance level of a hypothesis test is the probability that the null hypothesis (efficiency here) will be rejected purely by chance, even when it is true. Investigating data until a statistically significant relation is found is referred to as **data mining** or **data snooping**. Note that 1,000 analysts, each testing different hypotheses on the same data set, could produce the same results as a single researcher who performed 1,000 hypothesis tests.

To avoid data-mining bias, analysts should first ask if there is an economic basis for the relationships they find between certain variables and stock returns and then test the discovered relationships with a large sample of data to determine if the relationships are persistent and present in various subperiods.

Anomalies in Time-Series Data

Calendar anomalies. The **January effect** or **turn-of-the-year effect** is the finding that during the first five days of January, stock returns, especially for small firms, are significantly higher than they are the rest of the year. In an efficient market, traders would exploit this profit opportunity in January, and in so doing, eliminate it.

Possible explanations for the January effect are **tax-loss selling**, as investors sell losing positions in December to realize losses for tax purposes and then repurchase stocks in January, pushing their prices up, and **window dressing**, as portfolio managers sell risky stocks in December to remove them from their year-end statements and repurchase them in January. Evidence indicates that each of these explains only a portion of the January effect. However, after adjustments are made for risk, the January effect does not appear to persist over time.

Other calendar anomalies that were found at one time but no longer appear to persist are the *turn-of-the-month effect* (stock returns are higher in the days surrounding month end), the *day-of-the-week effect* (average Monday returns are negative), the *weekend effect* (positive Friday returns are followed by negative Monday returns), and the *holiday effect* (pre-holiday returns are higher).

Overreaction and momentum anomalies. The **overreaction effect** refers to the finding that firms with poor stock returns over the previous three or five years (losers) have better subsequent returns than firms that had high stock returns over the prior period. This pattern has been attributed to investor overreaction to both unexpected good news and unexpected bad news. This pattern is also present for bonds and in some international markets. **Momentum effects** have also been found where high short-term returns are followed by continued high returns. This pattern is present in some international markets as well.

Both the overreaction and momentum effects violate the weak form of market efficiency because they provide evidence of a profitable strategy based only on market data. Some researchers argue that the evidence of overreaction to new information is due to the nature of the statistical tests used and that evidence of momentum effects in securities prices reflects rational investor behavior.

Anomalies in Cross-Sectional Data

The **size effect** refers to initial findings that small-cap stocks outperform large-cap stocks. This effect could not be confirmed in later studies, suggesting that either investors had traded on, and thereby eliminated, this anomaly or that the initial finding was simply a random result for the time period examined.

The **value effect** refers to the finding that **value stocks** [those with lower price-to-earnings (P/E), lower market-to-book (M/B), and higher dividend yields] have outperformed **growth stocks** (those with higher P/E, higher M/B, and lower dividend yields). This violates the semi-strong form of market efficiency because the information necessary to classify stocks as value or growth is publicly available. However, some researchers attribute the value effect to greater risk of value stocks that is not captured in the risk adjustment procedure used in the studies.

Other Anomalies

Closed-end investment funds. The shares of **closed-end investment funds** trade at prices that sometimes deviate from the **net asset value** (NAV) of the fund shares, often trading at large discounts to NAV. Such large discounts are an anomaly because, by arbitrage, the value of the pool of assets should be the same as the market price for closed-end shares. Various explanations have been put forth to explain this anomaly, including management fees, taxes on future capital gains, and share illiquidity. None of these explanations fully explains the pricing discrepancy. However, transactions costs would eliminate any profits from exploiting the unexplained portion of closed-end fund discounts.

Earnings announcements. An **earnings surprise** is that portion of announced earnings that was not expected by the market. Positive earnings surprises (earnings higher than expected) precede periods of positive risk-adjusted post-announcement stock returns, and negative surprises lead to predictable negative risk-adjusted returns. The anomaly is that the adjustment process does not occur entirely on the announcement day. Investors could exploit this anomaly by buying positive earnings surprise firms and selling negative earnings surprise firms. Some researchers argue that evidence of predictable abnormal returns after earnings surprises is a result of estimating risk-adjusted returns incorrectly in the tests and that transactions costs would eliminate any abnormal profits from attempting to exploit this returns anomaly.

Initial public offerings. IPOs are typically underpriced, with the offer price below the market price once trading begins. However, the long-term performance of IPO shares as a group is below average. This suggests that investors overreact, in that they are too optimistic about a firm's prospects on the offer day. Some believe this is not an anomaly, but rather a result of the statistical methodologies used to estimate abnormal returns.

> *Professor's Note: The initial underpricing of IPOs is also discussed in the topic review of Market Organization and Structure.*

Economic fundamentals. Research has found that stock returns are related to known economic fundamentals such as dividend yields, stock volatility, and interest rates. However, we would expect stock returns to be related to economic fundamentals in efficient markets. The relationship between stock returns and dividend yields is also not consistent over all time periods.

Implications for Investors

The majority of the evidence suggests that reported anomalies are not violations of market efficiency but are due to the methodologies used in the tests of market efficiency. Furthermore, both underreaction and overreaction have been found in the markets, meaning that prices are efficient on average. Other explanations for the evidence of anomalies are that they are transient relations, too small to profit from, or simply reflect returns to risk that the researchers have failed to account for.

The bottom line for investors is that portfolio management based on previously identified anomalies will likely be unprofitable. Investment management based solely on anomalies has no sound economic basis.

LOS 47.g: Describe behavioral finance and its potential relevance to understanding market anomalies.

Behavioral finance examines the actual decision-making processes of investors. Many observers have concluded that investors are not the rational utility-maximizing decision makers with complete information that traditional finance assumes they are. Investors appear to exhibit bias in their decision making, base decisions on the actions of others, and not evaluate risk in the way traditional models assume they do.

Various types of investor irrationality have been proposed as explanations for reported pricing anomalies. Whether widespread investor irrationality is the underlying cause of reported returns anomalies is an open question. Market efficiency does not require an assumption that every investor acts rationally in accordance with traditional finance theory. Semi-strong form market efficiency requires that investors cannot earn positive abnormal returns on average (beat the market) using public information. The evidence on market efficiency certainly suggests that this is the case. Evidence that some investors exhibit bias, or other deviations from perfect rationality, in their investment decision making does not necessarily mean that market prices themselves are irrational, at least not in ways that lead to violations of market efficiency.

Observed investor behaviors and biases that are considered evidence of irrational behavior include:

- **Loss aversion**, which refers to the tendency of investors to be more risk averse when faced with potential losses than they are when faced with potential gains. Put another way, investors dislike a loss more than they like a gain of an equal amount.
- **Investor overconfidence**, which is a tendency of investors to overestimate their abilities to analyze security information and identify differences between securities' market prices and intrinsic values.
- **Herding**, which is a tendency of investors to act in concert on the same side of the market, acting not on private analysis, but mimicking the investment actions of other investors.

An **information cascade** results when investors mimic the decisions of others. The idea is that uninformed or less-informed traders watch the actions of informed traders and follow their investment actions. If those who act first are more knowledgeable investors, others following their actions may, in fact, be part of the process of incorporating new information into securities prices and actually move market prices toward their intrinsic values, improving informational efficiency.

Behavioral finance can explain how securities' market prices can deviate from rational prices and be biased estimates of intrinsic value. If investor rationality is viewed as a prerequisite for market efficiency, then markets are not efficient. If market efficiency only requires that investors cannot consistently earn abnormal risk-adjusted returns, then research supports the belief that markets are efficient.

Key Concepts

LOS 47.a
In an informationally efficient capital market, security prices reflect all available information fully, quickly, and rationally. The more efficient a market is, the quicker its reaction will be to new information. Only unexpected information should elicit a response from traders.

If the market is fully efficient, active investment strategies cannot earn positive risk-adjusted returns consistently, and investors should therefore use a passive strategy.

LOS 47.b
An asset's market value is the price at which it can currently be bought or sold.

An asset's intrinsic value is the price that investors with full knowledge of the asset's characteristics would place on the asset.

LOS 47.c
Large numbers of market participants and greater information availability tend to make markets more efficient.

Impediments to arbitrage and short selling and high costs of trading and gathering information tend to make markets less efficient.

LOS 47.d
The weak form of the efficient markets hypothesis (EMH) states that security prices fully reflect all past price and volume information.

The semi-strong form of the EMH states that security prices fully reflect all publicly available information.

The strong form of the EMH states that security prices fully reflect all public and private information.

LOS 47.e
If markets are weak-form efficient, technical analysis does not consistently result in abnormal profits.

If markets are semi-strong form efficient, fundamental analysis does not consistently result in abnormal profits. However, fundamental analysis is necessary if market prices are to be semi-strong form efficient.

If markets are strong-form efficient, active investment management does not consistently result in abnormal profits.

Even if markets are strong-form efficient, portfolio managers can add value by establishing and implementing portfolio risk and return objectives and assisting with portfolio diversification, asset allocation, and tax minimization.

LOS 47.f

A market anomaly is something that deviates from the efficient market hypothesis. Most evidence suggests anomalies are not violations of market efficiency but are due to the methodologies used in anomaly research, such as data mining or failing to adjust adequately for risk.

Anomalies that have been identified in time-series data include calendar anomalies such as the January effect (small firm stock returns are higher at the beginning of January), overreaction anomalies (stock returns subsequently reverse), and momentum anomalies (high short-term returns are followed by continued high returns).

Anomalies that have been identified in cross-sectional data include a size effect (small-cap stocks outperform large-cap stocks) and a value effect (value stocks outperform growth stocks).

Other identified anomalies involve closed-end investment funds selling at a discount to NAV, slow adjustments to earnings surprises, investor overreaction to and long-term underperformance of IPOs, and a relationship between stock returns and prior economic fundamentals.

LOS 47.g

Behavioral finance examines whether investors behave rationally, how investor behavior affects financial markets, and how cognitive biases may result in anomalies. Behavioral finance describes investor irrationality but does not necessarily refute market efficiency as long as investors cannot consistently earn abnormal risk-adjusted returns.

CONCEPT CHECKERS

1. In an informationally efficient capital market:
   A. active managers can generate abnormal profits.
   B. security prices quickly reflect new information.
   C. investors react to all information releases rapidly.

2. In terms of market efficiency, short selling *most likely*:
   A. leads to excess volatility, which reduces market efficiency.
   B. promotes market efficiency by making assets less likely to become overvalued.
   C. has little effect on market efficiency because short sellers face the risk of unlimited losses.

3. The intrinsic value of an asset:
   A. changes through time as new information is released.
   B. is the price at which the asset can be bought or sold at a given point in time.
   C. can be easily determined with a financial calculator, given investor risk preferences.

4. The weak-form EMH asserts that stock prices fully reflect which of the following types of information?
   A. Market only.
   B. Market and public.
   C. Public and private.

5. Research has revealed that the performance of professional money managers tends to be:
   A. equal to the performance of a passive investment strategy.
   B. inferior to the performance of a passive investment strategy.
   C. superior to the performance of a passive investment strategy.

6. Which of the following *best* describes the majority of the evidence regarding anomalies in stock returns?
   A. Weak-form market efficiency holds but semi-strong form efficiency does not.
   B. Neither weak-form nor semi-strong form market efficiency holds.
   C. Reported anomalies are not violations of market efficiency but are the result of research methodologies.

7. Investors who exhibit loss aversion *most likely*:
   A. have symmetric risk preferences.
   B. are highly risk averse.
   C. dislike losses more than they like equal gains.

For more questions related to this topic review, log in to your Schweser online account and launch SchweserPro™ QBank; and for video instruction covering each LOS in this topic review, log in to your Schweser online account and launch the OnDemand video lectures, if you have purchased these products.

Answers – Concept Checkers

1. **B** In informationally efficient capital markets, new information is quickly reflected in security prices. Investors react only to unexpected information releases because information releases that are expected will already be reflected in securities prices. Active strategies will underperform in an efficient market because they have greater transactions and management costs than passive strategies and will not consistently create positive abnormal returns after adjusting for risk.

2. **B** Short selling promotes market efficiency because the sales pressure from short selling can reduce the prices of assets that have become overvalued.

3. **A** Intrinsic value changes as new information arrives in the marketplace. It cannot be known with certainty and can only be estimated. The price of an asset at a given point in time is its market value, which will differ from its intrinsic value if markets are not fully efficient.

4. **A** Weak-form EMH states that stock prices fully reflect all market (i.e., price and volume) information.

5. **B** Tests indicate that mutual fund performance has been inferior to that of a passive index strategy.

6. **C** The majority of evidence is that anomalies are not violations of market efficiency but are due to the research methodologies used. Portfolio management based on anomalies will likely be unprofitable after transactions costs are considered.

7. **C** Loss aversion refers to the tendency of investors to be more risk averse when faced with potential losses and less risk averse when faced with potential gains. That is, they dislike losses more than they like gains of an equal amount. Their risk preferences are asymmetric.

The following is a review of the Equity Analysis and Valuation principles designed to address the learning outcome statements set forth by CFA Institute. Cross-Reference to CFA Institute Assigned Reading #48.

OVERVIEW OF EQUITY SECURITIES

Study Session 14

EXAM FOCUS

Equities have higher returns than bonds and bills, but also higher risk. Know the characteristics of common and preferred equity types, as well as the methods of investing in foreign stock. Understand the difference between the book value of equity and market value of equity and what this difference represents.

LOS 48.a: Describe characteristics of types of equity securities.

Common shares are the most common form of equity and represent an ownership interest. Common shareholders have a residual claim (after the claims of debtholders and preferred stockholders) on firm assets if the firm is liquidated and govern the corporation through voting rights. Firms are under no obligation to pay dividends on common equity; the firm determines what dividend will be paid periodically. Common stockholders are able to vote for the board of directors, on merger decisions, and on the selection of auditors. If they are unable to attend the annual meeting, shareholders can vote by **proxy** (having someone else vote as they direct them, on their behalf).

In a **statutory voting** system, each share held is assigned one vote in the election of each member of the board of directors. Under **cumulative voting**, shareholders can allocate their votes to one or more candidates as they choose. For example, consider a situation where a shareholder has 100 shares and three directors will be elected. Under statutory voting, the shareholder can vote 100 shares for his director choice in each election. Under cumulative voting, the shareholder has 300 votes, which can be cast for a single candidate or spread across multiple candidates. The three receiving the greatest number of votes are elected. Cumulative voting makes it possible for a minority shareholder to have more proportional representation on the board. The way the math works, a holder of 30% of the firm's shares could choose three of ten directors with cumulative voting but could elect no directors under statutory voting.

Callable common shares give the firm the right to repurchase the stock at a pre-specified call price. Investors receive a fixed amount when the firm calls the stock. The call feature benefits the firm because when the stock's market price is greater than the call price, the firm can call the shares and reissue them later at a higher price. Calling the shares, similarly to the repurchase of shares, allows the firm to reduce its dividend payments without changing its per-share dividend.

Putable common shares give the shareholder the right to sell the shares back to the firm at a specific price. A put option on the shares benefits the shareholder because it effectively places a floor under the share value. Shareholders pay for the put option because other things equal, putable shares are sold for higher prices than non-putable shares and raise more capital for the firm when they are issued.

Preference shares (or **preferred stock**) have features of both common stock and debt. As with common stock, preferred stock dividends are not a contractual obligation, the shares usually do not mature, and the shares can have put or call features. Like debt, preferred shares typically make fixed periodic payments to investors and do not usually have voting rights.

Cumulative preference shares are usually promised fixed dividends, and any dividends that are not paid must be made up before common shareholders can receive dividends. The dividends of **non-cumulative preference shares** do not accumulate over time when they are not paid, but dividends for any period must be paid before common shareholders can receive dividends.

Preferred shares have a stated par value and pay a percentage dividend based on the par value of the shares. An $80 par value preferred with a 10% dividend pays a dividend of $8 per year. Investors in **participating preference shares** receive extra dividends if firm profits exceed a predetermined level and may receive a value greater than the par value of the preferred stock if the firm is liquidated. **Non-participating preference shares** have a claim equal to par value in the event of liquidation and do not share in firm profits. Smaller and riskier firms whose investors may be concerned about the firm's future often issue participating preferred stock so investors can share in the upside potential of the firm.

Convertible preference shares can be exchanged for common stock at a conversion ratio determined when the shares are originally issued. It has the following advantages:

- The preferred dividend is higher than a common dividend.
- If the firm is profitable, the investor can share in the profits by converting his shares into common stock.
- The conversion option becomes more valuable when the common stock price increases.
- Preferred shares have less risk than common shares because the dividend is stable and they have priority over common stock in receiving dividends and in the event of liquidation of the firm.

Because of their upside potential, convertible preferred shares are often used to finance risky venture capital and private equity firms. The conversion feature compensates investors for the additional risk they take when investing in such firms.

LOS 48.b: Describe differences in voting rights and other ownership characteristics among different equity classes.

A firm may have different classes of common stock (e.g., "Class A" and "Class B" shares). One class may have greater voting power and seniority if the firm's assets are liquidated. The classes may also be treated differently with respect to dividends, stock splits, and other transactions with shareholders. Information on the ownership and voting rights of different classes of equity shares can be found in the company's filings with securities regulators, such as the Securities and Exchange Commission in the United States.

LOS 48.c: Distinguish between public and private equity securities.

The discussion so far has centered on equity that is publicly traded. **Private equity** is usually issued to institutional investors via private placements. Private equity markets are smaller than public markets but are growing rapidly.

Compared to public equity, private equity has the following characteristics:

- Less liquidity because no public market for the shares exists.
- Share price is negotiated between the firm and its investors, not determined in a market.
- More limited firm financial disclosure because there is no government or exchange requirement to do so.
- Lower reporting costs because of less onerous reporting requirements.
- Potentially weaker corporate governance because of reduced reporting requirements and less public scrutiny.
- Greater ability to focus on long-term prospects because there is no public pressure for short-term results.
- Potentially greater return for investors once the firm goes public.

The three main types of private equity investments are venture capital, leveraged buyouts, and private investments in public equity.

Venture capital refers to the capital provided to firms early in their life cycles to fund their development and growth. Venture capital financing at various stages of a firm's development is referred to as *seed* or *start-up*, *early stage*, or *mezzanine* financing. Investors can be family, friends, wealthy individuals, or private equity funds. Venture capital investments are illiquid and investors often have to commit funds for three to ten years before they can cash out (exit) their investment. Investors hope to profit when they can sell their shares after (or as part of) an initial public offering or to an established firm.

In a **leveraged buyout** (LBO), investors buy all of a firm's equity using debt financing (leverage). If the buyers are the firm's current management, the LBO is referred to as a **management buyout** (MBO). Firms in LBOs usually have cash flow that is adequate to service the issued debt or have undervalued assets that can be sold to pay down the debt over time.

In a **private investment in public equity** (PIPE), a public firm that needs capital quickly sells private equity to investors. The firm may have growth opportunities, be in distress, or have large amounts of debt. The investors can often buy the stock at a sizeable discount to its market price.

Study Session 14
Cross-Reference to CFA Institute Assigned Reading #48 – Overview of Equity Securities

LOS 48.d: Describe methods for investing in non-domestic equity securities.

When capital flows freely across borders, markets are said to be *integrated*. The world's financial markets have become more integrated over time, especially as a result of improved communications and trading technologies. However, barriers to global capital flows still exist. Some countries restrict foreign ownership of their domestic stocks, primarily to prevent foreign control of domestic companies and to reduce the variability of capital flows in and out of their countries.

An increasing number of countries have dropped foreign capital restrictions. Studies have shown that reducing capital barriers improves equity market performance. Furthermore, companies are increasingly turning to foreign investors for capital by listing their stocks on foreign stock exchanges or by encouraging foreign ownership of shares.

From the firm's perspective, listing on foreign stock exchanges increases publicity for the firm's products and the liquidity of the firm's shares. Foreign listing also increases firm transparency due to the stricter disclosure requirements of many foreign markets.

Direct investing in the securities of foreign companies simply refers to buying a foreign firm's securities in foreign markets. Some obstacles to direct foreign investment are that:

- The investment and return are denominated in a foreign currency.
- The foreign stock exchange may be illiquid.
- The reporting requirements of foreign stock exchanges may be less strict, impeding analysis.
- Investors must be familiar with the regulations and procedures of each market in which they invest.

Other methods for investing in foreign companies are provided by global depository receipts (GDRs), American depository receipts (ADRs), global registered shares (GRSs), and baskets of listed depository receipts (BLDRs).

Depository receipts (DRs) represent ownership in a foreign firm and are traded in the markets of other countries in local market currencies. A bank deposits shares of the foreign firm and then issues receipts representing ownership of a specific number of the foreign shares. The **depository bank** acts as a custodian and manages dividends, stock splits, and other events. Although the investor does not have to convert to the foreign currency, the value of the DR is affected by exchange rate changes, as well as firm fundamentals, economic events, and any other factors that affect the value of any stock.

If the firm is involved with the issue, the depository receipt is a **sponsored DR**; otherwise, it is an **unsponsored DR**. A sponsored DR provides the investor voting rights and is usually subject to greater disclosure requirements. In an unsponsored DR, the depository bank retains the voting rights.

Global depository receipts (GDRs) are issued outside the United States and the issuer's home country. Most GDRs are traded on the London and Luxembourg exchanges. Although not listed on U.S. exchanges, they are usually denominated in U.S. dollars and can be sold to U.S. institutional investors. GDRs are not subject to the capital flow restrictions imposed by governments and thus offer the firm and the investor greater opportunities for foreign investment. The firm usually chooses to list the GDR in a market where many investors are familiar with the firm.

American depository receipts (ADRs) are denominated in U.S. dollars and trade in the United States. The security on which the ADR is based is the **American depository share** (ADS), which trades in the firm's domestic market. Some ADRs allow firms to raise capital in the United States or use the shares to acquire other firms. Most require U.S. Securities and Exchange Commission (SEC) registration, but some are privately placed (Rule 144A or Regulation S receipts).

The four types of ADRs, with different levels of trading availability and firm requirements, are summarized in Figure 1.

Figure 1: Types of ADRs

	Level I	*Level II*	*Level III*	*Rule 144A*
Trading location	Over-the-counter (OTC)	NYSE, Nasdaq, and AMEX	NYSE, Nasdaq, and AMEX	Private
SEC registration required	Yes	Yes	Yes	No
Ability to raise capital in United States	No	No	Yes	Yes
Firm listing expenses	Low	High	High	Low

Global registered shares (GRS) are traded in different currencies on stock exchanges around the world.

A **basket of listed depository receipts** (BLDR) is an exchange-traded fund (ETF) that is a collection of DRs. ETF shares trade in markets just like common stocks.

LOS 48.e: Compare the risk and return characteristics of different types of equity securities.

The returns on equity investments consist of price changes, dividend payments, and, in the case of equities denominated in a foreign currency, gains or losses from changes in exchange rates. A Japanese investor who invests in euro-denominated shares will have greater yen-based returns if the euro appreciates relative to the yen.

Gains from dividends and the reinvestment of dividends have been an important part of equity investors' long-term returns. For example, $1 invested in U.S. stocks in 1900 would have been worth $834 in real terms in 2011 with dividends reinvested but only

$8.10 with price appreciation alone. Over the same time period, the terminal wealth for bonds and bills would have been $9.30 and $2.80, respectively.[1]

The risk of equity securities is most commonly measured as the standard deviation of returns. Preferred stock is less risky than common stock because preferred stock pays a known, fixed dividend to investors that is a large part of the return, whereas common dividends are variable and can vary with earnings. Also, preferred stockholders receive their distributions before common shareholders and have a claim in liquidation equal to the par value of their shares that has priority over the claims of common stock owners. Because it is less risky, preferred stock has a lower average return than common stock.

Cumulative preferred shares have less risk than non-cumulative preferred shares because they retain the right to receive any missed dividends before any common stock dividends can be paid.

For both common and preferred shares, putable shares are less risky and callable shares are more risky compared to shares with neither option. Putable shares are less risky because if the market price drops, the investor can put the shares back to the firm at a fixed price (assuming the firm has the capital to honor the put). Because of this feature, putable shares usually pay a lower dividend yield than non-putable shares.

Callable shares are the most risky because if the market price rises, the firm can call the shares, limiting the upside potential of the shares. Callable shares, therefore, usually have higher dividend yields than non-callable shares.

LOS 48.f: Explain the role of equity securities in the financing of a company's assets.

Equity capital is used for the purchase of long-term assets, equipment, research and development, and expansion into new businesses or geographic areas. Equity securities provide the firm with "currency" that can be used to buy other companies or that can be offered to employees as incentive compensation. Having publicly traded equity securities provides liquidity, which may be especially important to firms that need to meet regulatory requirements, capital adequacy ratios, and liquidity ratios.

LOS 48.g: Distinguish between the market value and book value of equity securities.

The primary goal of firm management is to increase the book value of the firm's equity and thereby increase the market value of its equity. The **book value of equity** is the value of the firm's assets on the balance sheet minus its liabilities. It increases when the firm has positive net income and retained earnings that flow into the equity account. When

---

1. Ryan C. Fuhrmann, CFA, and Asjeet S. Lamba, CFA, *Overview of Equity Securities*, CFA Program Level I 2017 Curriculum, Volume 5, (CFA Institute, 2016) p. 170.

management makes decisions that increase income and retained earnings, they increase the book value of equity.

The **market value of equity** is the total value of a firm's outstanding equity shares based on market prices and reflects the expectations of investors about the firm's future performance. Investors use their perceptions of the firm's risk and the amounts and timing of future cash flows to determine the market value of equity. The market value and book value of equity are seldom equal. Although management may be maximizing the book value of equity, this may not be reflected in the market value of equity because book value does not reflect investor expectations about future firm performance.

LOS 48.h: Compare a company's cost of equity, its (accounting) return on equity, and investors' required rates of return.

A key ratio used to determine management efficiency is the **accounting return on equity**, usually referred to simply as the **return on equity** (ROE). ROE is calculated as net income available to common (net income minus preferred dividends) divided by the average book value of common equity over the period:

$$\text{ROE}_t = \frac{\text{NI}_t}{\text{average BV}_t} = \frac{\text{NI}_t}{(\text{BV}_t + \text{BV}_{t-1})/2}$$

Alternatively, ROE is often calculated using only beginning-of-year book value of equity (i.e., book value of equity for end of year t – 1):

$$\text{ROE}_t = \frac{\text{NI}_t}{\text{BV}_{t-1}}$$

The first method is more appropriate when it is the industry convention or when book value is volatile. The latter method is more appropriate when examining ROE for a number of years or when book value is stable.

Higher ROE is generally viewed as a positive for a firm, but the reason for an increase should be examined. For example, if book value is decreasing more rapidly than net income, ROE will increase. This is not, however, a positive for the firm. A firm can also issue debt to repurchase equity, thereby decreasing the book value of equity. This would increase the ROE but also make the firm's shares riskier due to the increased financial leverage (debt).

Professor's Note: The DuPont formula discussed in the topic review of Financial Analysis Techniques can help the analyst determine the reasons for changes in ROE.

The book value of equity reflects a firm's financial decisions and operating results since its inception, whereas the market value of equity reflects the market's consensus view of a firm's future performance. The **price-to-book ratio** (also called the **market-to-book ratio**) is the market value of a firm's equity divided by the book value of its equity. The more optimistic investors are about the firm's future growth, the greater its price-to-book ratio. The price-to-book ratio is used as a measure of relative value. Often, firms with low price-to-book ratios are considered *value stocks*, while firms with high price-to-book ratios are considered *growth stocks*.

Example: ROE, market, and book value of equity calculations

Given the figures below for O'Grady Industries, calculate the return on average equity for 20X9 and the total market value of equity, the book value per share, and the price-to-book ratio at the end of 20X9.

Index Firm Data

Fiscal Year-End Dec. 31	20X9	20X8
Total stockholder's equity	18,503	17,143
Net income available to common	3,526	3,056
Stock price	$16.80	$15.30
Shares outstanding	3,710	2,790

Answer:

The return on average equity for 20X9 is:

$$ROE_t = \frac{NI_t}{\text{average BV}_t} = \frac{NI_t}{(BV_t + BV_{t-1})/2} = \frac{\$3,526}{(\$18,503 + \$17,143)/2} = 19.78\%$$

The total market value of the firm's equity at the end of 20X9 is:

$16.80 \times 3,710 = \$62,328$

The book value per share at the end of 20X9 is:

$= \frac{\$18,503}{3,710} = \$4.99$

The price-to-book ratio at the end of 20X9 is:

$= \frac{\$16.80}{\$4.99} = 3.37$

Investors' Required Return and the Cost of Equity

A firm's **cost of equity** is the expected equilibrium total return (including dividends) on its shares in the market. It is usually estimated in practice using a dividend-discount model or the capital asset pricing model. At any point in time, a decrease in share price will increase the expected return on the shares and an increase in share price will decrease expected returns, other things equal. Because the intrinsic value of a firm's shares is the discounted present value of its future cash flows, an increase (decrease) in the required return used to discount future cash flows will decrease (increase) intrinsic value.

Investors also estimate the expected market returns on equity shares and compare this to the minimum return they will accept for bearing the risk inherent in a particular stock.

If an investor estimates the expected return on a stock to be greater than her minimum required rate of return on the shares, given their risk, then the shares are an attractive investment. Investors can have different required rates of return for a given risk, different estimates of a firm's future cash flows, and different estimates of the risk of a firm's equity shares. A firm's cost of equity can be interpreted as the minimum rate of return required by investors (in the aggregate) to compensate them for the risk of the firm's equity shares.

Study Session 14
Cross-Reference to CFA Institute Assigned Reading #48 – Overview of Equity Securities

KEY CONCEPTS

LOS 48.a
Common shareholders have a residual claim on firm assets and govern the corporation through voting rights. Common shares have variable dividends which the firm is under no legal obligation to pay.

Callable common shares allow the firm the right to repurchase the shares at a pre-specified price. Putable common shares give the shareholder the right to sell the shares back to the firm at a pre-specified price.

Preferred stock typically does not mature, does not have voting rights, and has dividends that are fixed in amount but are not a contractual obligation of the firm.

Cumulative preferred shares require any dividends that were missed in the past (dividends in arrears) to be paid before common shareholders receive any dividends. Participating preferred shares receive extra dividends if firm profits exceed a pre-specified level and a value greater than the par value if the firm is liquidated. Convertible preferred stock can be converted to common stock at a pre-specified conversion ratio.

LOS 48.b
Some companies' equity shares are divided into different classes, such as Class A and Class B shares. Different classes of common equity may have different voting rights and priority in liquidation.

LOS 48.c
Compared to publicly traded firms, private equity firms have lower reporting costs, greater ability to focus on long-term prospects, and potentially greater return for investors once the firm goes public. However, private equity investments are illiquid, firm financial disclosure may be limited, and corporate governance may be weaker.

LOS 48.d
Investors who buy foreign stock directly on a foreign stock exchange receive a return denominated in a foreign currency, must abide by the foreign stock exchange's regulations and procedures, and may be faced with less liquidity and less transparency than is available in the investor's domestic markets. Investors can often avoid these disadvantages by purchasing depository receipts for the foreign stock that trade on their domestic exchange.

Global depository receipts are issued outside the United States and outside the issuer's home country. American depository receipts are denominated in U.S. dollars and are traded on U.S. exchanges.

Global registered shares are common shares of a firm that trade in different currencies on stock exchanges throughout the world.

Baskets of listed depository receipts are exchange-traded funds that invest in depository receipts.

LOS 48.e

Equity investor returns consist of dividends, capital gains or losses from changes in share prices, and any foreign exchange gains or losses on shares traded in a foreign currency. Compounding of reinvested dividends has been an important part of an equity investor's long-term return.

Preferred stock is less risky than common stock because preferred stock pays a known, fixed dividend to investors; preferred stockholders must receive dividends before common stock dividends can be paid; and preferred stockholders have a claim equal to par value if the firm is liquidated. Putable shares are the least risky and callable shares are the most risky. Cumulative preferred shares are less risky than non-cumulative preferred shares, as any dividends missed must be paid before a common stock dividend can be paid.

LOS 48.f

Equity securities provide funds to the firm to buy productive assets, to buy other companies, or to offer to employees as compensation. Equity securities provide liquidity that may be important when the firm must raise additional funds.

LOS 48.g

The book value of equity is the difference between the financial statement value of the firm's assets and liabilities. Positive retained earnings increase the book value of equity. Book values reflect the firm's past operating and financing choices.

The market value of equity is the share price multiplied by the number of shares outstanding. Market value reflects investors' expectations about the timing, amount, and risk of the firm's future cash flows.

LOS 48.h

The accounting return on equity (ROE) is calculated as the firm's net income divided by the book value of common equity. ROE measures whether management is generating a return on common equity but is affected by the firm's accounting methods.

The firm's cost of equity is the minimum rate of return that investors in the firm's equity require. Investors' required rates of return are reflected in the market prices of the firm's shares.

Study Session 14
Cross-Reference to CFA Institute Assigned Reading #48 – Overview of Equity Securities

CONCEPT CHECKERS

1. Which of the following *best* describes the benefit of cumulative share voting?
   A. It provides significant minority shareholders with proportional representation on the board.
   B. It prevents minority shareholders from exercising excessive control.
   C. If cumulative dividends are not paid, preferred shareholders are given voting rights.

2. The advantage of participating preferred shares versus non-participating preferred shares is that participating preferred shares can:
   A. obtain voting rights.
   B. receive extra dividends.
   C. be converted into common stock.

3. Compared to public equity, which of the following is *least likely* to characterize private equity?
   A. Lower reporting costs.
   B. Potentially weaker corporate governance.
   C. Lower returns because of its less liquid market.

4. Global depository receipts are most often denominated in:
   A. the currency of the country where they trade and issued outside the United States.
   B. U.S. dollars and issued in the United States.
   C. U.S. dollars and issued outside the United States.

5. Which of the following types of preferred shares has the *most* risk for investors?
   A. Putable shares.
   B. Callable shares.
   C. Non-putable, non-callable shares.

6. Which of the following *best* describes the book value of equity?
   A. Management should attempt to maximize book value of equity.
   B. Book value of equity decreases when retained earnings increase.
   C. Book value of equity reflects investors' perceptions of the firm's future.

7. Which of the following causes of an increase in return on equity is *most likely* a positive sign for a firm's equity investors?
   A. A firm issues debt to repurchase equity.
   B. Net income is increasing at a faster rate than book value of equity.
   C. Net income is decreasing at a slower rate than book value of equity.

For more questions related to this topic review, log in to your Schweser online account and launch SchweserPro™ QBank; and for video instruction covering each LOS in this topic review, log in to your Schweser online account and launch the OnDemand video lectures, if you have purchased these products.

Answers – Concept Checkers

1. **A** Cumulative voting allows minority shareholders to gain representation on the board because they can use all of their votes for specific board members.

2. **B** Participating preferred shares can receive extra dividends if firm profits exceed a pre-specified level and a value greater than the par value if the firm is liquidated.

3. **C** Private equity has less liquidity because no public market for it exists. The lower liquidity of private equity would increase required returns.

4. **C** Global Depository Receipts are not listed on U.S. exchanges and are most often denominated in U.S. dollars. They are not issued in the United States.

5. **B** Callable shares are the most risky because if the market price rises, the firm can call in the shares, limiting the investor's potential gains. Putable shares are the least risky because if the market price drops, the investor can put the shares back to the firm at a predetermined price. The risk of non-putable, non-callable shares falls in between.

6. **A** The primary goal of firm management is to increase the book value of equity. It *increases* when retained earnings are positive. The *market* value of equity reflects the collective expectations of investors about the firm's future performance.

7. **B** Net income increasing at a faster rate than book value of equity generally would be a positive sign. If a firm issues debt to repurchase equity, this decreases the book value of equity and increases the ROE. However, now the firm becomes riskier due to the increased debt. Net income decreasing at a slower rate than book value of equity would increase ROE, but decreasing net income is not a positive sign.

The following is a review of the Equity Analysis and Valuation principles designed to address the learning outcome statements set forth by CFA Institute. Cross-Reference to CFA Institute Assigned Reading #49.

Introduction to Industry and Company Analysis

Study Session 14

Exam Focus

This topic provides a great deal of material on industry analysis. Understand the effects of business cycles and the stage of an industry's life cycle. Porter's five forces and two competitive strategies are very important to know. Beyond these, make sure that you know the effects on price competition and profitability of the items considered in industry analysis and of the various firm characteristics discussed.

LOS 49.a: Explain uses of industry analysis and the relation of industry analysis to company analysis.

Industry analysis is important for company analysis because it provides a framework for understanding the firm. Analysts will often focus on a group of specific industries so that they can better understand the business conditions the firms in those industries face.

Understanding a firm's business environment can provide insight about the firm's potential growth, competition, and risks. For a credit analyst, industry conditions can provide important information about whether a firm will be able to meet its obligations during the next recession.

In an active management strategy, industry analysis can identify industries that are undervalued or overvalued in order to weight them appropriately. Some investors engage in **industry rotation**, which is overweighting or underweighting industries based on the current phase of the business cycle. A firm's industry has been found to be as important as its home country in determining its performance.

In performance attribution analysis, the sources of portfolio return are determined relative to a benchmark. The industry representation within a portfolio is often a significant component of attribution analysis.

LOS 49.b: Compare methods by which companies can be grouped, current industry classification systems, and classify a company, given a description of its activities and the classification system.

One way to group companies into an industry is by the *products and services* they offer. For example, the firms that produce automobiles constitute the auto industry. A **sector** is a group of similar industries. Hospitals, doctors, pharmaceutical firms, and other industries are included in the health care sector. Systems that are grouped by products and services usually use a firm's **principal business activity** (the largest source of sales or earnings) to classify firms. Examples of these systems are discussed in the following and include the Global Industry Classification Standard (GICS), Russell Global Sectors (RGS), and Industry Classification Benchmark.

Firms can also be classified by their *sensitivity to business cycles*. This system has two main classifications: cyclical and non-cyclical firms.

Statistical methods, such as cluster analysis, can also be used. This method groups firms that historically have had highly correlated returns. The groups (i.e., industries) formed will then have lower returns correlations between groups.

This method has several limitations:

- Historical correlations may not be the same as future correlations.
- The groupings of firms may differ over time and across countries.
- The grouping of firms is sometimes non-intuitive.
- The method is susceptible to statistical error (i.e., firms can be grouped by a relationship that occurs by chance, or not grouped together when they should be).

Industry Classification Systems

Classifying firms by industry provides a method of examining trends and firm valuations. It also allows analysts to compare firms in different countries on a similar basis. The following are the industry classification systems currently available to investors.

Commercial Classifications

Several index providers classify firms. Some use three levels of classification, while others use four levels. The providers generally use firm fundamentals such as revenue to classify firms. Although the nomenclature differs among providers, the broadest category is generally the sector level, followed by industry and sub-industry.

Commercial industry classifications include the Global Industry Classification Standard developed by Standard & Poor's and MSCI Barra, Russell Global Sectors, and the Industry Classification Benchmark developed by Dow Jones and FTSE.

Sectors and firm compositions representative of those used by commercial providers are as follows.

Basic materials and processing firms produce:

- Building materials.
- Chemicals.
- Paper and forest products.
- Containers and packaging.
- Metals, minerals, and mining.

Consumer discretionary firms are cyclical and sell goods and services in industries such as:

- Automotive.
- Apparel.
- Hotels and restaurants.

Consumer staples firms are less cyclical and sell goods and services in industries such as:

- Food.
- Beverage.
- Tobacco.
- Personal care products.

Energy firms are involved in:

- Energy exploration.
- Refining.
- Production.
- Energy equipment.
- Energy services.

Financial services firms include firms involved in:

- Banking.
- Insurance.
- Real estate.
- Asset management.
- Brokerage.

Health care includes:

- Pharmaceuticals.
- Biotech.
- Medical devices.
- Health care equipment.
- Medical supplies.
- Health care services.

Industrial and producer durables firms produce capital goods for commercial services industries including:

- Heavy machinery and equipment.
- Aerospace.
- Defense.
- Transportation.
- Commercial services and supplies.

Technology firms sell or produce:

- Computers.
- Software.
- Semiconductors.
- Communications equipment.
- Internet services.
- Electronic entertainment.
- Consulting and services.

Telecommunications firms include wired and wireless service providers. *Utilities* includes electric, gas, and water utilities. Some industry classification providers include telecommunication and utilities in the same group, while others separate them.

To classify a firm accurately, an analyst should have detailed knowledge about the firm and the delineation of industry classifications.

Government Classifications

Several government bodies also provide industry classification of firms. They frequently do so to organize the economic data they publish. A main thrust of their systems is to make comparisons of industries consistent across time and country. The main systems are similar to each other.

- *International Standard Industrial Classification of All Economic Activities* (ISIC) was produced by the United Nations in 1948 to increase global comparability of data.
- *Statistical Classification of Economic Activities in the European Community* is similar to the ISIC but is designed for Europe.
- *Australian and New Zealand Standard Industrial Classification* was jointly developed by those countries.
- *North American Industry Classification System* (NAICS) was jointly developed by the United States, Canada, and Mexico.

The methodologies that government providers use in their compilation of industry groups differ from those used by commercial providers. Most governments do not identify individual firms in a group, so an analyst cannot know the groups' exact composition. Commercial providers identify the constituent firms. Government systems are updated less frequently; for example, the NAICS is updated every five years. Governments do not distinguish between small and large firms, for-profit and not-for-profit organizations, or private and public firms. Commercial providers only include for-profit and public firms and can delineate by the size of the firm.

An analyst should not assume that two firms in the same narrowest industry classification can be compared with each other for fundamental analysis and valuation. Instead, the analyst should construct *peer groups*, as described later in this topic review.

LOS 49.c: Explain the factors that affect the sensitivity of a company to the business cycle and the uses and limitations of industry and company descriptors such as "growth," "defensive," and "cyclical".

A **cyclical firm** is one whose earnings are highly dependent on the stage of the business cycle. These firms have high earnings volatility and high operating leverage. Their products are often expensive, non-necessities whose purchase can be delayed until the economy improves. Examples of cyclical industries include basic materials and processing, consumer discretionary, energy, financial services, industrial and producer durables, and technology.

In contrast, a **non-cyclical firm** produces goods and services for which demand is relatively stable over the business cycle. Examples of non-cyclical industries include health care, utilities, telecommunications, and consumer staples.

Sectors can also be classified by their sensitivity to the phase of the business cycle. Cyclical sector examples include energy, financials, technology, materials, and consumer discretionary. Non-cyclical sector examples include health care, utilities, and consumer staples.

Non-cyclical industries can be further separated into defensive (stable) or growth industries. **Defensive industries** are those that are least affected by the stage of the business cycle and include utilities, consumer staples (such as food producers), and basic services (such as drug stores). **Growth industries** have demand so strong they are largely unaffected by the stage of the business cycle.

Descriptors such as "growth," "defensive," and "cyclical" should be used with caution. Cyclical industries, which are supposed to be dependent on the business cycle, often include growth firms that are less dependent on the business cycle. Non-cyclical industries can be affected by severe recessions, as was the case in the 2008–09 downturn. Defensive industries may not always be safe investments. For example, grocery stores are classified as defensive, but they are subject to intense price competition that reduces earnings. Defensive industries may also contain some truly defensive and some growth firms. Because business cycle phases differ across countries and regions, two cyclical firms operating in different countries may be simultaneously experiencing different cyclical effects on earnings growth.

LOS 49.d: Explain how a company's industry classification can be used to identify a potential "peer group" for equity valuation.

A **peer group** is a set of similar companies an analyst will use for valuation comparisons. More specifically, a peer group will consist of companies with similar business activities, demand drivers, cost structure drivers, and availability of capital.

To form a peer group, an analyst will often start by identifying companies in the same industry classification, using the commercial classification providers previously described. Usually, the analyst will use other information to verify that the firms in an industry are indeed peers. An analyst might include a company in more than one peer group.

The following are steps an analyst would use to form a peer group:

- Use commercial classification providers to determine which firms are in the same industry.
- Examine firms' annual reports to see if they identify key competitors.
- Examine competitors' annual reports to see if other competitors are named.
- Use industry trade publications to identify competitors.

- Confirm that comparable firms have similar sources of sales and earnings, have similar sources of demand, and are in similar geographic markets.
- Adjust financial statements of non-financial companies for any financing subsidiary data they include.

LOS 49.e: Describe the elements that need to be covered in a thorough industry analysis.

A thorough industry analysis should include the following elements:

- Evaluate the relationships between macroeconomic variables and industry trends using information from industry groups, firms in the industry, competitors, suppliers, and customers.
- Estimate industry variables using different approaches and scenarios.
- Compare with other analysts' forecasts of industry variables to confirm the validity of the analysis and potentially find industries that are misvalued as a result of consensus forecasts.
- Determine the relative valuation of different industries.
- Compare the valuations of industries across time to determine the volatility of their performance over the long run and during different phases of the business cycle. This is useful for long-term investing as well as short-term industry rotation based on the current economic environment.
- Analyze industry prospects based on **strategic groups**, which are groups of firms that are distinct from the rest of the industry due to the delivery or complexity of their products or barriers to entry. For example, full-service hotels are a distinct market segment within the hotel industry.
- Classify industries by **life-cycle stage**, whether it is embryonic, growth, shakeout, mature, or declining.
- Position the industry on the **experience curve**, which shows the cost per unit relative to output. The curve declines because of increases in productivity and economies of scale, especially in industries with high fixed costs.
- Consider the forces that affect industries, which include demographic, macroeconomic, governmental, social, and technological influences.
- Examine the forces that determine competition within an industry.

LOS 49.f: Describe the principles of strategic analysis of an industry.

Industries differ markedly in profitability because of differences in economic fundamentals, industry structure, and degree of competition. In some industries, competition is intense and few firms earn economic profits. **Economic profits**, the return on invested capital minus its cost, are greater than 20% in some industries and negative in others. The degree of economic profits depends in part on pricing power (elasticity of demand for the firm's products). An analyst should understand that industry conditions and profits can change dramatically over time, so industry analysis should be forward-looking.

One component of an analyst's industry analysis should be **strategic analysis**, which examines how an industry's competitive environment influences a firm's strategy. The analysis framework developed by Michael Porter[1] delineates five forces that determine industry competition.

1. *Rivalry among existing competitors.* Rivalry increases when many firms of relatively equal size compete within an industry. Slow growth leads to competition as firms fight for market share, and high fixed costs lead to price decreases as firms try to operate at full capacity. For example, the high fixed costs in the auto industry from capital investments and labor contracts force firms to produce a large number of vehicles that they can only sell at low margins. Industries with products that are undifferentiated or have barriers (are costly) to exit tend to have high levels of competition.

2. *Threat of entry.* Industries that have significant barriers to entry (e.g., large capital outlays for facilities) will find it easier to maintain premium pricing. It is costly to enter the steel or oil production industries. Those industries have large barriers to entry and thus less competition from newcomers. An analyst should identify factors that discourage new entrants, such as economies of scale.

3. *Threat of substitutes.* Substitute products limit the profit potential of an industry because they limit the prices firms can charge by increasing the elasticity of demand. Commodity-like products have high levels of competition and low profit margins. The more differentiated the products are within an industry, the less price competition there will be. For example, in the pharmaceutical industry, patents protect a producer from competition in the markets for patented drugs.

4. *Power of buyers.* Buyers' ability to bargain for lower prices or higher quality influences industry profitability. Bargaining by governments and ever-larger health care providers have put downward pressure even on patented drugs.

5. *Power of suppliers.* Suppliers' ability to raise prices or limit supply influences industry profitability. Suppliers are more powerful if there are just a few of them and their products are scarce. For example, Microsoft is one of the few suppliers of operating system software and thus has pricing power.

The first two forces deserve further attention because almost all firms must be concerned about the threat of new entrants and competition that would erode profits. Studying these forces also helps the analyst better understand the subject firm's competitors and prospects. The following summary describes how these two factors influence the competitive environment in an industry:

- Higher barriers to entry reduce competition.
- Greater concentration (a small number of firms control a large part of the market) reduces competition, whereas market fragmentation (a large number of firms, each with a small market share) increases competition.
- Unused capacity in an industry, especially if prolonged, results in intense price competition. For example, underutilized capacity in the auto industry has resulted in very competitive pricing.

---

1. Michael Porter, "The Five Competitive Forces That Shape Strategy," *Harvard Business Review*, Volume 86, No. 1: pp. 78–93.

- Stability in market share reduces competition. For example, loyalty of a firm's customers tends to stabilize market share and profits.
- More price sensitivity in customer buying decisions results in greater competition.
- Greater maturity of an industry results in slowing growth.

LOS 49.g: Explain the effects of barriers to entry, industry concentration, industry capacity, and market share stability on pricing power and price competition.

Barriers to Entry

High barriers to entry benefit existing industry firms because they prevent new competitors from competing for market share and reducing the existing firms' return on capital. In industries with low barriers to entry, firms have little pricing power and competition reduces existing firms' return on capital. To assess the ease of entry, the analyst should determine how easily a new entrant to the industry could obtain the capital, intellectual property, and customer base needed to be successful. One method of determining the ease of entry is to examine the composition of the industry over time. If the same firms dominate the industry today as ten years ago, entry is probably difficult.

High barriers to entry do not necessarily mean firm pricing power is high. Industries with high barriers to entry may have strong price competition among existing firms. This is more likely when the products sold are undifferentiated and commodity-like or when high barriers to exit result in overcapacity. For example, an automobile factory may have a low value in an alternative use, making firm owners less likely to exit the industry. They continue to operate even when losing money, hoping to turn things around, which can result in industry overcapacity and intense price competition.

Low barriers to entry do not ensure success for new entrants. Barriers to entry may change over time, and so might the competitive environment.

Industry Concentration

High industry concentration does not guarantee pricing power.

- Absolute market share may not matter as much as a firm's market share relative to its competitors. A firm may have a 50% market share, but if a single competitor has the other 50%, their 50% share would not result in a great degree of pricing power. Return on capital is limited by intense competition between the two firms.
- Conversely, a firm that has a 10% market share when no competitor has more than 2% may have a good degree of pricing power and high return on capital.
- If industry products are undifferentiated and commodity-like, then consumers will switch to the lowest-priced producer. The more importance consumers place on price, the greater the competition in an industry. Greater competition leads to lower return on capital.

- Industries with greater product differentiation in regard to features, reliability, and service after the sale will have greater pricing power. Return on capital can be higher for firms that can better differentiate their products.
- If the industry is capital intensive, and therefore costly to enter or exit, overcapacity can result in intense price competition.

Tobacco, alcohol, and confections are examples of highly concentrated industries in which firms' pricing power is relatively strong. Automobiles, aircraft, and oil refining are examples of highly concentrated industries with relatively weak pricing power.

Although industry concentration does not guarantee pricing power, a fragmented market does usually result in strong competition. When there are many industry members, firms cannot coordinate pricing, firms will act independently, and because each member has such a small market share, any incremental increase in market share may make a price decrease profitable.

Industry Capacity

Industry capacity has a clear impact on pricing power. Undercapacity, a situation in which demand exceeds supply at current prices, results in pricing power and higher return on capital. Overcapacity, with supply greater than demand at current prices, will result in downward pressure on price and lower return on capital.

An analyst should be familiar with the industry's current capacity and its planned investment in additional capacity. Capacity is fixed in the short run and variable in the long run. In other words, given enough time, producers will build enough factories and raise enough capital to meet demand at a price close to minimum average cost. However, producers may overshoot the optimal industry capacity, especially in cyclical markets. For example, producers may start to order new equipment during an economic expansion to increase capacity. By the time they bring the additional production on to the market, the economy may be in a recession with decreased demand. A diligent analyst can look for signs that the planned capacity increases of all producers (who may not take into account the capacity increases of other firms) sum to more output than industry demand will support.

Capacity is not necessarily physical. For example, an increase in demand for insurance can be more easily and quickly met than an increase in demand for a product requiring physical capacity, such as electricity or refined petroleum products.

If capacity is physical and specialized, overcapacity can exist for an extended period if producers expand too much over the course of a business cycle. Specialized physical capacity may have a low liquidation value and be costly to reallocate to a different product. Non-physical capacity (e.g., financial capital) can be reallocated more quickly to new industries than physical capacity.

Market Share Stability

An analyst should examine whether firms' market shares in an industry have been stable over time. Market shares that are highly variable likely indicate a highly competitive industry in which firms have little pricing power. More stable market shares likely indicate less intense competition in the industry.

Factors that affect market share stability include barriers to entry, introductions of new products and innovations, and the **switching costs** that customers face when changing from one firm's products to another. Switching costs, such as the time and expense of learning to use a competitor's product, tend to be higher for specialized or differentiated products. High switching costs contribute to market share stability and pricing power.

LOS 49.h: Describe industry life cycle models, classify an industry as to life cycle stage, and describe limitations of the life-cycle concept in forecasting industry performance.

Industry life cycle analysis should be a component of an analyst's strategic analysis. An industry's stage in the cycle has an impact on industry competition, growth, and profits. An industry's stage will change over time, so the analyst must monitor the industry on an ongoing basis. The five phases of the industry life-cycle model are illustrated in Figure 1.

Figure 1: Stages of the Industry Life Cycle

In the **embryonic stage**, the industry has just started. The characteristics of this stage are as follows:

- *Slow growth:* customers are unfamiliar with the product.
- *High prices:* the volume necessary for economies of scale has not been reached.
- *Large investment required:* to develop the product.
- *High risk of failure:* most embryonic firms fail.

In the **growth stage**, industry growth is rapid. The characteristics of this stage are as follows:

- *Rapid growth:* new consumers discover the product.
- *Limited competitive pressures:* the threat of new firms coming into the market peaks during the growth phase, but rapid growth allows firms to grow without competing on price.
- *Falling prices:* economies of scale are reached and distribution channels increase.
- *Increasing profitability:* due to economies of scale.

In the **shakeout stage**, industry growth and profitability are slowing due to strong competition. The characteristics of this stage are as follows:

- *Growth has slowed:* demand reaches saturation level with few new customers to be found.
- *Intense competition:* industry growth has slowed, so firm growth must come at the expense of competitors.
- *Increasing industry overcapacity:* firm investment exceeds increases in demand.
- *Declining profitability:* due to overcapacity.
- *Increased cost cutting:* firms restructure to survive and attempt to build brand loyalty.
- *Increased failures:* weaker firms liquidate or are acquired.

In the **mature stage**, there is little industry growth and firms begin to consolidate. The characteristics of this stage are as follows:

- *Slow growth:* market is saturated and demand is only for replacement.
- *Consolidation:* market evolves to an oligopoly.
- *High barriers to entry:* surviving firms have brand loyalty and low cost structures.
- *Stable pricing:* firms try to avoid price wars, although periodic price wars may occur during recessions.
- *Superior firms gain market share:* the firms with better products may grow faster than the industry average.

In the **decline stage**, industry growth is negative. The characteristics of this stage are as follows:

- *Negative growth:* due to development of substitute products, societal changes, or global competition.
- *Declining prices:* competition is intense and there are price wars due to overcapacity.
- *Consolidation:* failing firms exit or merge.

An analyst should determine whether a firm is "acting its age" or stage of industry development. Growth firms should be reinvesting in operations in an attempt to increase product offerings, increase economies of scale, and build brand loyalty. They are not yet worried about cost efficiency. They should not pay out cash flows to investors but save them for internal growth. On the other hand, mature firms focus on cost efficiency because demand is largely from replacement. They find few opportunities to introduce new products. These firms should typically pay out cash to investors as dividends or stock repurchases because cash flows are strong but internal growth is limited. An analyst should be concerned about firms that do not act their stage, such as a mature firm that is investing in low-return projects for the sake of increasing firm size.

Although life-cycle analysis is a useful tool, industries do not always conform to its framework. Life-cycle stages may not be as long or short as anticipated, or they might be skipped altogether. An industry's product may become obsolete quickly due to technological change, government regulation, societal change, or demographics. Life-cycle analysis is likely most useful during stable periods, not during periods of upheaval when conditions are changing rapidly. Furthermore, some firms will experience growth and profits that are dissimilar to others in their industries due to competitive advantages or disadvantages.

LOS 49.i: Compare characteristics of representative industries from the various economic sectors.

To illustrate the long list of factors to be considered in industry analysis, we use the following strategic analysis of the candy/confections industry.

- *Major firms*: Cadbury, Hershey, Mars, and Nestle.
- *Barriers to entry and success*: Very high. Low capital and technological barriers, but consumers have strong brand loyalty.
- *Industry concentration*: Very concentrated. Largest four firms dominate global market share.
- *Influence of industry capacity on pricing*: None. Pricing is determined by strength of brand, not production capacity.
- *Industry stability*: Very stable. Market share changes slowly.
- *Life cycle*: Very mature. Growth is driven by population changes.
- *Competition*: Low. Lack of unbranded candy makers in market reduces competition. Consumer decision is based on brand awareness, not price.
- *Demographic influences*: Not applicable.
- *Government influence*: Low. Industry is largely unregulated, but regulation arising from concerns about obesity is possible.
- *Social influence*: Not applicable.
- *Technological influence*: Very low. Limited impact from technology.
- *Business cycle sensitivity*: Non-cyclical and defensive. Demand for candy is very stable.

LOS 49.j: Describe macroeconomic, technological, demographic, governmental, and social influences on industry growth, profitability, and risk.

The external influences on industry growth, profitability, and risk should be a component of an analyst's strategic analysis. These external factors include macroeconomic, technological, demographic, governmental, and social influences.

Macroeconomic factors can be cyclical or structural (longer-term) trends, most notably economic output as measured by GDP or some other measure. Interest rates affect financing costs for firms and individuals, as well as financial institution profitability. Credit availability affects consumer and business expenditures and funding. Inflation affects costs, prices, interest rates, and business and consumer confidence. An example of a structural economic factor is the education level of the work force. More education can increase workers' productivity and real wages, which in turn can increase their demand for consumer goods.

Technology can change an industry dramatically through the introduction of new or improved products. Computer hardware is an example of an industry that has undergone dramatic transformation. Radical improvements in circuitry were assisted by transformations in other industries, including the computer software and telecommunications industries. Another example of an industry that has been changed by technology is photography, which has largely moved from film to digital media.

Demographic factors include age distribution and population size, as well as other changes in the composition of the population. As a large segment of the population reaches their twenties, residential construction, furniture, and related industries see increased demand. An aging of the overall population can mean significant growth for the health care industry and developers of retirement communities. For example, the aging of the post-World War II Baby Boomers is an example of demographics that will increase demand in these industries.

Governments have an important and widespread effect on businesses through various channels, including taxes and regulation. The level of tax rates certainly affects industries, but analysts should also be aware of the differential taxation applied to some goods. For example, tobacco is heavily taxed in the United States. Specific regulations apply to many industries. Entry into the health care industry, for example, is controlled by governments that license doctors and other providers. Governments can also empower self-regulatory organizations, such as stock exchanges that regulate their members. Some industries, such as the U.S. defense industry, depend heavily on government purchases of goods and services.

Social influences relate to how people work, play, spend their money, and conduct their lives; these factors can have a large impact on industries. For example, when women entered the U.S. workforce, the restaurant industry benefitted because there was less cooking at home. Child care, women's clothing, and other industries were also dramatically affected.

LOS 49.k: Describe the elements that should be covered in a thorough company analysis.

Having gained understanding of an industry's external environment, an analyst can then focus on **company analysis**. This involves analyzing the firm's financial condition, products and services, and **competitive strategy**. Competitive strategy is how a firm responds to the opportunities and threats of the external environment. The strategy may be defensive or offensive.

Porter has identified two important competitive strategies that can be employed by firms within an industry: a **cost leadership (low-cost) strategy** or a **product or service differentiation strategy**. According to Porter, a firm must decide to focus on one of these two areas to compete effectively.

In a *low-cost strategy*, the firm seeks to have the lowest costs of production in its industry, offer the lowest prices, and generate enough volume to make a superior return. The strategy can be used defensively to protect market share or offensively to gain market share. If industry competition is intense, pricing can be aggressive or even predatory. In **predatory pricing**, the firm hopes to drive out competitors and later increase prices. Although there are often laws prohibiting predatory pricing, it can be hard to prove if the firm's costs are not easily traced to a particular product. A low-cost strategy firm should have managerial incentives that are geared toward improving operating efficiency.

In a *differentiation strategy*, the firm's products and services should be distinctive in terms of type, quality, or delivery. For success, the firm's cost of differentiation must be less than the price premium buyers place on product differentiation. The price premium should also be sustainable over time. Successful differentiators will have outstanding marketing research teams and creative personnel.

A company analysis should include the following elements:

- Firm overview, including information on operations, governance, and strengths and weaknesses.
- Industry characteristics.
- Product demand.
- Product costs.
- Pricing environment.
- Financial ratios, with comparisons to other firms and over time.
- Projected financial statements and firm valuation.

A firm's return on equity (ROE) should be part of the financial analysis. The ROE is a function of profitability, total asset turnover, and financial leverage (debt).

Professor's Note: The DuPont formula discussed in the topic review of Financial Analysis Techniques can help an analyst understand what drives ROE.

Analysts often use **spreadsheet modeling** to analyze and forecast company fundamentals. The problem with this method is that the models' complexity can make their conclusions seem precise. However, estimation is performed with error that can compound over time. As a check on a spreadsheet model's output, an analyst should consider which factors are likely to be different going forward and how this will affect the firm. Analysts should also be able to explain the assumptions of a spreadsheet model.

KEY CONCEPTS

LOS 49.a
Industry analysis is necessary for understanding a company's business environment before engaging in analysis of the company. The industry environment can provide information about the firm's potential growth, competition, risks, appropriate debt levels, and credit risk.

Industry valuation can be used in an active management strategy to determine which industries to overweight or underweight in a portfolio.

Industry representation is often a component in a performance attribution analysis of a portfolio's return.

LOS 49.b
Firms can be grouped into industries according to their products and services or business cycle sensitivity, or through statistical methods that group firms with high historical correlation in returns.

Industry classification systems from commercial providers include the Global Industry Classification Standard (Standard & Poor's and MSCI Barra), Russell Global Sectors, and the Industry Classification Benchmark (Dow Jones and FTSE).

Industry classification systems developed by government agencies include the International Standard Industrial Classification (ISIC), the North American Industry Classification System (NAICS), and systems designed for the European Union and Australia/New Zealand.

LOS 49.c
A cyclical firm has earnings that are highly dependent on the business cycle. A non-cyclical firm has earnings that are less dependent on the business cycle. Industries can also be classified as cyclical or non-cyclical. Non-cyclical industries or firms can be classified as defensive (demand for the product tends not to fluctuate with the business cycle) or growth (demand is so strong that it is largely unaffected by the business cycle).

Limitations of descriptors such as growth, defensive, and cyclical include the facts that cyclical industries often include growth firms; even non-cyclical industries can be affected by severe recessions; defensive industries are not always safe investments; business cycle timing differs across countries and regions; and the classification of firms is somewhat arbitrary.

LOS 49.d
A peer group should consist of companies with similar business activities, demand drivers, cost structure drivers, and availability of capital. To form a peer group, the analyst will often start by identifying companies in the same industry, but the analyst should use other information to verify that the firms in an industry are comparable.

Study Session 14
Cross-Reference to CFA Institute Assigned Reading #49 – Introduction to Industry and Company Analysis

LOS 49.e
A thorough industry analysis should:
- Evaluate the relationships between macroeconomic variables and industry trends.
- Estimate industry variables using different approaches and scenarios.
- Check estimates against those from other analysts.
- Compare the valuation for different industries.
- Compare the valuation for industries across time to determine risk and rotation strategies.
- Analyze industry prospects based on strategic groups.
- Classify industries by their life-cycle stage.
- Position the industry on the experience curve.
- Consider demographic, macroeconomic, governmental, social, and technological influences.
- Examine the forces that determine industry competition.

LOS 49.f
Strategic analysis of an industry involves analyzing the competitive forces that determine the possibility of economic profits.

Porter's five forces that determine industry competition are:
1. Rivalry among existing competitors.
2. Threat of entry.
3. Threat of substitutes.
4. Power of buyers.
5. Power of suppliers.

LOS 49.g
High barriers to entry prevent new competitors from taking away market share, but they do not guarantee pricing power or high return on capital, especially if the products are undifferentiated or barriers to exit result in overcapacity. Barriers to entry may change over time.

While market fragmentation usually results in strong competition and low return on capital, high industry concentration may not guarantee pricing power. If industry products are undifferentiated, consumers will switch to the cheapest producer. Overcapacity may result in price wars.

Capacity is fixed in the short run and variable in the long run. Undercapacity typically results in pricing power. Producers may overinvest in new capacity, especially in cyclical industries or if the capacity is physical and specialized. Non-physical capacity comes into production and can be reallocated more quickly than physical capacity.

Highly variable market shares indicate a highly competitive industry. Stable market shares suggest less intense competition. High switching costs contribute to market share stability.

LOS 49.h
Phases of the industry life-cycle model are the embryonic, growth, shakeout, maturity, and decline stages.
- Embryonic stage: Slow growth; high prices; large investment required; high risk of failure.
- Growth stage: Rapid growth; little competition; falling prices; increasing profitability.
- Shakeout stage: Slowing growth; intense competition; industry overcapacity; declining profitability; cost cutting; increased failures.
- Mature stage: Slow growth; consolidation; high barriers to entry; stable pricing; superior firms gain market share.
- Decline stage: Negative growth; declining prices; consolidation.

A limitation of life-cycle analysis is that life-cycle stages may not be as long or short as anticipated or might be skipped altogether due to technological change, government regulation, societal change, or demographics. Firms in the same life-cycle stage will experience dissimilar growth and profits due to their competitive positions.

LOS 49.i
The elements of an industry strategic analysis are the major firms, barriers to entry, industry concentration, influence of industry capacity on pricing, industry stability, life cycle, competition, demographic influences, government influence, social influence, technological influence, and whether the industry is growth, defensive, or cyclical.

LOS 49.j
Macroeconomic influences on industries include long-term trends in factors such as GDP growth, interest rates, and inflation, as well as structural factors such as the education level of the workforce.

Demographic influences include the size and age distribution of the population.

Government factors include tax rates, regulations, empowerment of self-regulatory organizations, and government purchases of goods and services.

Social influences relate to how people interact and conduct their lives.

Technology can dramatically change an industry through the introduction of new or improved products.

LOS 49.k
Company analysis should include an overview of the firm, industry characteristics, and analysis of product demand, product costs, the pricing environment, the firm's financial ratios, and projected financial statements and firm valuation. The analysis should describe the company's competitive strategy.

Companies can employ a cost leadership (low-cost) strategy or a product or service differentiation strategy. A cost leadership firm seeks to have the lowest costs of production in its industry, offer the lowest prices, and generate enough volume to make a superior return. A differentiating firm's products and services should be distinctive in terms of type, quality, or delivery.

CONCEPT CHECKERS

1. Industry classification systems from commercial index providers typically classify firms by:
   A. statistical methods.
   B. products and services.
   C. business cycle sensitivity.

2. Firms and industries are *most appropriately* classified as cyclical or non-cyclical based on:
   A. their stock price fluctuations relative to the market.
   B. the sensitivity of their earnings to the business cycle.
   C. the volatility of their earnings relative to a peer group.

3. An analyst should *most likely* include two firms in the same peer group for analysis if the firms:
   A. are both grouped in the same industry classification.
   B. are similar in size, industry life-cycle stage, and cyclicality.
   C. derive their revenue and earnings from similar business activities.

4. The industry experience curve shows the cost per unit relative to:
   A. output.
   B. age of firms.
   C. industry life-cycle stage.

5. Greater pricing power is *most likely* to result from greater:
   A. unused capacity.
   B. market concentration.
   C. volatility in market share.

6. Which of the following statements *best* describes the relationship between pricing power and ease of entry and exit? Greater ease of entry:
   A. and greater ease of exit decrease pricing power.
   B. and greater ease of exit increase pricing power.
   C. decreases pricing power and greater ease of exit increases pricing power.

7. Industry overcapacity and increased cost cutting characterize which stage of the industry life cycle?
   A. Growth.
   B. Shakeout.
   C. Maturity.

8. Which of the following is *least likely* a significant external influence on industry growth?
   A. Social influences.
   B. Macroeconomic factors.
   C. Supplier bargaining power.

9. Which of the following is *least likely* an element of an industry strategic analysis?
   A. Market correlations.
   B. Demographic influences.
   C. Influence of industry capacity on pricing.

10. Which of the following *best* describes a low-cost competitive strategy?
    A. Volume sold is typically modest.
    B. Managerial incentives promote operational efficiency.
    C. Success depends heavily on creative marketing and product development.

For more questions related to this topic review, log in to your Schweser online account and launch SchweserPro™ QBank; and for video instruction covering each LOS in this topic review, log in to your Schweser online account and launch the OnDemand video lectures, if you have purchased these products.

ANSWERS – CONCEPT CHECKERS

1. **B** The classification systems provided by S&P/MSCI Barra, Russell, and Dow Jones/FTSE classify firms according to the product or service they produce.

2. **B** For industry analysis, cyclical firms and industries are those with earnings that are highly dependent on the business cycle, while non-cyclical firms and industries are those with earnings that are relatively less sensitive to the business cycle.

3. **C** Firms should be included in a peer group if their business activities are comparable. An analyst may begin with available industry classifications when forming peer groups but should refine them based on factors including the firms' sources of demand and earnings and the geographic markets in which they operate.

4. **A** The experience curve shows the cost per unit relative to output. Unit cost declines at higher output volume because of increases in productivity and economies of scale, especially in industries with high fixed costs.

5. **B** Greater concentration (a small number of firms control a large part of the market) typically reduces competition and results in greater pricing power. Greater unused capacity in an industry, especially if chronic, results in greater price competition and less pricing power. Greater stability in market share is typically associated with greater pricing power.

6. **C** In industries with greater ease of entry, firms have little pricing power because new competitors can take away market share. High costs of exiting result in overcapacity and likely price wars. Greater ease of exit (i.e., low costs of exit) increases pricing power.

7. **B** The shakeout stage is characterized by slowed growth, intense competition, industry overcapacity, increased cost cutting, declining profitability, and increased failures.

8. **C** Supplier bargaining power is best characterized as a force internal to the industry. External influences on industry growth, profitability, and risk include macroeconomic, technological, demographic, governmental, and social influences.

9. **A** Elements of an industry strategic analysis include the major firms, barriers to entry/success, industry concentration, influence of industry capacity on pricing, industry stability, life cycle, competition, demographic influences, government influence, social influence, technological influence, and whether the industry is growth, defensive, or cyclical.

10. **B** Firms that use a low-cost strategy should have managerial incentives suitable to create efficient operations. In a low-cost strategy, the firm seeks to generate high enough sales volume to make a superior return. Marketing and product development are key elements of a differentiation strategy.

The following is a review of the Equity Analysis and Valuation principles designed to address the learning outcome statements set forth by CFA Institute. Cross-Reference to CFA Institute Assigned Reading #50.

Equity Valuation: Concepts and Basic Tools

Study Session 14

Exam Focus

This topic review discusses the use of discounted cash flow models, price multiples, and asset-based models for stock valuation. Know when the various models are appropriate, how to apply them, and their advantages and disadvantages. This topic is foundational material for all three levels of the CFA exams. Be sure you understand these fundamental concepts.

LOS 50.a: Evaluate whether a security, given its current market price and a value estimate, is overvalued, fairly valued, or undervalued by the market.

Recall from the topic review of Market Efficiency that **intrinsic value** or **fundamental value** is defined as the rational value investors would place on the asset if they had full knowledge of the asset's characteristics. Analysts use valuation models to estimate the intrinsic values of stocks and compare them to the stocks' market prices to determine whether individual stocks are overvalued, undervalued, or fairly valued. In doing valuation analysis for stocks, analysts are assuming that some stocks' prices deviate significantly from their intrinsic values.

To the extent that market prices deviate from intrinsic values, analysts who can estimate a stock's intrinsic value better than the market can earn abnormal profits if the stock's market price moves toward its intrinsic value over time. There are several things to consider, however, in deciding whether to invest based on differences between market prices and estimated intrinsic values.

1. The larger the percentage difference between market prices and estimated values, the more likely the investor is to take a position based on the estimate of intrinsic value. Small differences between market prices and estimates of intrinsic values are to be expected.

2. The more confident the investor is about the appropriateness of the valuation model used, the more likely the investor is to take an investment position in a stock that is identified as overvalued or undervalued.

3. The more confident the investor is about the estimated inputs used in the valuation model, the more likely the investor is to take an investment position in a stock that is identified as overvalued or undervalued. Analysts must also consider the sensitivity of a model value to each of its inputs in deciding whether to act on a difference between model values and market prices. If a decrease of one-half percent in the long-term growth rate used in the valuation model would produce an estimated value equal to the market price, an analyst would have to be quite sure of the model's growth estimate to take a position in the stock based on its estimated value.

4. Even if we assume that market prices sometimes deviate from intrinsic values, market prices must be treated as fairly reliable indications of intrinsic value. Investors must consider why a stock is mispriced in the market. Investors may be more confident about estimates of value that differ from market prices when few analysts follow a particular security.

5. Finally, to take a position in a stock identified as mispriced in the market, an investor must believe that the market price will actually move toward (and certainly not away from) its estimated intrinsic value and that it will do so to a significant extent within the investment time horizon.

LOS 50.b: Describe major categories of equity valuation models.

Analysts use a variety of models to estimate the value of equities. Usually, an analyst will use more than one model with several different sets of inputs to determine a range of possible stock values.

In **discounted cash flow models** (or **present value models**), a stock's value is estimated as the present value of cash distributed to shareholders (*dividend discount models*) or the present value of cash available to shareholders after the firm meets its necessary capital expenditures and working capital expenses (*free cash flow to equity models*).

There are two basic types of **multiplier models** (or **market multiple models**) that can be used to estimate intrinsic values. In the first type, the ratio of stock price to such fundamentals as earnings, sales, book value, or cash flow per share is used to determine if a stock is fairly valued. For example, the price to earnings (P/E) ratio is frequently used by analysts.

The second type of multiplier model is based on the ratio of **enterprise value** to either earnings before interest, taxes, depreciation, and amortization (EBITDA) or revenue. Enterprise value is the market value of all a firm's outstanding securities minus cash and short-term investments. Common stock value can be estimated by subtracting the value of liabilities and preferred stock from an estimate of enterprise value.

In **asset-based models**, the intrinsic value of common stock is estimated as total asset value minus liabilities and preferred stock. Analysts typically adjust the book values of the firm's assets and liabilities to their fair values when estimating the market value of its equity with an asset-based model.

LOS 50.c: Explain the rationale for using present value models to value equity and describe the dividend discount and free-cash-flow-to-equity models.

The **dividend discount model** (DDM) is based on the rationale that the intrinsic value of stock is the present value of its future dividends.

The most general form of the model is as follows:

$$V_0 = \sum_{t=1}^{\infty} \frac{D_t}{(1+k_e)^t}$$

where:
V_0 = current stock value
D_t = dividend at time t
k_e = required rate of return on common equity

One-year holding period DDM. For a holding period of one year, the value of the stock today is the present value of any dividends during the year plus the present value of the expected price of the stock at the end of the year (referred to as its **terminal value**).

The one-year holding period DDM is simply:

$$\text{value} = \frac{\text{dividend to be received}}{(1+k_e)} + \frac{\text{year-end price}}{(1+k_e)}$$

> **Example: One-period DDM valuation**
>
> Calculate the value of a stock that paid a $1 dividend last year, if next year's dividend will be 5% higher and the stock will sell for $13.45 at year-end. The required return is 13.2%.
>
> **Answer:**
>
> The next dividend is the current dividend increased by the estimated growth rate. In this case, we have:
>
> $D_1 = D_0 \times (1 + \text{dividend growth rate}) = \$1.00 \times (1 + 0.05) = \$1.05$
>
> The present value of the expected future cash flows is:
>
> $\text{dividend: } \frac{\$1.05}{1.132} = \$0.93 \quad \text{year-end price: } \frac{\$13.45}{1.132} = \$11.88$
>
> The current value based on the investor's expectations is:
>
> stock value = $0.93 + $11.88 = $12.81

Multiple-year holding period DDM. With a multiple-year holding period, we simply sum the present values of the estimated dividends over the holding period and the estimated terminal value.

For a two-year holding period, we have:

$$\text{value} = \frac{D_1}{(1+k_e)} + \frac{D_2}{(1+k_e)^2} + \frac{P_2}{(1+k_e)^2}$$

Professor's Note: It is useful to think of the subscript t on dividends (D_t) and prices (P_t) as the end of period t. For example, in the preceding equation, P_2 is the price at the end of Year 2. Think of it as the selling price of a share, immediately after D_2 is received.

> **Example: Multiple-period DDM valuation**
>
> A stock recently paid a dividend of $1.00 which is expected to grow at 5% per year. The required rate of return of 13.2%. Calculate the value of this stock assuming that it will be priced at $14.12 two years from now.
>
> **Answer:**
>
> Find the PV of the future dividends:
>
> $$D_1: \frac{\$1.05}{1.132} = \$0.93$$
>
> $$D_2: \frac{\$1.05(1.05)}{(1.132)^2} = \frac{\$1.103}{1.2814} = \$0.86$$
>
> PV of dividends = 0.93 + 0.86 = $1.79
>
> Find the PV of the future price:
>
> $$\frac{\$14.12}{(1.132)^2} = \$11.02$$
>
> Add the present values. The current value based on the investor's expectations is $1.79 + $11.02 = $12.81.

The most general form of the DDM uses an infinite holding period because a corporation has an indefinite life. In an infinite-period DDM model, the present value of all expected future dividends is calculated and there is no explicit terminal value for the stock. In practice, as we will see, a terminal value can be calculated at a time in the future after which the growth rate of dividends is expected to be constant.

Free cash flow to equity (FCFE) is often used in discounted cash flow models instead of dividends because it represents the potential amount of cash that could be paid out to common shareholders. That is, FCFE reflects the firm's capacity to pay dividends. FCFE is also useful for firms that do not currently pay dividends.

FCFE is defined as the cash remaining after a firm meets all of its debt obligations and provides for the capital expenditures necessary to maintain existing assets and to purchase the new assets needed to support the assumed growth of the firm. In other words, it is the cash available to the firm's equity holders after a firm meets all of its other obligations. FCFE for a period is often calculated as:

FCFE = net income + depreciation − increase in working capital − fixed capital investment (FCInv) − debt principal repayments + new debt issues

FCFE can also be calculated as:

FCFE = cash flow from operations − FCInv + net borrowing

In the second formula, **net borrowing** is the increase in debt during the period (i.e., amount borrowed minus amount repaid) and is assumed to be available to shareholders. Fixed capital investment must be subtracted because the firm must invest in assets to sustain itself. FCFE is projected for future periods using the firm's financial statements.

Restating the general form of the DDM in terms of FCFE, we have:

$$V_0 = \sum_{t=1}^{\infty} \frac{FCFE_t}{(1+k_e)^t}$$

Estimating the Required Return for Equity

The capital asset pricing model (CAPM) provides an estimate of the required rate of return (k_i) for security *i* as a function of its systematic risk (β_i), the risk-free rate (R_f), and the expected return on the market [$E(R_{mkt})$] as:

$$k_i = R_f + \beta_i [E(R_{mkt}) - R_f]$$

There is some controversy over whether the CAPM is the best model to calculate the required return on equity. Also, different analysts will likely use different inputs, so there is no single number that is correct.

Professor's Note: The CAPM is discussed in detail in the Study Session on portfolio management.

Recall from the topic review of Cost of Capital that for firms with publicly traded debt, analysts often estimate the required return on the firm's common equity by adding a risk premium to the firm's current bond yield. If the firm does not have publicly traded debt, an analyst can add a larger risk premium to a government bond yield.

Study Session 14
Cross-Reference to CFA Institute Assigned Reading #50 – Equity Valuation: Concepts and Basic Tools

LOS 50.d: Calculate the intrinsic value of a non-callable, non-convertible preferred stock.

Preferred stock pays a dividend that is usually fixed and usually has an indefinite maturity. When the dividend is fixed and the stream of dividends is infinite, the infinite period dividend discount model reduces to a simple ratio:

$$\text{preferred stock value} = \frac{D_p}{(1+k_p)^1} + \frac{D_p}{(1+k_p)^2} + \ldots + \frac{D_p}{(1+k_p)^x} = \frac{D_p}{k_p}$$

> **Example: Preferred stock valuation**
>
> A company's $100 par preferred stock pays a $5.00 annual dividend and has a required return of 8%. Calculate the value of the preferred stock.
>
> **Answer:**
>
> Value of the preferred stock: D_p / k_p = $5.00 / 0.08 = $62.50

In the previous example, if the dividends were paid semiannually and the preferred stock had a maturity of one year, we would use a formula similar to the one we examined earlier for common stock. Instead of the price, we would use the par value (F) paid by the firm. Instead of the required return on common, we would use the required return on preferred:

$$\text{value} = \frac{D_1}{\left(1+\frac{k_p}{2}\right)^1} + \frac{D_2}{\left(1+\frac{k_p}{2}\right)^2} + \frac{F_2}{\left(1+\frac{k_p}{2}\right)^2}$$

With a 1-year maturity, there are two semiannual dividends of $2.50 remaining, and with a required semiannual return of 4% we have:

$$\text{value} = \frac{\$2.50}{(1+0.04)^1} + \frac{\$2.50}{(1+0.04)^2} + \frac{\$100}{(1+0.04)^2} = \$97.17$$

LOS 50.e: Calculate and interpret the intrinsic value of an equity security based on the Gordon (constant) growth dividend discount model or a two-stage dividend discount model, as appropriate.

The **Gordon growth model** (or **constant growth model**) assumes the annual growth rate of dividends, g_c, is constant. Hence, next period's dividend, D_1, is $D_0(1 + g_c)$, the second year's dividend, D_2, is $D_0(1 + g_c)^2$, and so on. The extended equation using this assumption gives the present value of the expected future dividends (V_0) as:

$$V_0 = \frac{D_0(1+g_c)}{(1+k_e)} + \frac{D_0(1+g_c)^2}{(1+k_e)^2} + \frac{D_0(1+g_c)^3}{(1+k_e)^3} + \ldots + \frac{D_0(1+g_c)^\infty}{(1+k_e)^\infty}$$

When the growth rate of dividends is constant, this equation simplifies to the Gordon (constant) growth model:

$$V_0 = \frac{D_0(1+g_c)}{k_e - g_c} = \frac{D_1}{k_e - g_c}$$

Professor's Note: In much of the finance literature, you will see this model referred to as the constant growth DDM, infinite period DDM, or the Gordon growth model. Whatever you call it, memorize D_1 over (k minus g). Note that our valuation model for preferred stock is the same as the constant growth model with no growth (g = 0).

The assumptions of the Gordon growth model are:

- Dividends are the appropriate measure of shareholder wealth.
- The constant dividend growth rate, g_c, and required return on stock, k_e, are never expected to change.
- k_e must be greater than g_c. If not, the math will not work.

If any one of these assumptions is not met, the model is not appropriate.

Example: Gordon growth model valuation

Calculate the value of a stock that paid a $2 dividend last year, if dividends are expected to grow at 5% forever and the required return on equity is 12%.

Answer:

Determine D_1: $D_0(1 + g_c)$ = $2(1.05) = $2.10

Calculate the stock's value = $D_1 / (k_e - g_c)$

= $2.10 / (0.12 − 0.05)
= $30.00

Professor's Note: When doing stock valuation problems on the exam, watch for words like "forever," "infinitely," "indefinitely," "for the foreseeable future," and so on. This will tell you that the Gordon growth model should be used. Also watch for words like "just paid" or "recently paid." These will refer to the last dividend, D_0. Words like "will pay" or "is expected to pay" refer to D_1.

This example demonstrates that the stock's value is determined by the relationship between the investor's required rate of return on equity, k_e, and the projected growth rate of dividends, g_c:

- As the difference between k_e and g_c widens, the value of the stock falls.
- As the difference narrows, the value of the stock rises.
- Small changes in the difference between k_e and g_c can cause large changes in the stock's value.

Because the estimated stock value is very sensitive to the denominator, an analyst should calculate several different value estimates using a range of required returns and growth rates.

An analyst can also use the Gordon growth model to determine how much of the estimated stock value is due to dividend growth. To do this, assume the growth rate is zero and calculate a value. Then, subtract this value from the stock value estimated using a positive growth rate.

Example: Amount of estimated stock value due to dividend growth

Using the data from the previous example, calculate how much of the estimated stock value is due to dividend growth.

Answer:

The estimated stock value with a growth rate of zero is:

$V_0 = D / k = \$2.00 / 0.12 = \$16.67$

The amount of the estimated stock value due to estimated dividend growth is:

$\$30.00 - \$16.67 = \$13.33$

Estimating the Growth Rate in Dividends

To estimate the growth rate in dividends, the analyst can use three methods:

1. Use the historical growth in dividends for the firm.
2. Use the median industry dividend growth rate.
3. Estimate the sustainable growth rate.

The **sustainable growth rate** is the rate at which equity, earnings, and dividends can continue to grow indefinitely assuming that ROE is constant, the dividend payout ratio is constant, and no new equity is sold.

sustainable growth = (1 − dividend payout ratio) × ROE

The quantity (1 − dividend payout ratio) is also referred to as the **retention rate**, the proportion of net income that is not paid out as dividends and goes to retained earnings, thus increasing equity.

> **Example: Sustainable growth rate**
>
> Green, Inc., is expected to pay dividends equal to 25% of earnings. Green's ROE is 21%. Calculate and interpret its sustainable growth rate.
>
> **Answer:**
>
> g = (1 − 0.25) × 21% = 15.75%
>
> With long-run economic growth typically in the single digits, it is unlikely that a firm could sustain 15.75% growth forever. The analyst should also examine the growth rate for the industry and the firm's historical growth rate to determine whether the estimate is reasonable.

Some firms do not currently pay dividends but are expected to begin paying dividends at some point in the future. A firm may not currently pay a dividend because it is in financial distress and cannot afford to pay out cash or because the return the firm can earn by reinvesting cash is greater than what stockholders could expect to earn by investing dividends elsewhere.

For these firms, an analyst must estimate the amount and timing of the first dividend in order to use the Gordon growth model. Because these parameters are highly uncertain, the analyst should check the estimate from the Gordon growth model against estimates made using other models.

> **Example: A firm with no current dividend**
>
> A firm currently pays no dividend but is expected to pay a dividend at the end of Year 4. Year 4 earnings are expected to be $1.64, and the firm will maintain a payout ratio of 50%. Assuming a constant growth rate of 5% and a required rate of return of 10%, estimate the current value of this stock.
>
> **Answer:**
>
> The first step is to find the value of the stock at the end of Year 3. Remember, P_3 is the present value of dividends in Years 4 through infinity, calculated at the end of Year 3, one period *before* the first dividend is paid.
>
> Calculate D_4, the estimate of the dividend that will be paid at the end of Year 4:
>
> D_4 = (dividend payout ratio)(E_4) = (0.5)(1.64) = $0.82
>
> Apply the constant growth model to estimate V_3:
>
> $V_3 = D_4 / (k_e - g_c)$ = $0.82 / (0.10 − 0.05) = $16.40
>
> The second step is to calculate the current value, V_0:
>
> $V_0 = 16.40 / 1.1^3 = \$12.32$

Multistage Dividend Growth Models

A firm may temporarily experience a growth rate that exceeds the required rate of return on the firm's equity, but no firm can maintain this relationship indefinitely. A firm with an extremely high growth rate will attract competition, and its growth rate will eventually fall. We must assume the firm will return to a more sustainable rate of growth at some point in the future in order to calculate the present value of expected future dividends.

One way to value a dividend-paying firm that is experiencing temporarily high growth is to add the present values of dividends expected during the high-growth period to the present value of the constant growth value of the firm at the end of the high-growth period. This is referred to as the **multistage dividend discount model**.

$$\text{value} = \frac{D_1}{(1+k_e)} + \frac{D_2}{(1+k_e)^2} + \ldots + \frac{D_n}{(1+k_e)^n} + \frac{P_n}{(1+k_e)^n}$$

where $P_n = \dfrac{D_{n+1}}{k_e - g_c}$ is the terminal stock value, assuming that dividends at t = n + 1 and beyond grow at a constant rate of g_c.

Steps in using the multistage model:

- Determine the discount rate, k_e.
- Project the size and duration of the high initial dividend growth rate, g^*.
- Estimate dividends during the high-growth period.
- Estimate the constant growth rate at the end of the high-growth period, g_c.
- Estimate the first dividend that will grow at the constant rate.
- Use the constant growth value to calculate the stock value at the end of the high-growth period.
- Add the PVs of all dividends to the PV of the terminal value of the stock.

Example: Multistage growth

Consider a stock with dividends that are expected to grow at 20% per year for four years, after which they are expected to grow at 5% per year, indefinitely. The last dividend paid was $1.00, and k_e = 10%. Calculate the value of this stock using the multistage growth model.

Answer:

Calculate the dividends over the high-growth period:

$$D_1 = D_0(1 + g^*) = 1.00(1.20) = \$1.20$$

$$D_2 = D_1(1 + g^*) = 1.20(1.20) = 1.2^2 = \$1.44$$

$$D_3 = D_2(1 + g^*) = 1.44(1.20) = 1.2^3 = \$1.73$$

$$D_4 = D_3(1 + g^*) = 1.73(1.20) = 1.2^4 = \$2.08 \text{ (rounded up)}$$

Although we increase D_3 by the high growth rate of 20% to get D_4, D_4 will grow at the constant growth rate of 5% for the foreseeable future. This property of D_4 allows us to use the constant growth model formula with D_4 to get P_3, a time = 3 value for all the (infinite) dividends expected from time = 4 onward.

$$P_3 = \frac{D_4}{k_e - g_c} = \frac{2.08}{0.10 - 0.05} = 41.60$$

Finally, we can sum the present values of dividends 1, 2, and 3 and of P_3 to get the present value of all the expected future dividends during both the high- and constant growth periods:

$$\frac{1.20}{1.1} + \frac{1.44}{1.1^2} + \frac{1.73}{1.1^3} + \frac{41.60}{1.1^3} = \$34.84$$

Professor's Note: Many finance textbooks solve multiple stage growth problems like this one by using the first dividend that has grown at the constant long-term rate to calculate the terminal value, one period after the dividend we have used. Except for rounding, this results in the same current stock value. In fact, the constant growth model can be employed using any dividend during the assumed constant growth period.

A common mistake with multistage growth problems is to calculate the future value, P_3 in this example, and then to either forget to discount it back to the present or to discount over the number of periods until the constant growth dividend is paid (four in this example) rather than using the correct number of periods for discounting the constant growth value (three periods in the example). Don't make these mistakes because question writers like to present these common errors as answer choices.

LOS 50.f: Identify characteristics of companies for which the constant growth or a multistage dividend discount model is appropriate.

The Gordon growth model uses a single constant growth rate of dividends and is most appropriate for valuing stable and mature, non-cyclical, dividend-paying firms.

For dividend-paying firms with dividends that are expected to grow rapidly, slowly, or erratically over some period, followed by constant dividend growth, some form of the multistage growth model should be employed. The important points are that dividends must be estimable and must grow at a constant rate after some initial period so that the constant growth model can be used to determine the terminal value of the stock. Thus, we can apply multistage dividend growth models to a firm with high current growth that will drop to a stable rate in the future or to a firm that is temporarily losing market share and growing slowly or getting smaller, as long as its growth is expected to stabilize to a constant rate at some point in the future.

One variant of a multistage growth model assumes that the firm has three stages of dividend growth, not just two. These three stages can be categorized as growth, transition, and maturity. A 3-stage model would be suitable for firms with an initial high growth rate, followed by a lower growth rate during a second, transitional period, followed by the constant growth rate in the long run, such as a young firm still in the high growth phase.

When a firm does not pay dividends, estimates of dividend payments some years in the future are highly speculative. In this case, and in any case where future dividends cannot be estimated with much confidence, valuation based on FCFE is appropriate as long as growth rates of earnings can be estimated. In other cases, valuation based on price multiples may be more appropriate.

LOS 50.g: Explain the rationale for using price multiples to value equity, how the price to earnings multiple relates to fundamentals, and the use of multiples based on comparables.

Because the dividend discount model is very sensitive to its inputs, many investors rely on other methods. In a **price multiple** approach, an analyst compares a stock's price multiple to a benchmark value based on an index, industry group of firms, or a peer group of firms within an industry. Common price multiples used for valuation include price-to-earnings, price-to-cash flow, price-to-sales, and price-to-book value ratios.

Price multiples are widely used by analysts and readily available in numerous media outlets. Price multiples are easily calculated and can be used in time series and cross-sectional comparisons. Many of these ratios have been shown to be useful for predicting stock returns, with low multiples associated with higher future returns.

A critique of price multiples is that they reflect only the past because historical (trailing) data are often used in the denominator. For this reason, many practitioners use forward (leading or prospective) values in the denominator (sales, book value, earnings, etc.). The use of projected values can result in much different ratios. An analyst should be sure to use price multiple calculations consistently across firms.

When we compare a price multiple, such as P/E, for a firm to those of other firms based on market prices, we are using **price multiples based on comparables**. By contrast, **price multiples based on fundamentals** tell us what a multiple should be based on some valuation model and therefore are not dependent on the current market prices of other companies to establish value.

LOS 50.h: Calculate and interpret the following multiples: price to earnings, price to an estimate of operating cash flow, price to sales, and price to book value.

Price multiples used for valuation include:

- **Price-earnings (P/E) ratio:** The P/E ratio is a firm's stock price divided by earnings per share and is widely used by analysts and cited in the press.
- **Price-sales (P/S) ratio:** The P/S ratio is a firm's stock price divided by sales per share.
- **Price-book value (P/B) ratio:** The P/B ratio is a firm's stock price divided by book value of equity per share.
- **Price-cash flow (P/CF) ratio:** The P/CF ratio is a firm's stock price divided by cash flow per share, where cash flow may be defined as operating cash flow or free cash flow.

Other multiples can be used that are industry specific. For example, in the cable television industry, stock market capitalization is compared to the number of subscribers.

Multiples Based on Fundamentals

To understand fundamental price multiples, consider the Gordon growth valuation model:

$$P_0 = \frac{D_1}{k - g}$$

If we divide both sides of the equation by next year's projected earnings, E_1, we get:

$\frac{P_0}{E_1} = \frac{D_1 / E_1}{k - g}$, which is the leading P/E for this stock if it is valued in the market according to the constant growth DDM.

This P/E based on fundamentals is also referred to as a **justified P/E**. It is "justified" because, assuming we have the correct inputs for D_1, E_1, k_e, and g, the equation above will provide a P/E ratio that is based on the present value of the future cash flows. We refer to this as a *leading P/E ratio* because it is based on expected earnings next period, not on actual earnings for the previous period, which would produce a lagging or *trailing P/E ratio*.

One advantage of this approach is that it makes clear how the firm's P/E ratio should be related to its fundamentals. It illustrates that the P/E ratio is a function of:

- D_1 / E_1 = expected dividend payout ratio.
- k = required rate of return on the stock.
- g = expected constant growth rate of dividends.

> **Example: P/E based on fundamentals**
>
> A firm has an expected dividend payout ratio of 60%, a required rate of return of 11%, and an expected dividend growth rate of 5%. Calculate the firm's fundamental (justified) leading P/E ratio.
>
> **Answer:**
>
> expected P/E ratio: 0.6 / (0.11 − 0.05) = 10

The justified P/E ratio serves as a benchmark for the price at which the stock should trade. In the previous example, if the firm's actual P/E ratio (based on the market price and expected earnings) was 16, the stock would be considered overvalued. If the firm's market P/E ratio was 7, the stock would be considered undervalued.

P/E ratios based on fundamentals are very sensitive to the inputs (especially the denominator, k − g), so the analyst should use several different sets of inputs to indicate a range for the justified P/E.

Because we started with the equation for the constant growth DDM, the P/E ratio calculated in this way is the P/E ratio consistent with the constant growth DDM. We can see from the formula that, *other things equal*, the P/E ratio we have defined here will increase with (1) a higher dividend payout rate, (2) a higher growth rate, or (3) a lower required rate of return. So, if the subject firm has a higher dividend payout ratio, higher growth rate, and lower required return than its peers, a higher P/E ratio may be justified.

In practice, other things are not equal. An increase in the dividend payout ratio, for example, will reduce the firm's sustainable growth rate. While higher dividends will increase firm value, a lower growth rate will decrease firm value. This relationship is referred to as the **dividend displacement of earnings**. The net effect on firm value of increasing the dividend payout ratio is ambiguous. As intuition would suggest, firms cannot continually increase their P/Es or market values by increasing the dividend payout ratio. Otherwise, all firms would have 100% payout ratios.

Professor's Note: Watch for the wording "other things equal" or "other variables unchanged" in any exam questions about the effect of changing one variable.

Example: Fundamental P/E ratio comparison

Holt Industries makes decorative items. The figures below are for Holt and its industry.

	Holt Industries	Industry Average
Dividend payout ratio	25%	16%
Sales growth	7.5%	3.9%
Total debt to equity	113%	68%

Which of these factors suggest a higher fundamental P/E ratio for Holt?

Answer:

- The higher dividend payout ratio supports Holt having a higher P/E ratio than the industry.
- Higher growth in sales suggests that Holt will be able to increase dividends at a faster rate, which supports Holt having a higher P/E ratio than the industry.
- The higher level of debt, however, indicates that Holt has higher risk and a higher required return on equity, which supports Holt having a lower P/E ratio than the industry.

Multiples Based on Comparables

Valuation based on price multiple comparables (or comps) involves using a price multiple to evaluate whether an asset is valued properly relative to a benchmark. Common benchmarks include the stock's historical average (a time series comparison) or similar stocks and industry averages (a cross-sectional comparison). Comparing firms within an industry is useful for analysts who are familiar with a particular industry. Price multiples are readily calculated and provided by many media outlets.

The economic principle guiding this method is the **law of one price**, which asserts that two identical assets should sell at the same price, or in this case, two comparable assets should have approximately the same multiple.

The analyst should be sure that any comparables used really are comparable. Price multiples may not be comparable across firms if the firms are different sizes, are in different industries, or will grow at different rates. Furthermore, using P/E ratios for cyclical firms is complicated due to their sensitivity to economic conditions. In this case, the P/S ratio may be favored over the P/E ratio because the sales are less volatile than earnings due to both operating and financial leverage.

The disadvantages of using price multiples based on comparables are (1) a stock may appear overvalued by the comparable method but undervalued by the fundamental method, or vice versa; (2) different accounting methods can result in price multiples that are not comparable across firms, especially internationally; and (3) price multiples for cyclical firms may be greatly affected by economic conditions at a given point in time.

> **Example: Valuation using comparables**
>
> The following figures are for Renee's Bakery. All figures except the stock price are in millions.
>
> | *Fiscal Year-End* | 20X3 | 20X2 | 20X1 |
> |---|---|---|---|
> | Total stockholder's equity | $55.60 | $54.10 | $52.60 |
> | Net revenues | $77.30 | $73.60 | $70.80 |
> | Net income | $3.20 | $1.10 | $0.40 |
> | Net cash flow from operations | $17.90 | $15.20 | $12.20 |
> | Stock price | $11.40 | $14.40 | $12.05 |
> | Shares outstanding | 4.476 | 3.994 | 3.823 |
>
> Calculate Renee's lagging P/E, P/CF, P/S, and P/B ratios. Judge whether the firm is undervalued or overvalued using the following relevant industry averages for 20X3 and the firm's historical trend.
>
> | *Lagging Industry Ratios* | 20X3 |
> |---|---|
> | Price-to-earnings | 8.6 |
> | Price-to-cash flow | 4.6 |
> | Price-to-sales | 1.4 |
> | Price-to-book value | 3.6 |
>
> **Answer:**
>
> To calculate the lagging price multiples, first divide the relevant financial statement items by the number of shares to get per-share amounts. Then, divide the stock price by this figure.

For example, for the P/S ratio for 20X3, divide net revenue (net sales) by the number of shares:

$$\frac{\text{sales}}{\text{number of shares}} = \frac{\$77.30}{4.476} = 17.270$$

Then, divide the stock price by sales per share:

$$\frac{P}{S} = \frac{\$11.40}{17.3} = 0.7$$

Using the net income for earnings, the net cash flow from operations for the cash flow, and stockholder's equity for book value, the ratios for Renee's Bakery are:

	20X3	20X2	20X1
P/E	15.9	52.3	115.2
P/CF	2.9	3.8	3.8
P/S	0.7	0.8	0.7
P/B	0.9	1.1	0.9

Comparing Renee's Bakery's ratios to the industry averages for 20X3, the price multiples are lower in all cases except for the P/E multiple. This cross-sectional evidence suggests that Renee's Bakery is undervalued.

The P/E ratio merits further investigation. Renee's Bakery may have a higher P/E because its earnings are depressed by high depreciation, interest expense, or taxes. Calculating the price-EBITDA ratio would provide an alternative measure that is unaffected by these expenses.

On a time series basis, the ratios are trending downward. This indicates that Renee's Bakery may be currently undervalued relative to its past valuations. We could also calculate average price multiples for the ratios over 20X1–20X3 as a benchmark for the current values:

Company average P/E 20X1–20X3	61.1
Company average P/CF 20X1–20X3	3.5
Company average P/S 20X1–20X3	0.7
Company average P/B 20X1–20X3	1.0

The current P/E, P/CF, and P/B ratios are lower than their 3-year averages. This indicates that Renee's Bakery may be currently undervalued. It also may be the case, however, that P/E ratios for the market as a whole have been decreasing over the period due to systematic factors.

LOS 50.i: Describe enterprise value multiples and their use in estimating equity value.

Enterprise value (EV) measures total company value. EV can be viewed as what it would cost to acquire the firm:

EV = market value of common and preferred stock + market value of debt − cash and short-term investments

Cash and short-term investments are subtracted because an acquirer's cost for a firm would be decreased by the amount of the target's liquid assets. Although an acquirer assumes the firm's debt, it also receives the firm's cash and short-term investments. Enterprise value is appropriate when an analyst wants to compare the values of firms that have significant differences in capital structure.

EBITDA (earnings before interest, taxes, depreciation, and amortization are subtracted) is probably the most frequently used denominator for EV multiples; operating income can also be used. Because the numerator represents total company value, it should be compared to earnings of both debt and equity owners. An advantage of using EBITDA instead of net income is that EBITDA is usually positive even when earnings are not. When net income is negative, value multiples based on earnings are meaningless. A disadvantage of using EBITDA is that it often includes non-cash revenues and expenses.

A potential problem with using enterprise value is that the market value of a firm's debt is often not available. In this case, the analyst can use the market values of similar bonds or can use their book values. Book value, however, may not be a good estimate of market value if firm and market conditions have changed significantly since the bonds were issued.

> **Example: Calculating EV/EBITDA multiples**
>
> Daniel, Inc., is a manufacturer of small refrigerators and other appliances. The following figures are from Daniel's most recent financial statements except for the market value of long-term debt, which has been estimated from financial market data.
>
> | | |
> |---|---|
> | Stock price | $30.00 |
> | Shares outstanding | 300,000 |
> | Market value of long-term debt | $800,000 |
> | Book value of long-term debt | $1,100,000 |
> | Book value of total debt | $2,600,000 |
> | Cash and marketable securities | $300,000 |
> | EBITDA | $1,200,000 |
>
> Calculate the EV/EBITDA multiple.

> **Answer:**
>
> First, we must estimate the market value of the firm's short-term debt and liabilities. To do so, subtract the book value of long-term debt from the book value of total debt: $2,600,000 − $1,100,000 = $1,500,000. This is the book value of the firm's short-term debt. We can assume the market value of these short-term items is close to their book value. (As we will see in the Study Session on fixed income valuation, the market values of debt instruments approach their face values as they get close to maturity.)
>
> Add the market value of long-term debt to get the market value of total debt: $800,000 + $1,500,000 = $2,300,000.
>
> The market value of equity is the stock price multiplied by the number of shares: $30 × 300,000 = $9,000,000.
>
> The enterprise value of the firm is the sum of debt and equity minus cash: $2,300,000 + $9,000,000 − $300,000 = $11,000,000.
>
> EV/EBITDA = $11,000,000 / $1,200,000 = 9.2.
>
> If the competitor or industry average EV/EBITDA is above 9.2, Daniel is relatively undervalued. If the competitor or industry average EV/EBITDA is below 9.2, Daniel is relatively overvalued.

LOS 50.j: Describe asset-based valuation models and their use in estimating equity value.

Our third category of valuation model is **asset-based models**, which are based on the idea that equity value is the market or fair value of assets minus the market or fair value of liabilities. Because market values of firm assets are usually difficult to obtain, the analyst typically starts with the balance sheet to determine the values of assets and liabilities. In most cases, market values are not equal to book values. Possible approaches to valuing assets are to value them at their depreciated values, inflation-adjusted depreciated values, or estimated replacement values.

Applying asset-based models is especially problematic for a firm that has a large amount of intangible assets, on or off the balance sheet. The effect of the loss of the current owners' talents and customer relationships on forward earnings may be quite difficult to measure. Analysts often consider asset-based model values as floor or minimum values when significant intangibles, such as business reputation, are involved. An analyst should consider supplementing an asset-based valuation with a more forward-looking valuation, such as one from a discounted cash flow model.

Asset-based model valuations are most reliable when the firm has primarily tangible short-term assets, assets with ready market values (e.g., financial or natural resource firms), or when the firm will cease to operate and is being liquidated. Asset-based models are often used to value private companies but may be increasingly useful for public firms as they move toward fair value reporting on the balance sheet.

Example: Using an asset-based model for a public firm

Williams Optical is a publicly traded firm. An analyst estimates that the market value of net fixed assets is 120% of book value. Liability and short-term asset market values are assumed to equal their book values. The firm has 2,000 shares outstanding.

Using the selected financial results in the table, calculate the value of the firm's net assets on a per-share basis.

Cash	$10,000
Accounts receivable	$20,000
Inventories	$50,000
Net fixed assets	$120,000
Total assets	$200,000
Accounts payable	$5,000
Notes payable	$30,000
Term loans	$45,000
Common stockholder equity	$120,000
Total assets	$200,000

Answer:

Estimate the market value of assets, adjusting the fixed assets for the analyst's estimates of their market values:

$10,000 + $20,000 + $50,000 + $120,000(1.20) = $224,000

Determine the market value of liabilities:

$5,000 + 30,000 + $45,000 = $80,000

Calculate the adjusted equity value:

$224,000 − $80,000 = $144,000

Calculate the adjusted equity value per share:

$144,000 / 2,000 = $72

LOS 50.k: Explain advantages and disadvantages of each category of valuation model.

Advantages of discounted cash flow models:

- They are based on the fundamental concept of discounted present value and are well grounded in finance theory.
- They are widely accepted in the analyst community.

Disadvantages of discounted cash flow models:

- Their inputs must be estimated.
- Value estimates are very sensitive to input values.

Advantages of comparable valuation using price multiples:

- Evidence that some price multiples are useful for predicting stock returns.
- Price multiples are widely used by analysts.
- Price multiples are readily available.
- They can be used in time series and cross-sectional comparisons.
- EV/EBITDA multiples are useful when comparing firm values independent of capital structure or when earnings are negative and the P/E ratio cannot be used.

Disadvantages of comparable valuation using price multiples:

- Lagging price multiples reflect the past.
- Price multiples may not be comparable across firms if the firms have different size, products, and growth.
- Price multiples for cyclical firms may be greatly affected by economic conditions at a given point in time.
- A stock may appear overvalued by the comparable method but undervalued by a fundamental method or vice versa.
- Different accounting methods can result in price multiples that are not comparable across firms, especially internationally.
- A negative denominator in a price multiple results in a meaningless ratio. The P/E ratio is especially susceptible to this problem.

Advantages of price multiple valuations based on fundamentals:

- They are based on theoretically sound valuation models.
- They correspond to widely accepted value metrics.

Disadvantage of price multiple valuations based on fundamentals:

- Price multiples based on fundamentals will be very sensitive to the inputs (especially the k − g denominator).

Advantages of asset-based models:

- They can provide floor values.
- They are most reliable when the firm has primarily tangible short-term assets, assets with ready market values, or when the firm is being liquidated.
- They are increasingly useful for valuing public firms that report fair values.

Study Session 14
Cross-Reference to CFA Institute Assigned Reading #50 – Equity Valuation: Concepts and Basic Tools

Disadvantages of asset-based models:

- Market values are often difficult to obtain.
- Market values are usually different than book values.
- They are inaccurate when a firm has a high proportion of intangible assets or future cash flows not reflected in asset values.
- Assets can be difficult to value during periods of hyperinflation.

KEY CONCEPTS

LOS 50.a
An asset is fairly valued if the market price is equal to its estimated intrinsic value, undervalued if the market price is less than its estimated value, and overvalued if the market price is greater than the estimated value.

For security valuation to be profitable, the security must be mispriced now and price must converge to intrinsic value over the investment horizon.

Securities that are followed by many investors are more likely to be fairly valued than securities that are neglected by analysts.

LOS 50.b
Discounted cash flow models estimate the present value of cash distributed to shareholders (dividend discount models) or the present value of cash available to shareholders after meeting capital expenditures and working capital expenses (free cash flow to equity models).

Multiplier models compare the stock price to earnings, sales, book value, or cash flow. Alternatively, enterprise value is compared to sales or EBITDA.

Asset-based models define a stock's value as the firm's total asset value minus liabilities and preferred stock, on a per-share basis.

LOS 50.c
The dividend discount model is based on the rationale that a corporation has an indefinite life, and a stock's value is the present value of its future cash dividends. The most general form of the model is:

$$V_0 = \sum_{t=1}^{\infty} \frac{D_t}{(1 + k_e)^t}$$

Free cash flow to equity (FCFE) can be used instead of dividends. FCFE is the cash remaining after a firm meets all of its debt obligations and provides for necessary capital expenditures. FCFE reflects the firm's capacity for dividends and is useful for firms that currently do not pay a dividend. By using FCFE, an analyst does not need to project the amount and timing of future dividends.

LOS 50.d
Preferred stock typically pays a fixed dividend and does not mature. It is valued as:

$$\text{preferred stock value} = \frac{D_p}{k_p}$$

LOS 50.e

The Gordon growth model assumes the growth rate in dividends is constant:

$$V_0 = \frac{D_1}{k_e - g_c}$$

The sustainable growth rate is the rate at which earnings and dividends can continue to grow indefinitely:

g = b × ROE

where:
b = earnings retention rate = 1 – dividend payout rate
ROE = return on equity

A firm with high growth over some number of periods followed by a constant growth rate of dividends forever can be valued using a multistage model:

$$\text{value} = \frac{D_1}{(1+k_e)} + \frac{D_2}{(1+k_e)^2} + \ldots + \frac{D_n}{(1+k_e)^n} + \frac{P_n}{(1+k_e)^n}$$

where:

$$P_n = \frac{D_{n+1}}{k_e - g_c}$$

g_c = constant growth rate of dividends
n = number of periods of supernormal growth

LOS 50.f

The constant growth model is most appropriate for firms that pay dividends that grow at a constant rate, such as stable and mature firms or noncyclical firms such as utilities and food producers in mature markets.

A 2-stage DDM would be most appropriate for a firm with high current growth that will drop to a stable rate in the future, an older firm that is experiencing a temporary high growth phase, or an older firm with a market share that is decreasing but expected to stabilize.

A 3-stage model would be appropriate for a young firm still in a high growth phase.

LOS 50.g

The P/E ratio based on fundamentals is calculated as:

$$\frac{P_0}{E_1} = \frac{D_1 / E_1}{k - g}$$

If the subject firm has a higher dividend payout ratio, higher growth rate, and lower required return than its peers, it may be justified in having a higher P/E ratio.

Price multiples are widely used by analysts, are easily calculated and readily available, and can be used in time series and cross-sectional comparisons.

LOS 50.h

The price-earnings (P/E) ratio is a firm's stock price divided by earnings per share.

The price-sales (P/S) ratio is a firm's stock price divided by sales per share.

The price-book value (P/B) ratio is a firm's stock price divided by book value per share.

The price-cash flow (P/CF) ratio is a firm's stock price divided by cash flow per share. Cash flow may be defined as operating cash flow or free cash flow.

LOS 50.i

Enterprise value (EV) measures total company value:

> EV = market value of common and preferred stock + market value of debt − cash and short-term investments

EBITDA is frequently used as the denominator in EV multiples because EV represents total company value, and EBITDA represents earnings available to all investors.

LOS 50.j

Asset-based models value equity as the market or fair value of assets minus liabilities. These models are most appropriate when a firm's assets are largely tangible and have fair values that can be established easily.

LOS 50.k

Advantages of discounted cash flow models:
- Easy to calculate.
- Widely accepted in the analyst community.
- FCFE model is useful for firms that currently do not pay a dividend.
- Gordon growth model is useful for stable, mature, noncyclical firms.
- Multistage models can be used for firms with nonconstant growth.

Disadvantages of discounted cash flow models:
- Inputs must be forecast.
- Estimates are very sensitive to inputs.
- For the Gordon growth model specifically:
  - Very sensitive to the k − g denominator.
  - Required return on equity must be greater than the growth rate.
  - Required return on equity and growth rate must remain constant.
  - Firm must pay dividends.

Advantages of price multiples:
- Often useful for predicting stock returns.
- Widely used by analysts.
- Easily calculated and readily available.
- Can be used in time series and cross-sectional comparisons.
- EV/EBITDA multiples are useful when comparing firm values independent of capital structure or when earnings are negative and the P/E ratio cannot be used.

Disadvantages of price multiples:
- P/E ratio based on fundamentals will be very sensitive to the inputs.
- May not be comparable across firms, especially internationally.
- Multiples for cyclical firms may be greatly affected by economic conditions. P/E ratio may be especially inappropriate. (The P/S multiple may be more appropriate for cyclical firms.)
- A stock may appear overvalued by the comparable method but undervalued by the fundamental method or vice versa.
- Negative denominator results in a meaningless ratio; the P/E ratio is especially susceptible to this problem.
- A potential problem with EV/EBITDA multiples is that the market value of a firm's debt is often not available.

Advantages of asset-based models:
- Can provide floor values.
- Most reliable when the firm has mostly tangible short-term assets, assets with a ready market value, or when the firm is being liquidated.
- May be increasingly useful for valuing public firms if they report fair values.

Disadvantages of asset-based models:
- Market values of assets can be difficult to obtain and are usually different than book values.
- Inaccurate when a firm has a large amount of intangible assets or future cash flows not reflected in asset value.
- Asset values can be difficult to value during periods of hyperinflation.

CONCEPT CHECKERS

1. An analyst estimates a value of $45 for a stock with a market price of $50. The analyst is *most likely* to conclude that a stock is overvalued if:
   A. few analysts follow the stock and the analyst has less confidence in his model inputs.
   B. few analysts follow the stock and the analyst is confident in his model inputs.
   C. many analysts follow the stock and the analyst is confident in his model inputs.

2. An analyst estimates that a stock will pay a $2 dividend next year and that it will sell for $40 at year-end. If the required rate of return is 15%, what is the value of the stock?
   A. $33.54.
   B. $36.52.
   C. $43.95.

3. What would an investor be willing to pay for a share of preferred stock that pays an annual $7 dividend if the required return is 7.75%?
   A. $77.50.
   B. $87.50.
   C. $90.32.

4. The constant growth model requires which of the following?
   A. $g < k$.
   B. $g > k$.
   C. $g \neq k$.

5. What is the intrinsic value of a company's stock if dividends are expected to grow at 5%, the most recent dividend was $1, and investors' required rate of return for this stock is 10%?
   A. $20.00.
   B. $21.00.
   C. $22.05.

6. Next year's dividend is expected to be $2, g = 7%, and k = 12%. What is the stock's intrinsic value?
   A. $28.57.
   B. $40.00.
   C. $42.80.

7. The XX Company paid a $1 dividend in the most recent period. The company is expecting dividends to grow at a 6% rate into the future. What is the value of this stock if an investor requires a 15% rate of return on stocks of this risk class?
   A. $10.60.
   B. $11.11.
   C. $11.78.

8. Assume that a stock is expected to pay dividends at the end of Year 1 and Year 2 of $1.25 and $1.56, respectively. Dividends are expected to grow at a 5% rate thereafter. Assuming that k_e is 11%, the value of the stock is *closest* to:
   A. $22.30.
   B. $23.42.
   C. $24.55.

9. An analyst feels that Brown Company's earnings and dividends will grow at 25% for two years, after which growth will fall to a constant rate of 6%. If the projected discount rate is 10%, and Brown's most recently paid dividend was $1, the value of Brown's stock using the multistage dividend discount model is *closest* to:
   A. $31.25.
   B. $33.54.
   C. $36.65.

10. A firm has an expected dividend payout ratio of 60% and an expected future growth rate of 7%. What should the firm's fundamental price-to-earnings (P/E) ratio be if the required rate of return on stocks of this type is 15%?
    A. 5.0×.
    B. 7.5×.
    C. 10.0×.

11. Which of the following firms would *most likely* be appropriately valued using the constant growth DDM?
    A. An auto manufacturer.
    B. A producer of bread and snack foods.
    C. A biotechnology firm in existence for two years.

12. Which of the following is *least likely* a rationale for using price multiples?
    A. Price multiples are easily calculated.
    B. The fundamental P/E ratio is insensitive to its inputs.
    C. The use of forward values in the divisor provides an incorporation of the future.

13. Which of the following firms would *most appropriately* be valued using an asset-based model?
    A. An energy exploration firm in financial distress that owns drilling rights for offshore areas.
    B. A paper firm located in a country that is experiencing high inflation.
    C. A software firm that invests heavily in research and development and frequently introduces new products.

For more questions related to this topic review, log in to your Schweser online account and launch SchweserPro™ QBank; and for video instruction covering each LOS in this topic review, log in to your Schweser online account and launch the OnDemand video lectures, if you have purchased these products.

ANSWERS – CONCEPT CHECKERS

1. **B** If the analyst is more confident of his input values, he is more likely to conclude that the security is overvalued. The market price is more likely to be correct for a security followed by many analysts and less likely correct when few analysts follow the security.

2. **B** ($40 + $2) / 1.15 = $36.52

3. **C** The share value is 7.0 / 0.0775 = $90.32.

4. **A** For the constant growth model, the constant growth rate (g) must be less than the required rate of return (k).

5. **B** Using the constant growth model, $1(1.05) / (0.10 – 0.05) = $21.00.

6. **B** Using the constant growth model, $2 / (0.12 – 0.07) = $40.00.

7. **C** Using the constant growth model, $1(1.06) / (0.15 – 0.06) = $11.78.

8. **C** ($1.25 / 1.11) + [1.56 / (0.11 – 0.05)] / 1.11 = $24.55.

9. **C** $1(1.25) / 1.1 + [$1(1.25)^2 / (0.10 – 0.06)] / 1.1 = $36.65.

10. **B** Using the earnings multiplier model, 0.6 / (0.15 – 0.07) = 7.5×.

11. **B** The constant growth DDM assumes that the dividend growth rate is constant. The most likely choice here is the bread and snack producer. Auto manufacturers are more likely to be cyclical than to experience constant growth. A biotechnology firm in existence for two years is unlikely to pay a dividend, and if it does, dividend growth is unlikely to be constant.

12. **B** The fundamental P/E ratio is sensitive to its inputs. It uses the DDM as its framework, and the denominator k – g in both has a large impact on the calculated P/E or stock value.

13. **A** The energy exploration firm would be most appropriately valued using an asset-based model. Its near-term cash flows are likely negative, so a forward-looking model is of limited use. Furthermore, it has valuable assets in the form of drilling rights that likely have a readily determined market value. The paper firm would likely not be appropriately valued using an asset-based model because high inflation makes the values of a firm's assets more difficult to estimate. An asset-based model would not be appropriate to value the software firm because the firm's value largely consists of internally developed intangible assets.

SELF-TEST: EQUITY INVESTMENTS

You have now finished the Equity Investments topic section. To get immediate feedback on how effective your study has been for this material, log in to your Schweser online account and take the self-test for this topic area. The number of questions on this test is equal to the number of questions for the topic on one-half of the actual Level I CFA exam. Questions are more exam-like than typical Concept Checkers or QBank questions; a score of less than 70% indicates that your study likely needs improvement. These tests are timed and allow 1.5 minutes per question.

FORMULAS

$$NPV = CF_0 + \frac{CF_1}{(1+k)^1} + \frac{CF_2}{(1+k)^2} + \cdots + \frac{CF_n}{(1+k)^n} = \sum_{t=0}^{n} \frac{CF_t}{(1+k)^t}$$

$$IRR: 0 = CF_0 + \frac{CF_1}{(1+IRR)^1} + \frac{CF_2}{(1+IRR)^2} + \cdots + \frac{CF_n}{(1+IRR)^n} = \sum_{t=0}^{n} \frac{CF_t}{(1+IRR)^t}$$

$$\text{payback period} = \text{full years until recovery} + \frac{\text{unrecovered cost at the beginning of the last year}}{\text{cash flow during the last year}}$$

$$PI = \frac{\text{PV of future cash flows}}{CF_0} = 1 + \frac{NPV}{CF_0}$$

$$WACC = (w_d)[k_d(1-t)] + (w_{ps})(k_{ps}) + (w_{ce})(k_{ce})$$

after-tax cost of debt = $k_d(1-t)$

cost of preferred stock = $k_{ps} = D_{ps} / P$

cost of common equity:

$$k_{ce} = \frac{D_1}{P_0} + g$$

$$k_{ce} = R_f + \beta[E(R_m) - R_f]$$

$$k_{ce} = \text{bond yield + risk premium}$$

unlevered asset beta:

$$\beta_{ASSET} = \beta_{EQUITY} \left[\frac{1}{1 + \left((1-t)\frac{D}{E}\right)} \right]$$

project beta:

$$\beta_{PROJECT} = \beta_{ASSET} \left[1 + \left((1-t)\frac{D}{E}\right) \right]$$

cost of common equity with a country risk premium:

$$k_{ce} = R_f + \beta\left[E(R_{MKT}) - R_f + \text{country risk premium}\right]$$

$$\text{break point} = \frac{\text{amount of capital at which the component's cost of capital changes}}{\text{weight of the component in the capital structure}}$$

$$\text{degree of operating leverage} = \frac{Q(P-V)}{Q(P-V)-F} = \frac{\%\Delta EBIT}{\%\Delta sales}$$

$$\text{degree of financial leverage} = \frac{EBIT}{EBIT - I} = \frac{\%\Delta EPS}{\%\Delta EBIT}$$

$$\text{degree of total leverage} = DOL \times DFL = \frac{\%\Delta EPS}{\%\Delta sales}$$

$$\text{breakeven quantity of sales} = \frac{\text{fixed operating costs} + \text{fixed financing costs}}{\text{price} - \text{variable cost per unit}}$$

$$\text{operating breakeven quantity of sales} = \frac{\text{fixed operating costs}}{\text{price} - \text{variable cost per unit}}$$

$$\text{current ratio} = \frac{\text{current assets}}{\text{current liabilities}}$$

$$\text{quick ratio} = \frac{\text{cash} + \text{short-term marketable securities} + \text{receivables}}{\text{current liabilities}}$$

$$\text{receivables turnover} = \frac{\text{credit sales}}{\text{average receivables}}$$

$$\text{number of days of receivables} = \frac{365}{\text{receivables turnover}} = \frac{\text{average receivables}}{\text{average day's credit sales}}$$

$$\text{inventory turnover} = \frac{\text{cost of goods sold}}{\text{average inventory}}$$

$$\text{number of days of inventory} = \frac{365}{\text{inventory turnover}} = \frac{\text{average inventory}}{\text{average day's COGS}}$$

$$\text{payables turnover ratio} = \frac{\text{purchases}}{\text{average trade payables}}$$

$$\text{number of days of payables} = \frac{365}{\text{payables turnover ratio}} = \frac{\text{average payables}}{\text{average day's purchases}}$$

operating cycle = average days of inventory + average days of receivables

$$\text{cash conversion cycle} = \begin{pmatrix} \text{average days} \\ \text{of receivables} \end{pmatrix} + \begin{pmatrix} \text{average days} \\ \text{of inventory} \end{pmatrix} - \begin{pmatrix} \text{average days} \\ \text{of payables} \end{pmatrix}$$

$$\% \text{ discount} = \left(\frac{\text{face value} - \text{price}}{\text{face value}} \right)$$

$$\text{discount-basis yield} = \left(\frac{\text{face value} - \text{price}}{\text{face value}} \right) \left(\frac{360}{\text{days}} \right) = \% \text{ discount} \times \left(\frac{360}{\text{days}} \right)$$

$$\text{money market yield} = \left(\frac{\text{face value} - \text{price}}{\text{price}} \right) \left(\frac{360}{\text{days}} \right) = \text{holding period yield} \times \left(\frac{360}{\text{days}} \right)$$

$$\text{bond equivalent yield} = \left(\frac{\text{face value} - \text{price}}{\text{price}} \right) \left(\frac{365}{\text{days to maturity}} \right)$$

$$= \text{holding period yield} \times \left(\frac{365}{\text{days}} \right)$$

$$\text{cost of trade credit} = \left(1 + \frac{\% \text{ discount}}{1 - \% \text{ discount}} \right)^{\frac{365}{\text{days past discount}}} - 1$$

where:
days past discount = number of days after the end of the discount period

$$\text{holding period return} = \frac{\text{end-of-period value}}{\text{beginning-of-period value}} - 1 = \frac{P_t + Div_t}{P_0} - 1 = \frac{P_t - P_0 + Div_t}{P_0}$$

$$\text{arithmetic mean return} = \frac{(R_1 + R_2 + R_3 + \ldots + R_n)}{n}$$

$$\text{geometric mean return} = \sqrt[n]{(1+R_1) \times (1+R_2) \times (1+R_3) \times \ldots \times (1+R_n)} - 1$$

$$\text{population variance from historical data: } \sigma^2 = \frac{\sum_{t=1}^{T}(R_t - \mu)^2}{T}$$

$$\text{sample variance from historical data: } s^2 = \frac{\sum_{t=1}^{T}(R_t - \bar{R})^2}{T-1}$$

$$\text{sample covariance from historical data: } Cov_{1,2} = \frac{\sum_{t=1}^{n}\{[R_{t,1} - \bar{R}_1][R_{t,2} - \bar{R}_2]\}}{n-1}$$

$$\text{correlation: } \rho_{1,2} = \frac{Cov_{1,2}}{\sigma_1 \times \sigma_2}$$

Book 4 – Corporate Finance, Portfolio Management, and Equity Investments
Formulas

standard deviation for a two-asset portfolio:

$$\sigma_p = \sqrt{w_1^2\sigma_1^2 + w_2^2\sigma_2^2 + 2w_1w_2\sigma_1\sigma_2\rho_{1,2}} \text{ or } \sqrt{w_1^2\sigma_1^2 + w_2^2\sigma_2^2 + 2w_1w_2\text{Cov}_{1,2}}$$

equation of the CML: $E(R_P) = R_f + \left(\dfrac{E(R_M) - R_f}{\sigma_M}\right)\sigma_P$

$$E(R_P) = R_f + \left(E(R_M) - R_f\right)\left(\dfrac{\sigma_P}{\sigma_M}\right)$$

total risk = systematic risk + unsystematic risk

$$\beta_i = \dfrac{\text{Cov}_{i,mkt}}{\sigma_{mkt}^2} = \rho_{i,mkt}\dfrac{\sigma_i}{\sigma_{mkt}}$$

capital asset pricing model (CAPM): $E(R_i) = R_f + \beta_i[E(R_{mkt}) - R_f]$

margin call price $= P_0\left(\dfrac{1 - \text{initial margin}}{1 - \text{maintenance margin}}\right)$

$$\text{price-weighted index} = \dfrac{\text{sum of stock prices}}{\text{number of stocks in index adjusted for splits}}$$

$$\text{market cap-weighted index} = \dfrac{\sum\left[(\text{price}_{today})(\text{number of shares outstanding})\right]}{\sum\left[(\text{price}_{base\ year})(\text{number of shares outstanding})\right]}$$

$\times$ base year index value

preferred stock valuation model: $P_0 = \dfrac{D_p}{k_p}$

one-period stock valuation model: $P_0 = \dfrac{D_1}{1 + k_e} + \dfrac{P_1}{1 + k_e}$

infinite period model: $P_0 = \dfrac{D_1}{k_e - g} = \dfrac{D_0 \times (1 + g)}{k_e - g}$

multistage model: $P_0 = \dfrac{D_1}{(1+k_e)} + \dfrac{D_2}{(1+k_e)^2} + \ldots + \dfrac{D_n}{(1+k_e)^n} + \dfrac{P_n}{(1+k_e)^n}$

where:

$P_n = \dfrac{D_{n+1}}{k_e - g_c}$, and D_{n+1} is a dividend that will grow at the constant rate of g_c forever

earnings multiplier: $\dfrac{P_0}{E_1} = \dfrac{\frac{D_1}{E_1}}{k - g}$

expected growth rate: g = (retention rate)(ROE)

$$\text{trailing P/E} = \dfrac{\text{market price per share}}{\text{EPS over previous 12 months}}$$

$$\text{leading P/E} = \dfrac{\text{market price per share}}{\text{forecast EPS over next 12 months}}$$

$$\text{P/B ratio} = \dfrac{\text{market value of equity}}{\text{book value of equity}} = \dfrac{\text{market price per share}}{\text{book value per share}}$$

where:
book value of equity = common shareholders' equity
= (total assets − total liabilities) − preferred stock

$$\text{P/S ratio} = \dfrac{\text{market value of equity}}{\text{total sales}} = \dfrac{\text{market price per share}}{\text{sales per share}}$$

$$\text{P/CF ratio} = \dfrac{\text{market value of equity}}{\text{cash flow}} = \dfrac{\text{market price per share}}{\text{cash flow per share}}$$

enterprise value = market value of common and preferred stock
+ market value of debt
− cash and short-term investments

INDEX

A

ability to bear risk 186
abnormal profit 247
accelerated book build 212
accounting return on equity 263
accounting risk 127
accounts payable management 103
acid-test ratio 96
active investment strategy 244
actively managed funds 116
active portfolio management 163
activist shareholders 7
adverse selection 204
after-tax cost of debt 45
after-tax nominal return 138
aging schedule 101
allocational efficiency 216
all-or-nothing orders 210
alternative markets 198
alternative trading systems (ATS) 202
American depository receipts (ADRs) 261
American depository share (ADS) 261
annual general meeting 4
arbitrage 204, 246
arithmetic mean return 135
ask price 208
ask size 209
asset-backed securities 200
asset-based models 291, 308
audit committee 6
average days' sales outstanding 97
average inventory processing period 97

B

bank 113
bank discount yield 100
banker's acceptances 105
basket of listed depository receipts (BLDR) 261
behavioral finance 251
best efforts 212
beta 127, 170
bias 117
bid-ask spread 209
bid price 208
bid size 209
blanket lien 105
block brokers 202
board of directors 2
bond equivalent yield 100

bond mutual funds 116
book runner 212
book value of equity 262
breakeven quantity of sales 72
break points 52
broker-dealers 203
brokered markets 215
brokers 202
business risk 66
buyout funds 117

C

calendar anomalies 249
callable common shares 257
call markets 213
call money rate 206
call option 201
cannibalization 20
capital allocation line (CAL) 149, 159
capital asset pricing model (CAPM) 47, 169
capital budgeting 18
capital components 41
capital market line (CML) 161
capital markets 198
capital rationing 21
cash conversion cycle 98
cash dividends 81
  liquidating 81
  regular 81
  special 81
cash management investment policy 100
characteristic line 168
civil law system 8
clearinghouses 205
closed-end funds 116, 250
commercial paper 105
commodities 201
commodity indexes 235
common-law system 8
common shares 257
common stock 199
company analysis 282
compensation committee 7
competitive strategy 282
complete markets 215
component cost of capital 41
conflicting project rankings 31
constant growth model 296
constituent securities 225
continuous markets 214

contracts 200
contractual infrastructure 4
contribution margin 72
conventional cash flow pattern 20
convertible bond arbitrage funds 117
convertible preference shares 258
core-satellite approach 190
correlation 141
cost leadership (low-cost) strategy 282
cost of debt capital 45, 46
cost of equity capital 47, 264
cost of preferred stock 46
counterparty risk 205
country risk premium 51
covariance 140
credit default swaps 201
creditors 2
credit risk 126
crossover rate 29
cumulative preference shares 258
cumulative voting 5, 257
currencies 200
current ratio 96
custodians 205
cyclical firm 273

D

daily cash position 98
data mining 248
day orders 210
dealer markets 214
debt securities 198
declaration date 84
decline stage 280
defensive industries 274
defined benefit pension plan 114
defined contribution pension plan 114
degree of financial leverage (DFL) 69
degree of operating leverage (DOL) 67
degree of total leverage (DTL) 70
delta 128
depository bank 260
depository institutions 203
depository receipts (DRs) 260
derivative contracts 198
derivatives risks 128
direct investing 260
disadvantages of the IRR method 31
discount-basis yield 100
discounted cash flow models 291
discounted payback method 26
diversifiable risk 163
diversification 129
diversification ratio 112

dividend discount model (DDM) 292
dividend displacement of earnings 304
dividend reinvestment plan 213
downside risk 128
dual class structure 10
duration 128

E

earnings surprise 250
economic profits 275
effect of a share repurchase on book value per share 88
efficient frontier 146
efficient market hypothesis (EMH) 246
electronic communication networks (ECNs) 202
embryonic stage 279
employees 2
endowment 113
enterprise value 291, 307
equal-weighted index 227
equilibrium interest rate 197
equity market-neutral funds 117
equity securities 198, 199
ESG integration 11
ESG investing 11
event-driven funds 117
event study 247
exchanges 202
exchange-traded funds (ETFs) 116, 200
exchange-traded notes (ETNs) 200
ex-dividend date 84
execution step 115
expansion projects 19
experience curve 275
externalities 20
extraordinary general meetings 5

F

factoring 105
factor loading 165
factor sensitivity 165
feedback step 115
fidelity bonds 130
fill-or-kill order 210
finance companies 105
financial assets 198
financial derivative contracts 198
financial intermediaries 202
financial leverage 206
financial risk 66, 126
firm-specific risk 163
fixed-income arbitrage funds 117
fixed income securities 199

float-adjusted market capitalization-weighted index 228
flotation costs 54
forward contract 200
foundation 113
free cash flow to equity (FCFE) 293
free float 227
fundamental analysis 247
fundamental value 245, 290
fundamental weighting 228
futures contract 200

G

gamma 128
geometric mean return 136
global depository receipts (GDRs) 260
global macro funds 117
global minimum-variance portfolio 146
global registered shares (GRS) 261
good-on-close orders 210
good-on-open orders 210
good-till-cancelled orders 210
Gordon growth model 296
governance committee 7
governmental infrastructure 4
governmental risk 126
gross return 137
growth industries 274
growth stage 279
growth stocks 249

H

hedge fund indexes 235
hedge funds 117, 200
herding 251
historical data 140
holder-of-record date 84
holding period return (HPR) 135
hostile takeover 8

I

immediate-or-cancel orders 210
impact investing 12
incremental cash flows 19
independent directors 5
independent projects 21
index funds 116
indications of interest 212
indifference curve 147
individual investors 113
industry life cycle 279
industry rotation 270
informational efficiency 215
informationally efficient capital market 244

information asymmetry 3
information cascade 251
initial margin requirement 206
initial public offerings (IPOs) 212, 250
institutions 113
insurance companies 113, 204
insurance contract 201
internal rate of return (IRR) 23
    disadvantages 31
    IRR decision rule 24
intrinsic value 245, 290
inventory management 102
inventory turnover 97
investment banks 202
investment committee 7
investment companies 114
investment constraints 186
investment opportunity schedule 44
investment policy statement (IPS) 115, 184
investor overconfidence 251

J

January effect 249
Jensen's alpha 177
justified P/E 303

L

lead independent director 6
legal and regulatory constraints 187
legal infrastructure 4
legal risk 127
leverage 66
leveraged buyout (LBO) 259
leveraged position 206
leveraged return 138
leverage ratio 207
life-cycle stage 275
lines of credit 105
liquidity 187
liquidity ratios 96
liquidity risk 126
load funds 116
longevity risk 127
long position 205
long/short funds 117
loss aversion 251

M

maintenance margin requirement 208
majority voting 5
mandatory projects 19
marginal cost of capital (MCC) 41, 52
marginal cost of capital schedule 44, 52
margin call 208

margin loan 206
market anomaly 248
market capitalization-weighted index 227
market float 227
market model 166
market multiple models 291
market-on-close orders 210
market portfolio 160
market risk 126, 163
market risk premium 161
market-to-book ratio 264
market value 245
market value of equity 263
market value-weighted index 230
matrix pricing 46
mature stage 280
minimum-variance frontier 146
minimum-variance portfolio 146
model risk 127
momentum effects 249
money market funds 116
money markets 198
money market yield 100
money-weighted rate of return 136
moral hazard 204
mortality risk 127
M-squared 176
multifactor models 165
multilateral trading facilities (MTFs) 202
"multiple IRR" and "no IRR" problems 32
multiplier models 291
mutual funds 114, 115, 200
mutually exclusive projects 21

N

negative screening 12
net asset value (NAV) 116, 250
net borrowing 294
net operating cycle 98
net present value (NPV) 21
    NPV and stock price 33
    NPV profile 29
net return 137
no-load funds 116
nominations committee 7
non-cumulative preference shares 258
non-cyclical firm 274
nondiversifiable risk 163
non-financial risks 126
non-participating preference shares 258
number of days of payables 98
number of days of receivables 97

O

offer price 208
one-tier board 5
open-end fund 116
operating breakeven quantity of sales 74
operating cycle 98
operating risk 66
operational efficiency 215
operational risk 126
opportunity costs 20
optimal capital budget 45
option contract 201
order-driven markets 214
order matching rules 214
organizational infrastructure 4
overreaction effect 249
over-the-counter markets 214

P

participating preference shares 258
passive investment strategy 163, 244
payables payment period 98
payables turnover ratio 98
payback period 25
payment date 84
payments-in-lieu 206
peer group 274
physical derivative contracts 198
planning step 115
political risk 126
pooled investments 115, 199
portfolio perspective 112
positive screening 12
post-trade transparent 215
predatory pricing 282
preference shares 258
preferred stock 199, 258, 295
present value models 291
pretax nominal return 138
pre-trade transparent 215
price-book value (P/B) ratio 264, 302
price-cash flow (P/CF) ratio 302
price-driven markets 214
price-earnings (P/E) ratio 302
price index 225
price multiple approach 302
price multiples based on comparables 302
price multiples based on fundamentals 302
price priority 214
price return 225
price-sales (P/S) ratio 302
price versus market value weighting 230
price-weighted index 226, 228
primary capital markets 212

primary dealers 203
primary market 198
primary sources of liquidity 95
principal-agent conflict 3
principal business activity 271
private equity funds 117
private investment in public equity (PIPE) 259
private placement 213
private securities 198
product or service differentiation strategy 282
profitability index 27, 28
project beta 49
project sequencing 21
proxy 5, 257
proxy fight 8
public securities 198
pure-play method 49
putable common shares 257
put option 201

Q

quick ratio 96
quote-driven markets 214

R

real assets 201
real estate indexes 235
real return 138
rebalancing 232
receivables turnover 96
reconstitution 232
regulatory risk 126
related party transactions 3
relative risk objectives 185
remuneration committee 7
replacement projects 19
responsible investing 11
return generating models 165
return index 225
return on equity (ROE) 263
reverse stock splits 84
rho 128
rights offering 213
risk-adjusted returns 247
risk-averse 142
risk aversion coefficient 148
risk budgeting 126, 190
risk committee 7
risk governance 125
risk management 124
risk management framework 125
risk-neutral 143
risk objectives 185
risk-seeking 143

risk shifting 130
risk tolerance 125
risk transfer 130

S

sales risk 66
scenario analysis 128
seasoned offerings 212
secondary financial markets 212
secondary issues 212
secondary market 198
secondary precedence rule 214
securities 199
security characteristic line 168
security market index 225
security market line (SML) 168
self-insurance 129
semi-strong form market efficiency 246
senior managers 2
separately managed account 117
shakeout stage 280
shareholders 2
shareholder theory 1
share repurchase 85
　using borrowed funds 87
Sharpe ratio 175
shelf registration 213
short position 205
short rebate rate 206
short sale 206
short-term funding 104
single-index model 166
size effect 249
socially responsible investing 11
solvency risk 126
sovereign wealth funds 114
sovereign yield spread 51
special resolutions 5
sponsored depository receipt 260
spot markets 198
spreadsheet modeling 283
staggered board 6
stakeholder management 4
stakeholder theory 1
standard deviation 127
standing limit orders 210
statutory voting 257
stock dividends 82
stock mutual funds 116
stock splits 82
stop-buy 210
stop loss orders 210
stop orders 210
stop-sell order 210

strategic analysis 276
strategic asset allocation 188
strategic groups 275
stress testing 128
strong-form market efficiency 246
sunk costs 19
suppliers 2
surety bond 130
sustainable growth rate 298
sustainable investing 11
swap contract 201
switching costs 279
systematic risk 163

T

tactical asset allocation 190
tail risk 127, 128
target capital structure 43
tax-loss selling 249
tax risk 126
tax situation 187
technical analysis 247
tender offer 8, 85
terminal value 292
thematic investing 12
time horizon 187
trade pricing rules 214
traditional investment markets 198
tranches 200
Treynor measure 177
turn-of-the-year effect 249
two-fund separation theorem 149
two-tier board 5

U

unconventional cash flow pattern 20
underwritten offering 212
unique circumstances 187
unique risk 163
unsponsored depository receipt 260
unsystematic risk 163
unweighted index bias 231
utility function 147

V

value at risk (VaR) 128
value effect 249
value stocks 249
value-weighted index 227
vega 128
venture capital 259
venture capital funds 118

W

warrants 199
weak-form market efficiency 246
weighted average collection period 101
weighted average cost of capital (WACC) 41
willingness to bear risk 186
window dressing 249
working capital 96

Notes

Notes

Notes

Notes

Notes

Notes

Notes

Notes